Constitutional Orphan

Constitutional Orphan

*Gender Equality and the
Nineteenth Amendment*

PAULA A. MONOPOLI

OXFORD
UNIVERSITY PRESS

Oxford University Press is a department of the University of Oxford. It furthers the
University's objective of excellence in research, scholarship, and education by publishing worldwide.
Oxford is a registered trademark of Oxford University Press in the UK and certain other countries.

Published in the United States of America by Oxford University Press
198 Madison Avenue, New York, NY 10016, United States of America.

© Paula A. Monopoli 2020

Library of Congress Cataloging-in-Publication Data
Names: Monopoli, Paula A., 1958– author.
Title: Constitutional orphan : gender equality and the Nineteenth Amendment / Paula A. Monopoli.
Description: New York, NY : Oxford University Press, [2020] | Includes bibliographical references
and index.
Identifiers: LCCN 2020021953 | ISBN 9780190092795 (hardback) | ISBN 9780190092825 (online) |
ISBN 9780190092801 (updf) | ISBN 9780190092818 (epub)
Subjects: LCSH: United States. Constitution. 19th Amendment. | Women's rights—United States. |
Women—Suffrage—United States—History. | Suffragists—United States—History |
Constitutional amendments—United States—History.
Classification: LCC KF4895 .M66 2020 | DDC 342.7308/78—dc23
LC record available at https://lccn.loc.gov/2020021953

1 3 5 7 9 8 6 4 2

Printed by Sheridan Books, Inc., United States of America

Note to Readers
This publication is designed to provide accurate and authoritative information in regard to the subject
matter covered. It is based upon sources believed to be accurate and reliable and is intended to be
current as of the time it was written. It is sold with the understanding that the publisher is not engaged
in rendering legal, accounting, or other professional services. If legal advice or other expert assistance is
required, the services of a competent professional person should be sought. Also, to confirm that the
information has not been affected or changed by recent developments, traditional legal research
techniques should be used, including checking primary sources where appropriate.

*(Based on the Declaration of Principles jointly adopted by a Committee of the
American Bar Association and a Committee of Publishers and Associations.)*

You may order this or any other Oxford University Press publication
by visiting the Oxford University Press website at www.oup.com.

To Marin, Richard, Victoria, Christopher, and Patrick.
And to my mother, Eileen; and in memory of my father, Richard.

Contents

Acknowledgments

As I write these Acknowledgments, we are in the midst of a global pandemic. The context is eerily similar to the period leading up to ratification of the Nineteenth Amendment in 1920, with the global flu pandemic of 1918 limiting suffragists' ability to gather for rallies and to lobby Congress. Despite that significant challenge, the suffragists persisted. The amendment's ratification has been described as "the single biggest democratizing event in American history." Yet the most common question I heard when writing this book was, "Which amendment is that?" And even when people knew that the Nineteenth Amendment to the United States Constitution was the woman suffrage amendment, they still questioned what more there could possibly be to say about it. The amendment simply meant that women must be allowed to cast a ballot, right? And it is true that it was this thin conception of the Nineteenth Amendment that emerged by the end of the decade following its ratification in 1920. The puzzle of how this thin conception emerged, as a mere non-discrimination-in-voting rule rather than a broader constitutional norm about women's citizenship and gender equality, is the primary focus of this book. In particular, I examine the role of two national suffrage organizations as institutional actors in that story, and how their strategic choices and divisions within the movement affected its outcome. My intellectual journey to understanding the complexity of that puzzle, as well as the full meaning and scope of the Nineteenth Amendment, has been long and challenging. And I have been supported by a number of family members, friends, and colleagues along the way.

I owe much to my colleagues at the University of Maryland Carey School of Law, including Jana Singer, Taunya Banks, Mark Graber, Jason Hawkins, Maxine Grosshans, Liz Graham, and Simon Canick, for reading drafts, suggesting relevant scholarship, and facilitating research and writing. Special thanks go to Sue McCarty, without whose expert editorial assistance the manuscript would not have been completed. Colleagues and friends at my February 2018 Sol & Carlyn Hubert Professorship lecture on the Nineteenth Amendment provided helpful perspectives, as well. And I am indebted to my dean and associate deans, including Donald Tobin, Barbara Gontrum, and Mike Pappas, for their support and research funding from the University of Maryland Carey Law Faculty Summer Research Grant Program. I am also grateful to my research assistants, including Alyssa Domzal, Medha Venugopal, Max Romanik, and Anamika Roy. And the support and friendship of my administrative assistant, Yvonne McMorris, has been invaluable.

Colleagues at other institutions have given me insights and feedback that have shaped, and often shifted, my thinking about the role of the suffragists in the emergence of a thin conception of the Nineteenth Amendment. These include Reva Siegel, whose foundational work inspired this book; and Tracy Thomas, Elizabeth Katz, Kimberly Hamlin, Ann Gordon, and other participants at the Center for Constitutional Law Akron's September 2019 Symposium on the Nineteenth Amendment. The Introduction to this book formed much of the basis of my remarks and the essay I wrote, as part of that symposium. I am grateful to Tracy Thomas for the invitation. The participants at the January 2020 AALS Section on Constitutional Law Panel on the Nineteenth Amendment, including Steven Calabresi, Reva Siegel, and Julie Suk, also gave me valuable insights through their panel remarks. I am grateful to the Executive Committee of the AALS Section on Constitutional Law and its chair, Lou Virelli, for selecting my paper for that panel. And I am grateful to Rick Hasen, Leah Litman, Neil Siegel, and Reva Siegel, who were willing to share drafts of their work on how more robust applications of the Nineteenth Amendment can emerge today. Sarah Hutcheon, at the Schlesinger Library, Radcliffe Institute for Advanced Study, Harvard University; and Bruce Kirby, at the Manuscript Division, Library of Congress, offered interest in and assistance with the project. And Eileen McDonagh and Georgia Sorenson have collaborated with me on prior projects that informed this book.

Many friends asked about my progress and offered moral support over the years that it took me to write this book. They know who they are and I am grateful to all of them. I am also grateful to my siblings, Beth, Chris, Rich, and Dan, for their continued love and support. And I owe special thanks to my mother, Eileen Monopoli, who read and commented on multiple drafts.

My husband and children tolerated my long days in archives and at the computer with humor and patience. My daughter, Victoria Scordato, provided exceptional research assistance. My son, Chris Scordato, provided excellent editing. My sons, Richard Scordato and Patrick Scordato, provided much appreciated moral support. My husband, Marin Scordato, listened to hours of discourse on legal history and theory, as he has for almost forty years, since we were law students. And he cared for us all, including our wonderful beagle, Sophia, as I worked on this book.

I am also very grateful to Jamie Berezin at Oxford for taking on this book, to the outside reviewers, who gave very helpful feedback, and to David Lipp, Arun Vasu, and others who helped bring it to fruition.

Finally, I am grateful to the suffragists who dedicated their lives to expand the scope of women's citizenship and our constitutional community. On the centennial of the Nineteenth Amendment, it is fitting to remember them.

Paula A. Monopoli

Bethesda, Maryland
May 2020

Abbreviations

AWSA	American Woman Suffrage Association
ERA	Equal Rights Amendment
IWSA	International Woman Suffrage Alliance
NAWSA	National American Woman Suffrage Association
NAACP	National Association for the Advancement of Colored People
NACW	National Association of Colored Women
NCL	National Consumers League
NLWV	National League of Women Voters
NOW	National Organization for Women
NWP	National Woman's Party
NWSA	National Woman Suffrage Association
SSWSC	Southern States Woman Suffrage Conference
WSPU	Women's Social and Political Union

Introduction

The right of citizens of the United States to vote shall not be denied
or abridged by the United States or by any state on account of sex.

Congress shall have power to enforce this article by appropriate
legislation.

—U.S. Const. amend. XIX

On August 26, 1920, these words became part of the United States
Constitution as its Nineteenth Amendment. The requisite thirty-six states
had ratified the amendment in the year since its enactment by Congress on
June 4, 1919. A revolution in women's rights, spanning over seventy years,
came to a quiet conclusion as Secretary of State Bainbridge Colby signed the
measure into law in the privacy of his home at eight o'clock in the morning.[1]
None of the prominent suffrage leaders of the day, including the National
American Woman Suffrage Association (NAWSA) president, Carrie
Chapman Catt; or the National Woman's Party (NWP) chair, Alice Paul, were
at the signing.[2] Catt was later invited to go to the State Department to see the
proclamation, but no similar invitation was extended to the more militant
Paul. Paul had been a thorn in the side of President Woodrow Wilson, with
her White House picketing and willingness to be imprisoned for the vote.[3]

Ratification was followed by ten years of litigation—most of it in state
courts—during which the meaning and scope of the Nineteenth Amendment
was contested. In its most literal sense, the Nineteenth Amendment did
not confer a "right" to vote per se. Rather, it simply prohibited the states or
the federal government from using sex as a criterion for voter eligibility.[4]
In other words, its ratification meant that state and federal impediments
to voting based on sex were now unconstitutional. It did not mean that all
women in the United States could vote.[5] As a matter of law, the Nineteenth
Amendment meant that states could not prevent African American women
from voting based solely on their sex. Yet vast numbers of African American

Constitutional Orphan. Paula A. Monopoli, Oxford University Press (2020). © Paula A. Monopoli.
DOI: 10.1093/oso/9780190092795.001.0001

women were prevented from voting in the November 1920 presidential election that followed on the heels of ratification.[6] They faced the same impediments—poll taxes, literacy tests, grandfather clauses, and physical intimidation—used to prevent their male counterparts from voting after ratification of the Fourteenth and Fifteenth Amendments.[7] Those amendments conferred citizenship on previously enslaved persons and barred state or federal restrictions on voting based on race, color, and previous condition of servitude.

Inspired by Reva Siegel's article, "She the People: The Nineteenth Amendment, Sex Equality, Federalism and the Family," this book examines the meaning and scope of the Nineteenth Amendment in the decade after its ratification. It traces the journey of the Nineteenth Amendment through the federal and state courts, and the fate of its pending enforcement legislation in Congress. The chapters highlight how the amendment implicated three areas of constitutional import: federalism, the scope of women's citizenship, and the constitutional meaning of equality. In the book, I argue that the Nineteenth Amendment represented an important moment in American history that held the promise of significant change in the political, civil, and social status of women in our republic. However, what emerged from a decade of contestation was a "thin" rather than a robust conception of the Nineteenth Amendment's constitutional meaning.

The post-ratification story of the Nineteenth Amendment presents a puzzle as to why its impact on women's equal citizenship was so limited. Drawing on original historical sources, legal scholarship, and case analysis, the book illuminates a piece of that puzzle and highlights how the meaning of the amendment was shaped by the intersection of race, gender, and class. While Congress and the courts are significant sites of constitutional interpretation, social movements within civil society play important roles as well. Through their efforts to enfranchise American women, suffragists assumed that role. Yet, they made strategic choices post-ratification that took them away from the Nineteenth Amendment as a focus of energy and resources. That pivot meant that there was a less consistent, unified pressure on state courts as they parsed the corollary legal questions that arose in the wake of ratification. Those questions included the extent of the Nineteenth Amendment's impact on state law regulating obstacles to voting like poll taxes, as well as political rights like jury service and holding public office. There was a similar absence of unified pressure on Congress to enact enforcement legislation under the Nineteenth Amendment, as well as an acrimonious split in the former suffrage movement over the Equal Rights Amendment (ERA). Exploring this history helps us understand the puzzle as to why the Nineteenth Amendment did not develop a more robust, or "thick," constitutional meaning in the decade after its ratification.

The book focuses on the role suffragists played in this multi-institutional puzzle, including the strategic choices made by two national suffrage organizations, NAWSA and the NWP, post-ratification.[8] The NWP played a central role in the final passage of this sweeping federal ban on sex-based discrimination in voting. But the NWP pivoted as soon as it secured this protection for women to vote in all state and federal elections. In early 1921, the NWP essentially disbanded and reconstituted itself with a new mission. No longer focused on the singular purpose of achieving a federal amendment securing suffrage, it chose a much broader mission, "adopting a program to remove all remaining forms of the subjection of women."[9]

Similarly, NAWSA ceased its active operations in 1920, after being instrumental in achieving ratification of the Nineteenth Amendment. In February 1920, NAWSA established the National League of Women Voters (NLWV) as a successor organization.[10] The NLWV shifted the focus of its former suffragist members to voter education and advocacy for progressive social welfare legislation like the Sheppard-Towner Act, which provided federal funding for maternal and child health.

Immediately after ratification, both national suffrage organizations continued to put time and money into the federal cases that involved challenges to the validity of the Nineteenth Amendment and its pending enforcement legislation. But outside of those cases, the NWP and NAWSA (as the NLWV), turned their resources to other issues. This shift in goals did not mean that they ceased to advocate for reform that improved the lives of American women. They did not. But by easing up on the pressure for Congress to enforce the amendment, they played a part in leaving a vacuum around the Nineteenth Amendment. It developed in state courts untethered by much, if any, federal enforcement or civil rights legislation. Few, if any, courts analyzed the relationship between the Nineteenth and Fourteenth Amendments in the decade following ratification. And the Nineteenth Amendment became a constitutional orphan in American jurisprudence, cited substantively by only a handful of federal and state courts over the course of almost one hundred years.[11]

The post-ratification story of the Nineteenth Amendment implicates larger, philosophical issues like the relationship between the individual and the state. In the pages that follow, I identify three areas in which the Nineteenth Amendment had an impact, albeit perhaps not as great an impact as it might have had. The first was federalism. The role of the national government in state issues like the general taxing power, voter eligibility criteria, and other political rights, such as juror eligibility and the right to hold public office, were all implicated by ratification of the Nineteenth Amendment. The precise boundary lines between federal and state sovereignty in these areas were at the very heart of the state and federal litigation that followed ratification of the Nineteenth Amendment. Federal constitutional amendments, constructed like the Nineteenth, were generally presumed to be "self-executing" as a legal matter, and were seen as preemptive of contrary state laws or constitutional provisions. But there were widely disparate state court approaches to construction of the Nineteenth Amendment. Some courts adopted an expansive view of the Nineteenth Amendment, deciding that other political rights like jury service were "coextensive" with voting. Perhaps fearing the broad social change the Nineteenth Amendment might signal in the role of women, or its political impact on state sovereignty, other courts cabined the impact of the Nineteenth by adopting a constrictive interpretation of its scope, declaring it narrowly applicable to the ballot only.

The membership of the NWP included a number of experienced women lawyers, like social feminist Florence Kelley, head of the National Consumers League (NCL), who had deep roots in strategic, test case litigation around protective legislation for women workers. And both the NWP and NAWSA had an extensive political infrastructure, developed over decades of successful lobbying of Congress and state legislatures. Both suffrage organizations, and their successor organizations, could have chosen to work more closely with the National Association for the Advancement of Colored People (NAACP) and the National Association of Colored Women (NACW) to push enforcement legislation out of Congress and challenge the barriers to African American women voting in southern states after ratification. The implementation of such enforcement legislation could have provided a federal forum for courts to interpret the Nineteenth Amendment in a way that gave it a more robust meaning, extending it beyond a mere non-discrimination rule governing voting.[12] Enforcement legislation enacted pursuant to the Fourteenth and the Fifteenth Amendments gave federal courts the opportunity in cases like *Strauder v. West Virginia* and *Neal v. State of Delaware* to parse congressional intent around jury service.[13] Similar enforcement legislation, enacted pursuant to the Nineteenth Amendment, would have allowed for more federal court litigation and, consequently, more interpretation of specific congressional intent around the Nineteenth. And such federal litigation might have engendered more judicial consideration of the relationship between the Nineteenth, the Fourteenth and the Fifteenth Amendments, providing more extensive judicial insight with which to reason about the civil, political, and legal rights of women.

The pervasive concerns of many white southern suffragists about states' rights and extending the vote to African American women played a role in truncating the development of the Nineteenth Amendment. As always, race, gender, and class have a significant impact on how law develops. The Nineteenth Amendment was no different, with race and the legacy of the Civil War playing a central role in its constitutional development. Southern states' resistance to giving women the vote was, in large part, connected to the perceived risk of enforcement legislation, akin to that enacted in the wake of ratification of the Fourteenth and Fifteenth Amendments, and its potential to lead to a "Second Reconstruction."[14]

Second, the Nineteenth Amendment implicated the scope of women's citizenship under the federal Constitution. The state cases described earlier, which sought a resolution as to how far the Nineteenth Amendment extended into state control of jury service eligibility and the right to hold public office, implicated more than federalism. They determined how the Nineteenth Amendment would affect the scope of women's citizenship. Some state courts determined that the Nineteenth Amendment meant that women must be allowed to serve on juries and hold public office, while others used strict statutory construction to limit women's place in the constitutional order, holding that voting was not coextensive with jury service and holding public office. In so doing, social norms around separate spheres and institutional concerns about expanding women's political power continued to play a role in limiting women's citizenship.

Third, ratification of the Nineteenth Amendment implicated the definition of gender equality under the Constitution. In *Adkins v. Children's Hospital*, the United States Supreme Court invoked the Nineteenth Amendment when grappling with the constitutionality of protective labor legislation that regulated wages for women, but not for men.[15] This issue was informed not only by gender, but by class in the first decades of the twentieth century. Many professional and upper-class neutrality feminists tended to support formal equality and a *laissez-faire* view of the relationship between the State and the individual.[16] Such a view favored limitations on the government's power to intrude into spheres like the employer-employee relationship. Those feminists saw protective legislation as a civil rights issue, in that such legislation limited a woman's liberty to contract for her labor. Alternatively, other upper-class social feminists and working-class women tended to embrace government intervention in such relationships, supporting laws that required minimum wages and maximum hours. Judges embracing a *laissez-faire* approach were more likely to find unconstitutional those governmental regulations that interfered with or limited an individual's right to negotiate a wage contract with an employer.[17]

Much of the debate between the neutrality feminists and the social feminists split along these lines. It was focused on the potential impact of the proposed ERA on the validity of protective legislation. Today's courts are still grappling with how they should interpret statutes that protect against sex discrimination in the workplace, for example, when the case involves differential treatment based on pregnancy.[18] These cases raise the question of whether courts should apply law as if men and women are the same (a neutrality view) or different (acknowledging that effectuating women's equality in the workplace may actually require different treatment of pregnant women).[19] This neutrality versus difference debate about the meaning of constitutional equality was at the heart of the battle for and against the ERA. The neutrality feminists' battle with social feminists and legal progressives, who opposed the ERA, distracted either side from extensive involvement in the post-ratification development of the Nineteenth Amendment. And social feminists would have been wary of a robust view of the Nineteenth Amendment, given the *Adkins* court's invocation of the amendment in striking down protective legislation.

We still have no federal equal rights amendment today. In her seminal article, "She the People: The Nineteenth Amendment, Sex Equality, Federalism and the Family," Reva Siegel notes that "[m]odern sex discrimination doctrine is built on this 'thin' conception of the Nineteenth Amendment—on the assumption that the Nineteenth Amendment is a nondiscrimination rule governing voting that has no bearing on questions of equal citizenship for women outside the franchise."[20] Siegel goes on to describe the US Supreme Court's approach to sex discrimination doctrine as one that ignores the constitutional history embodied in the debates leading up to ratification of the Nineteenth Amendment. She suggests that the court's reliance on the Fourteenth Amendment alone signals a view that the source of constitutional law governing the scope of women's citizenship is derived solely from an analogy to race. Siegel concludes that "[t]hese assumptions have given rise to a body of sex discrimination doctrine that is limited in legitimacy and acuity by the ahistorical manner in which it was derived from the law of race discrimination."[21]

This book offers an account of *how* that thin conception of the Nineteenth Amendment emerged and the role that suffragists played in that process. With Congress, state legislatures, and state and federal courts important sites of constitutional enforcement and interpretation, the suffrage movement faced powerful patriarchal agents that were, as a matter of institutional self-interest, likely to be inclined to limit the impact of women's enfranchisement.[22] Even if former suffragists had been more engaged in applying pressure to develop an expansive meaning of the Nineteenth Amendment, it is unlikely that a more robust interpretation would have emerged from such entrenched institutions, until it was expedient for them to embrace one.[23] But the choice made by the suffragists who secured ratification of the Nineteenth Amendment—to turn away from both lobbying for enforcement legislation and engaging in litigation that might have deepened its meaning as law—played an important role in the thin conception that emerged in subsequent years. As Vicki Schultz has pointed out in the context of Title VII, when activists stop advocating, at best, the law fails to develop and; at worst, it develops in a counterproductive way: "In areas of law where feminists did not campaign to challenge difference, or where they later took a less decisive or divided stance as the women's movement began to fade and fracture, the absence of visible, unified feminist pressure permitted judges to retain or retreat back to older, biased views that attribute workplace inequality to women's own preferences."[24] Schultz suggests that it is therefore important to examine "not only the influence of a social movement overall, but also the rise of internal divisions *within* the movement and changes in its presence, visibility, and strength over time, in shaping legal developments."[25] Thus, this book also explores the post-ratification divisions between the neutrality feminists and the social feminists, and what role those divisions played in the constitutional development of the Nineteenth Amendment.

The book concludes by suggesting some of the ways that the Nineteenth could be used either directly, or synthetically with the Fourteenth Amendment, to reason differently about current cases involving sex discrimination and women's equal citizenship.[26] Given the uncertainty about the status of the ERA, revisiting the potential of the Nineteenth Amendment can shed light on how we may better secure women's constitutional equality today.

Organization

The book proceeds in eight chapters. Chapter 1, "Ratification," examines the role of two national suffrage organizations, the NWP and NAWSA, in the final years leading up to ratification of the Nineteenth Amendment in 1920. This account highlights the strategic and tactical differences between the organizations and the women who led them. The major difference was adopting a state-by-state approach to enacting suffrage versus a federal amendment. This difference was papered over when NAWSA changed its position in 1916 and joined in the call for a federal amendment. But the acrimony between the organizations' leaders remained deep in the decade after ratification of the Nineteenth Amendment.

Chapter 2, "Validity," describes how each group disbanded as soon as the Nineteenth Amendment was ratified and reinvented themselves as the new NWP and the NLWV. Debates within the new organizations, focused on their new missions, tell us much about why the former suffragists moved away from the Nineteenth Amendment. The chapter analyzes the cases challenging the validity of the Nineteenth Amendment, *Leser v. Garnett* and *Fairchild v. Hughes*, which were pursued by lawyers committed to a states' rights philosophy.[27] Rejecting the concept of an "unconstitutional constitutional amendment," both state and federal courts upheld the legitimacy of the amendment.

Chapter 3, "Enforcement Legislation," offers an account of the failure of Congress to enact enforcement legislation pursuant to section two of the Nineteenth Amendment. The lack of enforcement legislation makes the Nineteenth different in structure and effect than the Fifteenth Amendment, even though the text of both amendments is virtually the same. The NWP was instrumental in having enforcement legislation introduced into Congress in December 1920. But such legislation raised the specter of a Second Reconstruction among white southerners. White southern suffragists and politicians pushed back hard on possible enforcement legislation, as they had against inclusion of the enforcement clause of the Nineteenth Amendment prior to its enactment. While the NWP's initial support for the enforcement legislation was public and strong, within six months the organization had effectively walked away from lobbying for its passage. Both the NWP and NAWSA failed to respond to the post-ratification requests of African American suffragists, like Ida B. Wells-Barnett and Mary Church Terrell, to help combat voter suppression in the South. The chapter suggests that the NWP's perceived need for white southern votes, both in Congress and state legislatures, for its new mission—passage of an equal rights amendment and reform of state legislation discriminating against women—helps explain why its strong support for enforcement legislation faded. But without such legislation, state courts were left to interpret the scope of the Nineteenth Amendment without specific federal legislation defining that scope. And no broader federal judicial forum was created to parse questions like which political rights, beyond voting, should be included within its scope.

Chapter 4, "A Self-Executing Amendment," examines federalism in the context of state cases brought in the decade after ratification. These cases determined the impact of the Nineteenth Amendment on state constitutional and legislative doctrine, such as the right to impose poll taxes as a condition of voting. They shed light on how those courts viewed what it meant for an amendment to be "self-executing," and how much a federal amendment could intrude upon or alter state law.

Chapter 5, "Voting and Jury Service," evaluates how those same state courts assessed whether voting was "coextensive" with jury service. These cases had an impact on whether the Nineteenth Amendment would expand the scope of women's citizenship beyond the partialized version that had existed prior to ratification. Similarly, Chapter 6, "Voting and Holding Public Office," explores how state courts interpreted the impact of the Nineteenth Amendment on their own state constitutions and legislation governing who was eligible to run for and hold public office. Chapters 5 and 6 explore the scope of women's citizenship and their place in the constitutional order. The case analysis in these chapters illustrates what we mean by the thin conception of the Nineteenth Amendment. If voting was understood to be the apex of political rights, why did some state courts find that other political rights, like serving on a jury and holding public office, were not automatically extended to women upon its ratification? Some state courts did construe their constitutional provisions and statutes expansively in light of the passage of the federal suffrage amendment. But others used statutory interpretation to cabin the impact of the federal amendment on state law. In the wake of the Civil War, Congress enacted enforcement legislation pursuant to the Fourteenth and Fifteenth Amendments. That legislation provided for criminal penalties if local officials prevented citizens from serving on juries or holding public office, based on their race, color, or previous condition of servitude. In the absence of similar legislation pursuant to the Nineteenth Amendment, state courts were left on their own to parse whether Congress intended the Nineteenth Amendment to extend to political rights beyond voting. And the NWP and the NLWV did not play a significant role in most of these state cases, at least until the end of the decade.[28]

In Chapter 7, "Defining Equality," the book examines the Nineteenth Amendment's impact on the constitutional meaning of gender equality. After ratification, the NWP turned to drafting an equal rights amendment. It faced opposition from social feminists and legal progressives concerned about the impact such an amendment might have on the constitutional validity of protective legislation. In 1923, the US Supreme Court's decision in *Adkins v. Children's Hospital* invoked the Nineteenth Amendment, as it struck down minimum wage legislation for women under the Fifth Amendment's due process clause. One of the few cases to link the Nineteenth Amendment to other constitutional provisions, *Adkins* signaled the high water mark for a thicker understanding of the Nineteenth as an amendment that had an impact on other constitutional doctrine.[29] Later cases retreated from such an understanding and a thin conception prevailed by the end of the decade.

Chapter 8, "The Nineteenth Amendment Today," proposes that a thicker understanding of the Nineteenth could be used, either directly or synthetically with the Fourteenth and Fifteenth Amendments, to further women's equality today. It reviews new scholarship suggesting more robust direct applications of the amendment to voting rights, including enactment of enforcement legislation by Congress. And it describes how scholars have argued that the Nineteenth Amendment should be read synthetically with other amendments to extend congressional authority over areas of law beyond voting rights. Given the current uncertainty about the validity of the ERA, the chapter suggests that the Nineteenth Amendment can be revitalized as a constitutional tool to better secure women's equality today.

1

Ratification

Never say Die. We are the People.
——Letter from Louise McKay to Alice Paul (August 22, 1920)

Immediately after ratification of the Nineteenth Amendment, letters and telegrams poured into the headquarters of the major suffrage organizations. The letter from Louise McKay quoted above reflected the belief of many American women that their status in the constitutional order had undergone a fundamental change.[1] They had become more fully part of "the People" as described in the Preamble to the United States Constitution, in that they now had a direct relationship with the government established thereunder. Those letters also reflected another truth. That change in women's citizenship had been won after a long battle, and at a significant price. In a heartfelt letter to Alice Paul on August 20, 1920, J. E. Milholland captured the sentiments of many Americans upon hearing the news that the seventy-two-year-old struggle for woman suffrage was over when he wrote, "You suffered personal violence . . . Punishment, humiliating attacks and disgraceful imprisonment only made you stronger and more daring. I congratulate you one and all. Every honor to you!"[2] Tennessee, the final state needed for ratification, had voted in favor of the Nineteenth Amendment to the US Constitution two days before Milholland wrote to Paul. Milholland continued to laud Paul's NWP members in his letter, writing "a braver body of Women never engaged upon any crusade in the whole history of civilization."[3] The quest for suffrage required such courage, in large part, because it threatened the existing social order and raised the specter of a democratic reconstruction of the family.[4] The venerable *New York Times* characterized women's suffrage as "repugnant to instincts that strike their roots deep in the order of nature," and as a development that would " 'derange' the social and political structure" of the nation.[5] The NWP and NAWSA, along with organizations like the NACW, had challenged that national social and political structure in their suffrage

Constitutional Orphan. Paula A. Monopoli, Oxford University Press (2020). © Paula A. Monopoli.
DOI: 10.1093/oso/9780190092795.001.0001

campaigns. And those organizations had brought the battle for the vote to a successful close with ratification of a federal amendment, prohibiting the states and the federal government from barring them from voting based solely on their sex. Or so they thought.

Why suffrage?[6] What did the vote mean to these generations of women who lectured in the public sphere when such behavior was derided as outside the bounds of acceptable behavior, who testified before congressional committees when the male legislators "yawned and read newspapers," and who traveled endless miles across the United States to persuade state legislators and voters to embrace woman suffrage? As the apex of political rights in a representative democracy, the vote was the gateway to the broader social and economic freedom these women sought to unlock. If consent of the governed was the hallmark of republican government, then withholding the right to vote for one's representatives contravened the social compact on which the nation had been founded. And suffragists believed that social and economic equality would flow from exercising that political right.[7]

Over the course of the nineteenth century, the broad women's rights movement in the United States narrowed as it evolved into the woman suffrage movement. This occurred as activists began to argue that the vote was the key to securing equal rights and creating better lives for women through legislation. They adopted the view that equality within the family and society as a whole required the political clout to unseat politicians who refused to reform laws that reified the subordination of women. Laws that governed marriage and divorce, the right to contract, and property rights needed to be changed. New laws protecting equal pay for equal work and ensuring civil and political rights, like jury service and holding public office, needed to be passed. Suffragists believed that the power of the vote could be wielded to force such legislative reform. And they believed that legal reform would translate into a change in the social order, where gender norms about the proper role of women kept them subordinated within the family, out of the public sphere, and outside of the professions in any meaningful way. Note that suffragists were not all aligned, and the movement was not a monolith. They diverged in their views of what equality meant, and in terms of their arguments in favor of the vote. Some suffragists made political arguments about the hypocrisy of a republican government denying half the adult population the central instrument of the vote. Others emphasized the fact that women voting would bring a higher moral sensibility to law and society. And some did both.[8]

Along the path, there were grave injustices perpetrated by white suffragists against African American suffragists, as well as virulent racist and nativist arguments made against black men and male immigrants for why educated white women deserved the vote more than they did. Despite these significant moral failings of the leading suffragists, the movement saw women from disparate classes, races, and religions focused on a singular purpose—securing the right to vote in all state and federal elections. Though their ideologies and strategies diverged, with some following a state-by-state approach and others a federal amendment that would sweep away state limitations at once, the belief that political liberty lay in the franchise was shared by all. This commonality of purpose held the movement together long enough to achieve victory in 1920. But those divisions quickly reappeared after ratification of the Nineteenth Amendment and, as later chapters describe, they blunted the potential impact the Nineteenth Amendment might have had on constitutional doctrines like federalism, women's citizenship, and equality norms.

The history of the organized woman suffrage movement in the United States is traditionally dated from 1848, when Lucretia Mott and Elizabeth Cady Stanton convened a group of activists in Seneca Falls, New York.[9] That convention produced the Declaration of Sentiments, a document modeled on the Declaration of Independence, which called for a panoply of reforms to laws that disadvantaged women, as well as the right to vote. Asking for the vote was heavily contested by many of those attending the convention as far too radical. And the motion to include it in the Declaration of Sentiments passed by only a narrow margin.[10]

In the years that followed Seneca Falls, there were several more conventions, including one in Worcester, Massachusetts, in 1850. Much of the energy of women like Stanton, Lucy Stone, Susan B. Anthony, and African American suffragists like Sojourner Truth after 1850 and before the Civil War was focused on abolition and the woman's rights movement. Those efforts lay dormant during the war years. After the war, these women hit the lecture circuit for woman suffrage and pushed for women to be included in two of the three amendments that constituted the Reconstruction Amendments, the Thirteenth, Fourteenth, and Fifteenth Amendments. Together, these amendments held the potential for sweeping change in the constitutional order. The Thirteenth Amendment (1865) outlawed slavery, the Fourteenth Amendment (1868) guaranteed equal application of the law and due process for all citizens. And the Fifteenth Amendment (1870) prohibited the states and the federal government from preventing citizens from voting based on race, color, or previous condition of servitude.

Stone, Stanton, and Anthony lobbied Congress to include women in the Fourteenth and the Fifteenth Amendments to no avail. Along the way, Stanton and Anthony split with Stone over the Fifteenth Amendment. A long-time abolitionist, Stone supported the amendment. While Stone hoped that woman suffrage would be included, she continued to support the Fifteenth Amendment even when it became clear that sex would not be one of the prohibited criteria in determining voter eligibility. In contrast, Stanton and Anthony vehemently opposed the Fifteenth Amendment when the final version did not include sex but rather only race, color, and previous condition of servitude as prohibited voting criteria, thus enfranchising African American men but not white women—nor African American women. In 1869, Stanton and Anthony split with Stone. Stone and Julia Ward Howe formed the American Woman Suffrage Association (AWSA), while Stanton and Anthony formed the National Woman Suffrage Association (NWSA).[11]

After failing to persuade Congress to include women in the Fourteenth and Fifteenth Amendments, and after the United States Supreme Court refused to construe the Fourteenth Amendment to include women, Stanton and Anthony eventually turned to advocating for a Sixteenth Amendment. That amendment was modeled on the Fifteenth Amendment, and it would have barred the states and the federal government from denying women the vote based solely on their sex. This shift away from their efforts to include women in the Reconstruction Amendments, toward lobbying for Congress to enact a separate amendment to ensure women the vote, produced the earliest textual version of what was to become known as the "Susan B. Anthony Amendment" in 1920—the Nineteenth Amendment to the US Constitution.[12]

Establishing the criteria for who is eligible to vote in both state and federal elections is a power generally left to the states as a constitutional matter. The Fourteenth and Fifteenth Amendments intruded on that authority by prohibiting states from abridging the right to vote based on race, color, or previous condition of servitude; and punishing states that did so with a reduction in congressional representation. But the constitutional authority to set other conditions of voting, like sex, poll taxes, and literacy tests remained in the hands of the states in the wake of the Reconstruction Amendments. So while NWSA pursued a federal suffrage amendment like the Fifteenth Amendment, AWSA pursued a state-by-state strategy. AWSA hoped that each state that granted woman suffrage would add new electors to the rolls. Their voting power to unseat incumbents could be used as leverage to push Congress to adopt a suffrage amendment. But that strategy proved to be very slow. Only four states in the West had enacted full suffrage for women by the end of the nineteenth century.[13] These states included Wyoming (1869), Colorado (1893), Utah (1896), and Idaho (1896). That trend came to a halt in 1896, and it would be another fourteen years before another state extended the franchise to women.[14] By that time, the NWSA and the AWSA had merged into a single, national suffrage organization, NAWSA, in 1890.

In 1896, Mary Church Terrell and Ida B. Wells-Barnett founded the NACW. Terrell served as its first president. The NACW was formed to advocate for a wide range of reforms, including the abolition of Jim Crow laws in the South that enshrined second-class citizenship for African Americans in state law. In addition to these reforms, the NACW advocated for woman suffrage.[15] Their efforts, detailed in later chapters, were a significant part of the overall suffrage movement, activating women in a variety of cities to push for the right to vote as a means to alleviating not only gender but racial subordination. While African American men had achieved the right to vote under the Fifteenth Amendment in 1870, state law and practice had essentially blocked them from exercising that right. Impediments like poll taxes, literacy tests, and so-called grandfather clauses had effectively deprived them of the ability to cast a ballot. The NACW's efforts to organize support for universal suffrage lent much needed heft to the work of NAWSA. Despite this help from the NACW and similar groups, some white suffragists used racial fearmongering—especially in the southern states—as a means to push white men into voting for suffrage. The shockingly overt public discourse around making southern politicians feel that woman suffrage would benefit them reveals some members of NAWSA's strategy in this regard. They stressed that white women voters would "neutralize" African American voters and maintain the regime of white supremacy. If white women could vote, they could support the continued states' rights policies that prevented African American men from voting. The racism inherent in these arguments was manifested in white suffragists' refusal to allow African American suffragists a seat at the table, barring them from speaking at, or even attending, meetings and conventions. This racial exclusion continued throughout the suffrage campaign and beyond.[16] And as later chapters lay out, it was not only a moral failing but a strategic one as well.

The failure of white suffragists to heed the calls of African American suffragists to help strike down poll taxes and literacy tests, and to enforce the Nineteenth Amendment after ratification, was a missed constitutional opportunity. Such action offered the chance to strengthen the power and impact of the Nineteenth Amendment, as a matter of federalism. But the NWP's perceived need for white southern political support for a new equal rights amendment, and state legislation abolishing sex-based discrimination, helps explain how that opportunity was missed.

Susan B. Anthony was the first suffragist to lead NAWSA in 1890. Anthony was followed by Carrie Chapman Catt in 1900 and Anna Howard Shaw in 1904. Catt succeeded Shaw again from 1915–1920. Twenty-five-year-old Alice Paul, already well known for being arrested and jailed in England for her suffrage work, became involved in NAWSA in 1910, when she returned from England and was invited to give a lecture to the local Philadelphia chapter.[17]

Paul was the daughter of devout Quakers, William Paul and Tacie Parry Paul. She was born in Mt. Laurel Township, New Jersey, in 1885. Just thirty-five years old when she engineered one of the most significant constitutional reforms in American history, Paul had long fought for suffrage. After graduating from Swarthmore, working as a social worker in New York City and earning a master's degree in sociology at the University of Pennsylvania, Paul traveled to England in 1907 to study at a Quaker institution in Birmingham.[18] While in England, Paul became involved with Emmeline Pankhurst and the militant British "suffragettes" of the time.[19] Her attraction to equal rights for women was not surprising, given her Quaker background. The Quaker tradition had long included a commitment to women's equality:

> At sessions held every two weeks in most congregations, women discussed church accounts and records, philanthropic efforts, and the proper behavior of members . . . Women also became traveling ministers, going out to faraway sites to interact with established groups and to form new meetings, often at great physical risk . . . This women's rights tradition within Quakerism, so influential to Alice Paul, had flourished in the United States from the colonial period.[20]

Repeatedly jailed, Paul's activities made the American papers. On learning that Paul had been arrested, her uncle Mickle invoked their Quaker ancestors, who had been jailed for their refusal to pay taxes to support a militia. Mickle wrote to Paul's mother, "It is cause for pride to find that there is yet the spirit of progress [and] independent thought and individual responsibility that marked the family in earlier days still in the head and heart of one of its members." But Mickle added that he hoped that Paul would "return home."[21] Tacie Paul pled with Emmeline's daughter, Christabel Pankhurst, to encourage Paul to come home as well when she was released.[22]

Paul did eventually return to the United States, where she began suffrage work with NAWSA, the largest national woman suffrage organization of the time, in 1910. In 1912, Paul was named chair of NAWSA's congressional committee and moved to Washington, DC, with her friend Lucy Burns, to lobby Congress for a federal amendment.[23] The committee grew into the Congressional Union in 1913, which in turn became an independent organization in 1914, when Paul broke with NAWSA over making the organization's top priority a federal constitutional amendment granting women the right to vote.[24] At that point, NAWSA was still focused on a state-by-state strategy, hoping to build up support among federal legislators as more states gave women the vote. But Paul was impatient. She had seen the militancy of the Pankhursts and their Women's Social and Political Union (WSPU). Paul was inclined to use similar tactics: tactics that NAWSA thought were counterproductive, to say the least.[25]

In the push for a federal amendment, the Congressional Union became the National Woman's Party (NWP) in 1916.[26] With Paul as its chair, it developed a strategy of nonviolent picketing of the White House and President Woodrow Wilson. Derided as anti-patriotic for continuing the pickets even after the nation had entered World War I, Paul and many other well-connected picketers were jailed at Virginia's Occoquan Workhouse and Washington's District Jail, where they protested with hunger strikes and were subsequently force-fed. In the face of growing public alarm at the manner in which these middle- and upper-class women were being treated, Wilson finally changed his anti-federal amendment stance in 1918 and threw his weight behind the proposed suffrage amendment in Congress. On June 4, 1919, the bill passed both houses and it went to the states for ratification. Tennessee was the thirty-sixth state to ratify on August 18, 1920, giving the legislation the requisite three-fourths of the states for ratification. On August 26, 1920, US Secretary of State Bainbridge Colby certified the ratification, and the Nineteenth Amendment became law.[27]

NAWSA's long battle for woman suffrage predated the NWP's fairly late entry into the fight. Although it chose a more conciliatory approach to

Wilson and congressional leaders, its efforts, too, were central to passage and ratification of the Nineteenth Amendment. NAWSA's leader, Carrie Lane Chapman Catt, was born in Wisconsin in 1859, many years before Alice Paul. She was raised on a farm in Iowa and became a teacher and then a superintendent of schools in Mason City, Iowa. Catt had begun the study of law but broke off when she received a well-paid offer to teach. She met and married her first husband, Leo Chapman, in Mason City in 1885, and together they edited the newspaper he owned there. Five years after losing Chapman to an untimely death, Carrie Lane Chapman married George W. Catt in 1890. Carrie Chapman Catt was a powerful speaker and an exceptional organizer. Her skills caught the attention of Susan B. Anthony, and Catt became one of a group of young suffragists who were central to the operation of Anthony's NAWSA. When an elderly Anthony stepped down as the president of NAWSA in 1890, she handed the reins to Catt.[28]

As the two-time president of NAWSA (Catt had to step down the first time to care for her ailing second husband), Catt "reorganized the suffrage forces on election district lines, giving political structure to the movement . . . Two million organized women took part under Mrs. Catt's direction in the National American Woman Suffrage Association."[29] Over the years, NAWSA had rejected calls to lobby directly for a federal amendment, choosing to pursue a state-by-state strategy that appeased many of NAWSA's most prominent white southern members. The state-by-state strategy was acceptable to white southerners because it was grounded in a vision of federalism that reserved significant sovereignty to the states. That states' rights approach to constitutional issues was particularly salient when it came to voting. As noted earlier, the Constitution reserves to the states the power to set eligibility criteria for voting—for both state and federal elections. The legacy of the Reconstruction Amendments was to intrude on that explicitly reserved power via federal constitutional amendments. The Fourteenth and the Fifteenth Amendments explicitly limited state control of voter eligibility criteria, and that intrusion was anathema to white southern suffragists. NAWSA leaders also felt that it was particularly problematic to those white southern politicians whose votes were needed to achieve woman suffrage. Thus, the strategy of moving slowly, state by state, was, in part, to keep white southern suffragists and politicians in the fold. NAWSA's adherence to this strategy persisted well into the second decade of the twentieth century.

But by 1916, when Catt took over a second time as president, she pivoted from NAWSA's previous state-by-state strategy to a focused push for the federal amendment, "ending [NAWSA's] long period of almost exclusive concentration on the states." Catt's new strategic approach was dubbed the "Winning Plan" and was submitted to NAWSA members at the group's 1916 convention.[30] This shift in NAWSA's focus put the two national suffrage organizations on the same path. While Paul and Catt remained personally antagonistic toward each other, they shared a common goal—full suffrage for American women. And NAWSA's shift toward a federal amendment likely accelerated the fulfillment of that goal in 1920.

After ratification in 1920, NAWSA "ceased operations," and its successor, the NLWV, had a different goal: educating voters and pursuing progressive legislation. Similarly, the NWP disbanded at its February 1921 convention and reconstituted itself with a new mission, the elimination of all legal disabilities for women. Both groups monitored and put resources into defending post-ratification legal challenges to the validity of the Nineteenth Amendment. Those efforts were successful and the United States Supreme Court upheld the validity of the Nineteenth Amendment in *Leser v. Garnett* in 1922.[31] The hard work around the Nineteenth Amendment seemed to be done. The following chapters trace the constitutional development of the Nineteenth Amendment that began as soon as ratification was complete and continued throughout the decade following ratification. That decade saw bitter philosophical and political divides among former suffragists that affected its development, including debates about what equality meant, whether to help African American women in the south actually vote, how expansively state courts should interpret the text of the Nineteenth Amendment, and whether to lobby for legislation that would flesh out the bare bones of the amendment. As a constitutional amendment, the Nineteenth emerged from the decade after its ratification undertheorized and rarely cited in American jurisprudence. And its underlying history has disappeared from our collective constitutional consciousness. The following chapters help illuminate the puzzle as to how that occurred and the role of two national suffrage organizations in that puzzle.

2

Validity

[The Nineteenth Amendment] brings another class of citizens
within the reach of the prohibition against discrimination on the
part of the states or of the United States in conferring suffrage.
If . . . the Fifteenth Amendment was a valid exercise of the amending
power, it is impossible to conceive that the Nineteenth Amendment
was not likewise a valid exercise of that power, because it is not possible to distinguish the two in principle.
                    —Leser v. Garnett (Maryland Court of Appeals 1921)

Legal challenges to the validity of the Nineteenth Amendment came immediately in the wake of ratification.[1] NAWSA and the NWP closely monitored this litigation. At the same time, both groups began to debate what they
should do, now that the goal of woman suffrage had been achieved. Their
mission as suffrage organizations—to ensure the franchise for women in
every state—was now seemingly obsolete. Those internal debates, which reflected philosophical, ideological, and cultural divides in the broader society,
foreshadowed three significant constitutional questions the amendment was
to raise in the decade of litigation that followed. Shaped by race, gender, and
class, those debates implicated (1) the balance of power between the federal
and state governments, (2) the scope of women's citizenship, and (3) the constitutional meaning of equality. Those three areas proved to be the terrain
upon which the meaning and scope of the Nineteenth was parsed in federal
and state courts post-ratification.

The year that followed ratification saw the NWP debate whether it should
completely disband now that suffrage had been achieved or whether it
should reconstitute itself with a new mission. Its February 1921 convention was a pivotal moment in that sense, one that was to have a significant
impact on the eventual interpretation of the Nineteenth Amendment.[2]
Similarly, NAWSA wound down operations and established a successor

Constitutional Orphan. Paula A. Monopoli, Oxford University Press (2020). © Paula A. Monopoli.
DOI: 10.1093/oso/9780190092795.001.0001

organization in February 1920, even before ratification was achieved.[3] While the national suffrage organizations remained actively involved in the initial litigation around the validity of the Nineteenth Amendment, like *Leser v. Garnett* and its companion case, *Fairchild v. Hughes*, neither national group appears to have been as involved in the state court litigation over the decade that followed.[4] That state court litigation put some flesh on the bare bones of the Nineteenth Amendment. And the task of interpreting the Nineteenth Amendment, and its relationship to other amendments like the Fourteenth and Fifteenth Amendments, was left to those state courts without much apparent unified pressure from national suffrage organizations to extend the vote to jury service, holding public office, and similar political rights.

State court judges held the power to cabin the meaning of the Nineteenth Amendment. Many of those judges presumably had concerns about the amendment's effect on women's role in the social order and its impact on state sovereignty. These fears had been expressed throughout the seventy-two years of collective American conversation about woman suffrage. For example, opponents of woman suffrage wrote books that equated woman suffrage with socialism, communism, and atheism and railed against its impact on the family.[5] Others wrote about suffragists as temptresses, who had been tainted by the serpent in the Garden of Eden, and who could only be redeemed by Christ.[6] Suffrage threatened to undermine carefully crafted narratives around female subordination.

At the time the Nineteenth Amendment was enacted, NAWSA claimed two million or so members around the country. Even before thirty-six states had ratified the Nineteenth Amendment, NAWSA chose to wind down operations as a suffrage organization and initiated plans for a successor organization, the National League of Women Voters (NLWV), at its "Jubilee Convention" in 1919.[7] The following year, Carrie Chapman Catt called the NAWSA state auxiliaries to order at the Congress Hotel in Chicago on February 13, 1920, at the "Victory Convention," which also served as the First National Congress of the NLWV.[8] Catt read a statement from President Woodrow Wilson, who wrote:

> Permit me to congratulate your Association upon the fact that its great work is so near its triumphant end that you can now merge it into a League of Women Voters to carry on the development of good citizenship and real democracy, and to wish for the new organization the same success and wise leadership.
>
> Woodrow Wilson[9]

Having previously formed a committee of NAWSA to begin planning for post-ratification issues, like educating citizens and supporting progressive legislation, Catt presided over both the NAWSA convention itself and over meetings of the NLWV during that week.[10] Without much apparent objection by state delegates, NAWSA voted to make the NLWV committee of NAWSA a permanent and separate successor organization to the parent organization. NAWSA itself would be wound down on a graduated schedule, allowing it to marshal resources needed for any remaining ratification litigation.[11]

The newly permanent NLWV passed a series of resolutions that week in February 1920, signaling its direction post-ratification. These resolutions ranged from endorsing federal legislation in the traditionally state realm of marriage and divorce to citizenship schools designed to better educate women and men about their civic duty.[12] Supporting federal intrusion into the state realm implicated issues of federalism. The NLWV committees included a committee on Women and Industry, which reported out specific support for minimum wage and maximum hour laws. That kind of protective legislation had long been contested in the nation's courts and at its dinner tables. It implicated the long-contested view of what the Constitution promised—neutrality or substantive equality.

After the Victory Convention, Catt turned her attention back to the organization she had founded to secure woman suffrage around the world, the International Woman Suffrage Alliance (IWSA). She also focused on the larger question of world peace in the wake of a horrific war in Europe. Catt reasoned that now that women could vote, they should turn that political power to improving the lot of all human beings by alleviating the severe suffering caused by war.[13]

Six months after the NAWSA convention, in the immediate aftermath of ratification, the question for Alice Paul and the NWP was the twelve-thousand-dollar debt the NWP had incurred in its final push for ratification.[14] But a longer term question was also on her mind—the future of the NWP. On August 28, 1920, Paul wrote a letter to a supporter seeking contributions to offset the debt:

> As soon as all the bills are paid and all litigation disposed of, we shall hold our final convention at which the work will be formally brought to an end. At this convention it will be decided whether the Woman's Party shall

disband or whether it shall take up a new program for the welfare of women and continue as a permanent organization.[15]

The days that followed that letter in August 1920 until February 1921, when that convention finally took place, were pivotal.[16] During this time, the women in the NWP had fierce debates about which direction the NWP should take now that the federal amendment had been ratified. In the months between ratification in August 1920 and the NWP convention in February 1921, Paul had a number of exchanges with her colleagues about whether the NWP should disband permanently or whether it should end as a suffrage organization and reconstitute itself as a new organization. The NWP's hierarchy included Paul as president, a national executive committee, a national advisory council, and state chairs for each state-level branch. Paul convened a meeting of the executive committee of the NWP on September 10, 1920 (less than a month after ratification) that included some members of the national advisory council and some state chairmen as guests of the executive committee. Paul first, "outlined the legal situation" and gave those assembled, "a summary of the five lawsuits attacking the validity of ratification that were pending . . ." The committee unanimously agreed to "continue to work in every line possible" for ratification.[17] Paul then opened the floor for a general discussion of the future of the party:

> While Doris Stevens took notes, some of the biggest names in feminism held forth. Alva Belmont favored a full-fledged political NWP, and Harriot [Stanton] Blatch . . . agreed that the world needed an independent feminist force. Author Charlotte Perkins Gilman spoke loftily of an organization with mass power and a flexible program in the hands of a NWP with brains. Socialist Crystal Eastman called for a feminist movement focused on education, freedom in occupational choice, and birth control.[18]

In that September 10, 1920, meeting, Paul argued for "equal rights for women, shaped by legislation at both the state and national levels."[19] She clearly intended that the convention bring together the women's groups who had helped lobby for the vote to create a new, unified movement with this as its focus. In furtherance of this goal, she invited dozens of women's groups and told them at the beginning of the convention that "We have called this convention together to close up the work connected with the suffrage campaign and to turn over to you the question of the next step." Paul indicated to those at the convention, "that their input would be crucial in determining whether the NWP would continue the battle for women's political equality along different lines or if it would disband."[20]

Given her comments during the September 1920 executive committee meeting, Paul clearly intended to push for some kind of federal legislation that would ensure what she called "equal rights" for women. In that phrase, lay the seeds of such legislation's eventual failure. There was no consensus about what "equal rights" meant. Did it mean that the state must adopt a "neutrality principle" when enacting and enforcing laws? In other words, did it mean a level playing field in terms of opportunity in the workforce and in civic life? Or did it mean that differences shouldered primarily by women, like childbearing and childrearing, should be accommodated by the state in order to give women a supportive workplace in which to earn a living wage? Where one came out on this philosophical debate about the meaning of equality was determined in large part by where one stood in society. Upper- and middle-class women stood to benefit most from the neutrality principle, while working-class (often immigrant) women arguably needed "protective" legislation that set minimum wages and maximum hours. Professional women often saw such protective legislation as a hindrance to women and their ability to work in certain industries that required long hours and night work. This intellectual split, and the infinite variety of possible goals for a new NWP, were reflected in the convention itself in February 1921. The impact of this split on the constitutional development of the Nineteenth Amendment is explored in depth in Chapter 7.

One of the most prominent advocates for protective legislation for women was lawyer Florence Kelley of the National Consumers League (NCL). Kelley was born in Philadelphia in 1859 to abolitionist and Congressman William Kelley and Caroline Bartram Bonsall. Kelley's mother's family also had Quaker connections. Kelley "[rose] from a researcher and resident at Chicago's Hull House to the powerful position of General Secretary of the NCL."[21] During her time at prominent social worker Jane Addams's Hull House, Kelley earned a law degree from Northwestern University in 1894. After moving to New York City in 1899, Kelley became one of the legal architects of a series of test cases to uphold the constitutionality of minimum wage and maximum hour legislation for women. Kelley was one of those who authored the famous Brandeis brief filed in *Muller v. Oregon*, working with Louis Brandeis and later Felix Frankfurter to enshrine such protective legislation in the American constitutional order.[22] Kelley was involved in the formation of Paul and Burns's Congressional Union, the precursor to the NWP. She was a member of the Union's national advisory council, formed when the Union broke with NAWSA in 1914.[23] Kelley was present at the NWP's national executive committee meeting when it met in 1920 to debate the future of the NWP after ratification. At the first meeting of the executive committee after ratification in September 1920, Kelley argued that the NWP had a "sublime opportunity to appeal to the conscience of all the women of the world," presumably by supporting legislation that protected women workers.[24]

As the NWP's leadership continued to meet in the months before the February 1921 convention, a second issue—continuing barriers to African American women voting—also surfaced. As discussed more fully in Chapter 3, "Enforcement Legislation," National Advisory Council member Mary White Ovington called on the NWP to allow African American suffragist and NACW president, Mary C. Talbert, to address the upcoming convention. Ovington also called on the NWP to put resources behind enforcing the Nineteenth Amendment in the southern states, where voter suppression had been rampant in the November 1920 presidential elections. The repeated requests of Ovington and others for assistance with voter suppression, and for Mary Talbert to speak, were ignored. And a resolution at the national advisory council's meeting on January 28, 1921, to bring "pressure to bear on Congress for a special Congressional Committee to investigate the violation of the . . . 19th Amendment,"[25] was not included in the minutes of the meeting nor a subsequent issue of the NWP's newspaper, *The Suffragist*, describing the convention.[26]

Even though Paul asked those invited to attend the convention to help decide the focus of the new NWP, she had already made the decision to focus on getting a federal equal rights amendment passed and ratified.[27] Both her decision about which path to take, even before hearing from the hundreds of women invited to share their views, and her failure to vigorously pursue enforcement of the Nineteenth Amendment shed light on the puzzle of how the amendment came to be viewed as no more than a narrow, non-discrimination rule about voting.[28]

The February 1921 convention to decide the future of the NWP began with a memorial service on Tuesday evening, February 15, 1921, at 8:15 p.m. in the Capitol Rotunda. The ceremony had been engineered by Paul, a master in terms of the power of pageantry to move women to action.[29] The NWP had commissioned sculptor Adelaide Johnson to complete a marble statue of the founding mothers of the suffrage movement, Elizabeth Cady Stanton, Susan B. Anthony, and Lucretia Mott. The convention began with an unveiling and presentation of that statue to the speaker of the House of Representatives. Presenting the statue as deeply symbolic, Jane Addams, the chair of the ceremony, said, "These women will stand for all time as the great emancipators of women all over the world."[30] Emancipation, defined as freedom and liberty, were the goals of these, "[w]omen [who] rebelled particularly against their exclusion from the central mechanism of self-governance in a democracy: the right to vote."[31]

That broad or "emancipatory" view of the Nineteenth Amendment was held by many of the women who had fought for its passage. The next speaker, poet Sarah Bard Field, echoed that broad vision of the work engaged in by the suffrage movement:

> I do not feel I arrogate to my faith in women too much when I say that with the dedication of these busts of our pioneers there is presented tonight the renewed dedication of the women of this Land to the vast work of a greater freedom which lies before us. It is Universal Freedom for which the movement represented by these women has ever stood.[32]

Yet, in accepting the statue on behalf of the congressional committee that had authorized it, the speaker of the House of Representatives, Frederick Gillett, seemed to express the more limited view that the vote itself had been the goal, rather than a greater vision of women's emancipation. The speaker evoked a narrow vision of the suffrage movement when he said, "[W]e must the more glorify those who have brought to a successful termination your great struggle which is now settled forever."[33]

The memorial service was followed by the first business session of the convention the next morning, Wednesday, February 16th. With seven hundred delegates and alternates in attendance, the NWP began the process of wrapping up its existence as a suffrage organization. It now turned to the issue of whether it should continue, in a new form with new goals.[34] The majority report of the executive committee, which was eventually adopted, recommended disbanding the old NWP. A new NWP should be formed to protect the hard-won "political freedom of women" by removing their legal disabilities.[35] The divisions within the NWP about this new goal were reflected in the minority report of the national advisory council, which was voted down. That report included the same request sought by Ella Rush

Murray at a January 1921 national advisory council meeting, the request to create a special committee to lobby Congress to investigate Nineteenth Amendment violations in the southern states.[36] This division about race and the division about protective legislation at the convention help explain the role of the suffragists in the emergence of a thin conception of the Nineteenth Amendment in the decade following ratification.[37]

At the convention, Ella Rush Murray asked that there be a discussion of voting rights violations in the southern states. By the time she stood up to present the minority report of the council, Murray understood that she had to frame the issue as a "feminist" issue rather than a racial one. It was clear from the procedural maneuvering before and during the convention that Paul was using that frame as a rationale for excluding any other potential new NWP goal that might be proposed by the convention's speakers.[38] Paul's message, channeled through the leadership on the executive committee, the national advisory council, and the majority resolutions of both, was clear. The NWP should stick to a single issue and let the other social organizations of the time pursue world peace, child labor, birth control, or one of the other myriad goals proposed by the organizations represented at the convention. Murray deftly reframed the question of southern states preventing African American women from voting, using intimidation tactics, as a feminist and not a racial issue. One might also read Murray's words as subtly suggesting that this issue of enforcement was being suppressed by the NWP. Although Murray diplomatically noted in her speech that the omission of her resolution from both the minutes of the meeting and *The Suffragist* report of the meeting had been done "in error":

> Mrs. Murray: (delegate from New York) . . . At the meeting of the Advisory council January 28th, the last official meeting, I made this motion, "That the Advisory Council recommend to the National Woman's Party, in the event of its reorganization, the appointment of a special committee to bring pressure to bear on Congress to investigate the violation of the intent and purposes of the 19th amendment." This action was seconded and defeated by the Advisory Council. Under the ruling we have just heard, I find I am allotted 10 minutes to explain this report, because it may not be understood by all of you, I want you to understand it because the motion was by error left out of the minutes and was also left out of the last edition of The Suffragist, so there has been no chance for consideration of the part of the delegates at large.

Murray tried to maneuver around Paul's strategic separation of women's issues and racial issues, as she continued:

> I feel a responsibility in having brought up this matter, because I have
> regarded it as a purely feminist matter, and not as a racial matter. In other
> words, the violation of the intent and purposes of the 19th Amendment,
> while confined to one section of the country, nevertheless, contains a germ
> in establishing a legal rule which may spread from one end of the country to
> the other. I heard Mr. Hughes make a speech on this. He said, "my friends,
> remember that perversion or evasion of a law taking place in a little town
> in Florida may effect [sic] the people in other sections because [they are]
> allowed to go unprotected." I feel very, very deeply that this splendid body of
> women should not go on record as ignoring the fact that the very thing for
> which it sprang into existence, and for which it suffered dislike, contempt,
> opposition and imprisonment, is being derided by that very portion of the
> country that fought us the hardest. It is not a question of race, my friends,
> because what is being done in one portion of the country now, namely, in
> the Southern States,—Georgia, Mississippi, South Carolina, portions of
> Virginia,—sometimes effect [sic] both. In this effort being brought about to
> keep one race out, they are willing that white women shouldn't vote in order
> to keep out the colored. Can't you see they are keeping us out?[39]

Murray was followed by a delegate from Massachusetts who endorsed
Murray's remarks by adding, "I hope that this matter will come up tomorrow
and that the majority will go on record as not ignoring this vital matter."[40]
This was followed by audience applause, indicating significant support for
the motion.[41] At several points during the proceedings, the chairman assured
the audience that there would be plenty of time for discussion of resolutions
in the coming days. But when the final resolutions were presented, motions
were made to limit debate to three minutes and to restrict discussion
to simply whether a speaker was for or against a resolution. A number of
delegates were deeply disturbed by these parliamentary restrictions and Ella
Murray said, "Madam Chairman, there has been no possibility in this great
convention which has assembled together from all over the country for a
chance to vote for free discussion. We pretend to stand for democracy. I ask
in the name of democracy that this meeting of women should have a chance
to speak for more than three minutes for whatever they may believe."[42] In
the end, the time was extended to five minutes, but new matters not in the

report could only be discussed as amendments to the resolution. In a final effort to push for recognition of the ongoing violations of the Nineteenth Amendment in the southern states, Murray responded to the chairman's call for debate. She rose to say, "I am against the report . . . because it does not include this, that women are not yet free . . . Just as long as there is a portion of this country where women cannot vote,—north, south, east or west,— as long as they cannot, there is an entering wedge by which other women cannot vote . . ."[43]

Florence Kelley also pushed for attention to the "negro question."[44] But her primary concern at the convention was support for protective legisla- tion.[45] Kelley, "represented the first shot fired in the disagreement over the protective legislation issue that would split the women's movement for more than two decades. Women had to be protected, Kelley asserted, whether they 'demanded it for themselves or not.'"[46] On the floor of the convention, Kelley argued:

> The National Consumers League a year ago adopted a new 10 year's pro- gram which is to continue the work begun one and 20 years ago. For the last 10 years we have been at work, men and women, white and colored, establishing legislative standards and defending in the courts of last resort of the States and Nation especially statutes intended to establish a level of pay for unskilled women workers below which no employer, no matter how unscrupulous, or incompetent can pay his humblest worker. These statutes have been challenged as being expressions of a desire for unequal legisla- tion between men and women but so long as our industry presses so heavily upon such a large body of self-supporting women, innumerable numbers of whom are responsible for other dependent persons, so long this Republic must furnish, whether they demand it for themselves or not, the power or right of those most defenceless [sic] workers, colored and white women alike the opportunity guarded by law, the right to express their conscience and their will as to the remuneration they will accept for their work.[47]

Kelley concluded by questioning the value of equality, when all were not equal. "Let's not begin by meaningless words. 'Equality' where there is no equality is as terrible a thing for the defenseless workers as the cry of 'peace' where there is no peace."[48] In her remarks, Kelley alluded to the comments of opposing speakers. These included Elizabeth Cady Stanton's granddaughter, Nora Stanton Barney, who spoke on behalf of the Equal Rights Association and the Woman's League for Equal Opportunity. In her remarks, Barney decried the same protective legislation that Kelley lauded:

> I have during the past three days been standing side by side with a big group of working women in New York State representing many different trades and occupations. They have felt the full depressing effect of having laid on them laws which prevent them dealing directly as free agents with their employers. I have seen not hundreds, but thousands, of women thrown out of work due to these laws, which are supposed to protect them but which really handicap them and I beseech you here of the National Woman's Party to pause before going headlong down the given task of heaping more protective legislation on adult women.[49]

Barney concluded by asking the delegates to:

> [R]eally stand for what the platform recommended by Mrs. Hooker stands for, verbatim,—that we will henceforth try to remedy conditions by legislating, trade by trade, and putting equal laws upon the statute books, and urge the industrial and business women to gain better wages, shorter hours and better working conditions in the same way that her brother worker is gaining his.[50]

Barney had previously questioned the head of the NWP's Research Department, Sue Shelton White, to clarify whether the NWP stood for "absolute equality of the law." White had replied, "'Absolutely' is the word I would use."[51] In questioning White, Barney's goal was to pin the NWP's leaders down, to make sure their agenda would be to oppose protective legislation that treated working women differently from working men. She wanted to ensure that the new NWP's goal would be to, "equalize the law no matter which way it swings . . . [that] adult women shall be free to make their own contracts in their own way and to work through the same organizations as the men."[52] There could be no more stark illustration of the split that came to haunt the NWP's campaign for an equal rights amendment than the Kelley-Barney statements at the convention—a split that dogs feminists to this day. What does equality under the law mean—neutrality or accommodation to the unique circumstances of women?[53]

In the end, on Friday, February 18, 1921, the delegates voted to disband and to reconstitute the NWP with the goal of "the removal of all those discriminations which exist in the law against women."[54] As Paul described this pivot:

> The Woman's Party was disbanded as a suffrage organization, having accomplished its work, at our national convention in February. It immediately reorganized under the same name to work for the welfare of women in other ways. The new organization, of which Miss Elsie Hill is in the national chairman, is taking as its first work, the removal of all the legal disabilities of women.[55]

The scope of this goal is breathtaking. As law professor and NWP adviser Albert Levitt characterized it, the NWP was, "revolutionizing the legal tradition of eleven centuries."[56] And Paul had to have been aware of its reach.[57] But she had played a central role in taking a seventy-two-year social movement across the finish line, in the face of strong opposition from a president and members of Congress, pushing back against them even while the country was at war. So she may well have believed that this new goal was also well within her reach. It was certainly important to her. As Anita Pollitzer, the temporary secretary of the new NWP wrote:

> [T]he Woman's Party is going along one step at a time to do another gigantic job. We are going to introduce an amendment in Congress this session saying that under the laws of the United States, the rights of women with men shall not be denied or abridged on account of sex or marriage.[58] Miss Paul came in to me last night and said in the funny little way she has when she is deeply interested and in earnest, her eyes and voice emotion-filled, "you know, I think I would rather get this principle established than anything I know of in the whole world."[59]

While the original NWP had as many as fifty thousand members, the new NWP had to begin from scratch to solicit members.[60] Their efforts to remove all the legal disabilities of women included introducing uniform legislation in all the states as well as an effort to get women elected to Congress. But the vehicle they focused on most was the Equal Rights Amendment. And, as described more fully in Chapter 7, "Defining Equality," it was here that Alice Paul met opponents she could not convert to her cause—legal progressives of early twentieth-century America, many of whom, like Florence Kelley and the social feminists, were former allies in the woman suffrage movement.

Why was the new NWP so focused on another constitutional amendment? Anita Pollitzer explained:

> This is not only far better because it means that we have thirty-eight [*sic*] state legislatures instead of forty-eight to struggle with, but it means that we can once again keep the women of the country on one issue. It is also better to have a constitutional amendment because a bill can be superseded by another bill at any time, while a constitutional amendment writes the position of women into the laws of the land.[61]

But with progressive legal lights like Felix Frankfurter, then on the faculty of Harvard Law School, writing that the NWP's amendment, "may bring into question a permissive field of legislation such as the minimum wage in favor of women which cannot be based solely on the basis of the physical constitution of women"; that it might inadvertently restrict the "so-called 'police power'"; and that it was "fraught with mischief,"[62] the neutrality feminists like Paul were in for a long battle. At first, they tried to work with these prominent legal figures like Frankfurter and Roscoe Pound, dean of Harvard Law School. Elsie Hill, the new NWP's national chairman, wrote that "We are determined that we shall not have the measure in a form which will prevent future or present protective legislation for women, such as mothers' pensions, or interfere with the validity of existing legislation such as minimum wage law, eight-hour day, and others."[63] Despite these early efforts, Paul and the NWP's new leadership never got active support from Frankfurter or Pound for their amendment. Nor did Paul ever openly support protective legislation for women and, eventually, the NWP took an official position against it.[64] While this negotiation was going on, neither the social feminists like Kelley, nor the neutrality feminists like Paul, were attending to the Nineteenth Amendment. The consequence was a lack of unified pressure on Congress to enact legislation and on courts to interpret the amendment in ways that extended its reach.

As a movement leader, Paul's strength was her singularity of purpose. But after ratification, that attribute contributed to the deep divide in the former suffrage movement and its fracture. Paul commanded loyalty among the thousands of women who had fought for a federal amendment and were now seeking a new goal.[65] If Paul had signaled to the leadership of the new NWP that they should continue to pay attention to the Nineteenth Amendment around issues like pushing for Congress to enact enforcement legislation, a more robust conception might have emerged. But it appears that her view of the scope of the Nineteenth Amendment was that, at most, it extended political rights, and that it did not reach many of the statutory legal disabilities suffered by women. Only an equal rights amendment could remove those.[66]

If the social feminists and the neutrality feminists had been able to work together post-ratification, they might have found common ground in the cases percolating up in the states. Kelley's experience and strategic legal prowess in bringing test cases, in the protective legislation sphere, would have been a powerful tool for Paul to use in expanding the scope and meaning of the Nineteenth Amendment, case by case. Much like Kelley, Brandeis, and Frankfurter in the 1910s, Thurgood Marshall in the 1940s and Ruth Bader Ginsburg in the 1970s, this incremental approach could have been used to push courts, one step at a time, into a thicker interpretation of constitutional provisions. The relationship between the Nineteenth and the Fourteenth Amendments might have been more deeply explored. That, in turn, would have given courts a more solid foundation for a synthetic reading of the amendments over the decades following ratification.[67] "Compromise would have allowed women to strengthen their ranks and consolidate their new power. In this way, women in the 1920s, in the short run could have preserved the gains made by them over the past two decades . . . that in the long run, would have provided the foundation to launch an effective equal rights campaign supported by a majority."[68]

Personally, Paul was simply not inclined to go in this direction. She was a lawyer, but only in the most academic sense.[69] Paul had three law degrees but she was not a legal practitioner.[70] In the years following ratification of the Nineteenth Amendment, Paul was essentially a newly minted legal scholar, interested in understanding the law and writing about how the common law and statutory law historically disadvantaged women and allowed differential treatment.[71] As previously noted, much more experienced lawyers, like Florence Kelley, had skillfully used litigation to establish a more expansive view of the police power in cases like *Muller v. Oregon*.[72] But Paul had little litigation experience. She did not show much inclination to bring test cases as an instrument for shaping the law. While she was familiar with researching and analyzing appellate cases, Paul had never been a practicing lawyer who had experience making those arguments in a courtroom. As a consequence, she did not speak or write much about using litigation to flesh out the bare bones of the Nineteenth Amendment. And the single-minded strategy that had brought such success in terms of ratification left her unable to shift gears and see the importance of test cases in fully developing the amendment's potential.

Politically, Paul's post-ratification agenda was being pursued as anti-socialist fervor swept the country in the 1920s. There was also a new wave of racism in the twenties. Many of the NWP's social feminists, like Kelley, were founders and members of the National Association for the Advancement of Colored People (NAACP) and involved in the anti-lynching movement. Paul's reluctance to support "socialist" legislation like minimum wage and maximum hour statutes, and her reluctance to pursue vigorous enforcement of the Nineteenth Amendment in the face of racist barriers to voting, reflected her continuing personal and political desire to avoid those contentious issues in American political life.

In addition to a personal and political reluctance to become embroiled in contentious social issues, Paul was only too familiar with the financial drain of a successful constitutional reform movement. The NWP was always short of funds, despite significant support from socialite and suffragist Alva Belmont. NAWSA had many more members and had received a significant "legacy from Mrs. Frank Leslie to further women's suffrage" in 1917.[73] Much of the correspondence sent and received by NWP officials involved requests for contributions, requests for reimbursements from the young women sent to the provinces to stump for suffrage, and the overdue bills that always seemed to plague the NWP. Its frequent office moves during this period were, in some part, due to a need to be attentive to the cost of rent. The NWP finally purchased a building "on the front lawn of the Capitol" after years of soliciting contributions for the acquisition of a permanent home.[74] A federal amendment, as opposed to a state-by-state strategy, had been a more cost-effective approach to woman suffrage.[75] And presumably the same principle applied to the new Equal Rights Amendment (ERA) Paul proposed.

Both the NWP and NAWSA continued to closely monitor and financially support the validity challenges to the Nineteenth Amendment that came even before ratification was complete.[76] Article V of the US Constitution grants Congress the power to amend the Constitution. It provides several avenues for Congress to amend. When either two-thirds of both houses of Congress propose amendments or two-thirds of the states call a convention proposing amendments, such amendments will be valid if either (1) ratified by three-fourths of the state legislatures, or (2) if by state convention, by three-fourths of those conventions.[77] Despite having been passed by two-thirds of the House and the Senate as of June 4, 1919, and ratified by three-fourths of the states by the time it was certified by Secretary of State Colby on August 26, 1920, the validity of the Nineteenth Amendment was attacked in the courts. During the 1921 NWP Convention, Sue Shelton White noted in her report as chair of the Research Department, "Throughout the year, perhaps the most important work . . . has been trying to maintain an intelligent contact with the mass of litigation which has arisen. Four suits have been brought against the suffrage amendment. They are known as the Ohio Referendum Case, the Injunction Suit, the Tennessee Case, and the Maryland case . . ."[78]

The Maryland case, which went all the way to the US Supreme Court, was *Leser v. Garnett*.[79] Justice Brandeis wrote the unanimous opinion and gave the following history of the case that, notably, involved both a white woman and a black woman seeking to register to vote after ratification of the Nineteenth Amendment:

> On October 12, 1920, Cecilia Streett Waters and Mary D. Randolph, cit-
> izens of Maryland, applied for and were granted registration as qualified
> voters in Baltimore City. To have their names stricken from the list Oscar
> Leser and others brought this suit in the court of common pleas. The only
> ground of disqualification alleged was that the applicants for registration
> were women, whereas the Constitution of Maryland limits the suffrage to
> men. Ratification of the proposed amendment to the federal Constitution,
> now known as the Nineteenth, 41 Stat. 362, had been proclaimed on
> August 26, 1920, 41 Stat. 1823, pursuant to Revised Statutes, 205 (Comp. St.
> 303). The Legislature of Maryland had refused to ratify it. The petitioners
> contended, on several grounds, that the amendment had not become part
> of the federal Constitution. The trial court overruled the contentions and
> dismissed the petition. Its judgment was affirmed by the Court of Appeals
> of the state (Md.) 114 Atl. 840; and the case comes here on writ of error. That
> writ must be dismissed; but the petition for a writ of certiorari, also duly
> filed, is granted. The laws of Maryland authorize such a suit by a qualified
> voter against the board of registry. Whether the Nineteenth Amendment
> has become part of the federal Constitution is the question presented for
> decision.

As Justice Brandeis noted, the highest court in Maryland, its Court of Appeals, had previously upheld the validity of the Nineteenth Amendment. In finding the Nineteenth Amendment valid, the Court of Appeals analogized to cases implicating the Fifteenth Amendment to the US Constitution, forbidding a state or the United States from preventing a citizen from voting based on his race, color, or condition of previous servitude. Citing *Neal v. Delaware*, the Court of Appeals noted that:

> [I]n Neal v. Delaware, the court said:
> "Beyond question the adoption of the Fifteenth Amendment had the effect, in law, to remove from the state Constitution, or render inoperative, that provision which restricts the right of suffrage to the white race. Thenceforward, the statute which prescribed the qualification of jurors was, itself, enlarged in its operation, so as to embrace all who by the state Constitution, as modified by the supreme law of the land, were qualified to vote at a general election. The presumption should be indulged, in the first instance, that the state recognizes, as is its plain duty, an amendment of the federal Constitution, from the time of its adoption, as binding on all of its citizens and every department of its government, and to be enforced, within its limits, without reference to any inconsistent provisions in its own Constitution or statutes."[80]

The Maryland Court of Appeals decision was upheld by the US Supreme Court on appeal. The court dealt with the three arguments by the plaintiff as follows:

> The first contention is that the power of amendment conferred by the federal Constitution and sought to be exercised does not extend to this amendment because of its character. The argument is that so great an addition to the electorate, if made without the state's consent, destroys its autonomy as a political body. This amendment is in character and phraseology precisely similar to the Fifteenth. For each the same method of adoption was pursued. One cannot be valid and the other invalid. That the Fifteenth is valid, although rejected by six states, including Maryland, has been recognized and acted on for half a century . . . The suggestion that the Fifteenth was incorporated in the Constitution, not in accordance with law, but practically as a war measure which has been validated by acquiescence, cannot be entertained.
>
> The second contention is that in the Constitutions of several of the 36 states named in the proclamation of the Secretary of State there are provisions which render inoperative the alleged ratifications by their

Legislatures. The argument is that by reason of these specific provisions the Legislatures were without power to ratify. But the function of a state Legislature in ratifying a proposed amendment to the federal Constitution, like the function of Congress in proposing the amendment, is a federal function derived from the federal Constitution; and it transcends any limitations sought to be imposed by the people of a state.

The remaining contention is that the ratifying resolutions of Tennessee and of West Virginia are inoperative, because adopted in violation of the rules of legislative procedure prevailing in the respective states. The question raised may have been rendered immaterial by the fact that since the proclamation the Legislatures of two other states—Connecticut and Vermont—have adopted resolutions of ratification. But a broader answer should be given to the contention. The proclamation by the Secretary certified that from official documents on file in the Department of State it appeared that the proposed amendment was ratified by the Legislatures of 36 states, and that it 'has become valid to all intents and purposes as a part of the Constitution of the United States.' As the Legislatures of Tennessee and of West Virginia had power to adopt the resolutions of ratification, official notice to the Secretary, duly authenticated, that they had done so, was conclusive upon him, and, being certified to by his proclamation, is conclusive upon the courts . . .

Affirmed.[81]

Where had this theory that an amendment to the Constitution could itself be unconstitutional come from? The decade that led up to ratification of the Nineteenth Amendment was a time of heightened popular constitutional discourse. More amendments to the Constitution were ratified between 1913 and 1920 than during any other period of our constitutional history (other than in 1791 when the first ten amendments that constitute the Bill of Rights were ratified). There was a robust public discussion about the Sixteenth Amendment (Income Tax—1913), the Seventeenth Amendment (Direct Election of Senators—1913), the Eighteenth Amendment (Prohibition—1919), and the Nineteenth Amendment (Woman Suffrage—1920). Like the three amendments that immediately preceded it, the Nineteenth Amendment was covered extensively by the major newspapers of the time, including the *New York Times*. Elite lawyers and legal academics, in particular, had a continuing conversation about the challenges such amendments posed to traditional constitutional doctrines and norms. Baltimore lawyer William L. Marbury Jr. played a central role in *Leser v. Garnett*, representing Oscar Leser and the other petitioners on the Supreme Court brief. Marbury was a descendant of the named plaintiff in the seminal American case, *Marbury v. Madison*, which enshrined the principle of judicial review in 1803.[82] Marbury was also a prominent lawyer involved in the eugenics movement embraced by scientists (and some legal progressives) in the early twentieth century.[83] He had led an effort to disenfranchise black voters in Baltimore.[84] And he had previously challenged the Fifteenth Amendment, after which the Nineteenth Amendment was modeled almost verbatim. In *Myers v. Anderson*, Marbury had first deployed this theory of the unconstitutional amendment.[85] In that case, the US Supreme Court simply affirmed the lower court's upholding of the amendment as valid, without opinion. In his 1919 *Harvard Law Review* article, Marbury tried to rationalize the court's decision by suggesting that, after forty-five years, the country, and not just the state legislatures, had tacitly affirmed the amendment.[86] He tried to distinguish newer amendments like the Eighteenth and the Nineteenth Amendments from the Fifteenth Amendment in that manner. One can see Marbury's vision of states' rights, or "local self-government," in the following passage:

> If the framers of the Constitution had been told that the time would ever come in the United States when a comparatively small but highly organized and determined minority could cause the legislatures of numbers of states to ratify amendments to the Constitution of the United States contrary to the well-known sentiments and wishes of a vast majority of the people of those states, recently manifested at the polls, the suggestion would probably have been received with absolute incredulity; and if the further suggestion had been made that the ratification of amendments could be secured in that way, which would strip the people of the states of an important part of their legislative powers, such as the right to determine who should be qualified to vote for state officers, or the right to regulate their own habits in regard to eating and drinking, that incredulity would have been still greater. Nevertheless, the American people are now witnessing exactly such a spectacle . . . [This] has occurred in a number of states in connection with the ratification of both the Woman Suffrage and the Prohibition Amendments.[87]

In a vigorous response, also in the *Harvard Law Review*, United States Assistant Attorney General (who soon became US Solicitor General) William L. Frierson noted that:

> Mr. Marbury frankly concedes that the objection he urges against the validity of the amendments now under consideration would, if seasonably made, have been equally effective against the Thirteenth and the Fifteenth Amendments. He thinks, however, that the court would not hold that, as an original proposition, the ratification by the legislatures of three fourths of the states made the Thirteenth and the Fifteenth Amendments a part of the Constitution, but that because no one saw fit to challenge their validity for forty-five years the court would be justified in treating this acquiescence by the people as the equivalent of a solemn action by a constitutional convention . . . This theory introduces a startling innovation as to the means by which laws may be adopted . . . The requirement that the Constitution shall be obeyed surely cannot be evaded by saying that a violation of constitutional provisions may become effective through the lapse of time.[88]

The idea that a constitutional amendment could be declared unconstitutional by the US Supreme Court is still unresolved and the subject of extensive scholarly debate.[89] But Frierson clearly thought no such power lay in the court:

> It is said [by William Marbury] that if the courts cannot pass upon a question of this kind, then the framers of the Constitution have failed in their efforts to establish and secure to their posterity forever the benefits of a perpetual union, by failing to clothe the Supreme Court of the United States with the power necessary to insure that perpetuity by preserving the integrity of the states . . . [T]he Supreme Court clearly was not clothed with any such power. The Eighteenth Amendment [Prohibition] has been proposed in the regular way, has received the approval of those bodies to whom alone has been committed the right to approve or disapprove, and its validity as a part of the Constitution is therefore not open to question in any court.[90]

After the Nineteenth Amendment was ratified, Marbury continued his attack, in a *Virginia Law Review* article, where he wrote that "It may well be that in some States [the Nineteenth Amendment] will produce all the good results which its most ardent advocates predict . . . It might not have any tendency to destroy the unity of the family, to increase the frequency of divorce, to affect injuriously the training and welfare of children, to prevent in times of national peril the enactment of those severe, sometimes cruelly severe laws necessary for the safety of the people and the State or Nation."[91] Marbury's rhetoric made clear the view of many Americans, that upholding the validity of the Nineteenth Amendment was disruptive to the social order and the nation's security. His "local self-government" rule or states' rights argument was to animate the action of many government officials, in southern states, after ratification.

Despite ratification of the Nineteenth Amendment in August 1920, African American women were widely denied the right to register and vote in the November 1920 presidential election. When local officials had engaged in similar behavior toward African American men after ratification of the Fifteenth Amendment, Congress had responded with enforcement legislation, and federal officials indicted and tried those local officials, for a time. But no similar enforcement legislation followed ratification of the Nineteenth Amendment. As the next chapter delineates, race played a central role in that story. The lack of enforcement legislation, and the subsequent federal forum for litigation that may well have been created as a result of such legislation, proved to be a missed opportunity to develop a thicker conception of the Nineteenth Amendment.

3

Enforcement Legislation

> [A] denial to citizens of the African race, because of their color, of
> the right or privilege accorded to white citizens, of participating, as
> jurors, in the administration of justice, is a discrimination against the
> former inconsistent with the [Fourteenth] amendment, and within
> the power of Congress, by appropriate legislation, to prevent[.]
> —*Neal v. State of Delaware* (United States Supreme Court 1881)

After the Civil War, the United States Supreme Court engaged in extensive
interpretation of the meaning and scope of the Fourteenth and Fifteenth
Amendments, as well as the enforcement legislation that had followed the
ratification of those amendments.[1] Cases like *Neal v. State of Delaware* (cited
by the Supreme Court in upholding the Nineteenth Amendment's validity in
Leser v. Garnett) and *Strauder v. West Virginia* were vehicles for the federal
courts to parse the text of the Reconstruction Amendments. Such cases often
got into to the federal courts, as a result of procedural provisions included
in the enforcement legislation enacted pursuant to those amendments.[2] But
there was to be no similar enforcement legislation, which might have triggered federal litigation around the scope of the Nineteenth Amendment—
litigation that might have provided a federal forum in which to develop a
more robust meaning of the Nineteenth Amendment. There was no *Strauder*
or *Neal* for women in the US Supreme Court. State courts were left to
parse the meaning of the Nineteenth Amendment for political rights, like
jury service and holding public office, without federal constraint. The enforcement legislation that was introduced in Congress following ratification of the Nineteenth Amendment was destined to die in committee. This
chapter offers an account of the former suffragists' role in how and why that
happened. And it lays out some of the consequences for the post-ratification
development of the Nineteenth Amendment.

Constitutional Orphan. Paula A. Monopoli, Oxford University Press (2020). © Paula A. Monopoli.
DOI: 10.1093/oso/9780190092795.001.0001

The Nineteenth Amendment enfranchised an entirely new class of cit-izens, previously ineligible to vote.[3] The twenty-six million new women voters included three million African American women. Three-quarters of those African American women lived in southern states.[4] In the November 1920 election, state and local governments across the South failed to enforce the new suffrage amendment for those women.[5] Even before the Nineteenth Amendment was ratified, African American women who tried to exer-cise their vote in the few states that had already enfranchised women faced resistance:

> Texas was the first southern state to provide full woman suffrage be-fore the ratification of the Nineteenth Amendment. With the need for an intelligent female electorate in mind, Black women organ-ized voter leagues there in 1917, the year Texas women won the right to vote . . . The women of Austin held voter education classes, and the women of Galveston held mass meetings to arouse interest in voter reg-istration. Fear of Black female voters resulted in immediate discrimina-tion against them. Six African American women were refused the right to register at Fort Worth on the ground that the primaries were open to white Democrats only.[6]

This resistance in the South was not surprising. In the wake of the Civil War, and despite enactment of the Fourteenth Amendment, African American men had been effectively disenfranchised. Congress felt compelled to enact the Fifteenth Amendment in 1870 to protect their voting rights.[7] As noted earlier, it also passed enforcement legislation under section five of the Fourteenth Amendment and section two of the Fifteenth Amendment. At first, the federal government actually used the enforcement power granted by this legislation.

> Under these laws the Department of Justice made a determined effort to enforce the Fifteenth Amendment. . . . In 1870 the government won 74% of its enforcement cases; in 1871, 41%; in 1872, 49%; and in 1873, 36%. After 1874 . . . convictions seldom passed the 10% mark and were often consider-ably below it.[8]

A number of factors conspired to limit, and then eventually stop, enforce-ment efforts altogether. One of the reasons that enforcement declined after

1874 was the interpretation of the scope of section two of the Fifteenth Amendment by the federal courts:

> At the April 1874 term of the circuit court for the district of Louisiana more than one hundred persons were indicted under sections five and six of the First Enforcement Act. Supreme Court Justice Joseph P. Bradley, who was reputed to believe the law unconstitutional, sat in on the trial . . . In a closely-reasoned opinion Bradley questioned the scope of the Fifteenth Amendment. It was clear, he said, that Congress has the power to enforce "every right and privilege given or guaranteed by the constitution" but that the mode of enforcement depends upon the character of the right. Where the right is guaranteed by the Constitution "only by a declaration that the State or the United States shall not violate it," as in the Fifteenth Amendment, the power of affirmative enforcement is retained by the state "as part of its residuary sovereignty." Hence, "the power of Congress . . . to legislate for the enforcement of such a guarantee, does not extend to the passage of laws for the suppression of ordinary crime within the States." The other trial justice, Circuit Judge William B. Woods, did not agree, and the case went to the Supreme Court on a division of opinion.[9]

The upshot was that in 1876, in *United States v. Cruikshank*, the US Supreme Court reiterated that the Fifteenth Amendment, did "not confer the right of suffrage upon any one," citing Minor v. Happersett.[10] Cruikshank involved the same enforcement act as another cased decided during the same term, United States v. Reese, 92 U.S. 214 (1875). Reese held that the third and fourth sections of the 1870 Act were "beyond the limit of the Fifteenth Amendment" and were thus "unauthorized." As scholars have noted, "[t]echnically, just two sections of the act were declared unconstitutional, but the whole law had been brought under a shadow. The effect of the decisions was to bring to a close the active policy of the government to enforce the Fifteenth Amendment."[11] After enforcement failed, conditions in the southern states continued to deteriorate for African Americans:

> Southern legislatures passed new election laws in the 1890s that were not discriminatory at face value, with Mississippi leading the way. New tools to keep blacks from casting their ballots in the Magnolia State included residence requirements, literacy and understanding tests, and poll taxes. Other states soon followed suit, adopting similar measures as well as new ones,

including the disqualification of voters who did not have vouchers of "good character" and who had committed crimes of "moral turpitude."[12]

Many predicted that, after ratification of the Nineteenth Amendment, the same disenfranchisement of African American women would occur as had occurred for African American men after ratification of the Fifteenth Amendment.[13] In fact, white southern politicians were particularly concerned about African American women getting the vote. South Carolina Senator Ben Tillman wrote, "A moment's thought will show you that if women were given the ballot, the negro woman would vote as well as the white women . . . Experience has taught us that negro women are much more aggressive in asserting the 'rights of the race' than the negro men are." And Mississippi Senator J. K. Vardaman concurred, arguing that "the negro woman . . . will be more offensive, more difficult to handle at the polls than the negro man."[14]

Indeed, after the Nineteenth Amendment was ratified, disenfranchisement continued across the southern states. "As a result of the 1920 election . . . Black women had registered in large numbers throughout the South, especially in Georgia and Louisiana, despite deliberate attempts to discourage them."[15] While African American women rallied to form voter education groups and register in large numbers, there were myriad ways of discouraging them from voting since they "posed a major threat to white supremacy" by their sheer numbers. For example, African American women made up the largest group in South Carolina.[16] On the first day of voting:

> Black women in Columbia, South Carolina, apparently took the white male registrars by surprise, and no plan to disqualify them was in effect. Many Black women reported to the registrar's office, but the only discrimination was in that whites were registered first. As a result some African Americans were kept standing for hours . . . Some Black women waited in line nearly twelve hours, such was their determination. The following day, property tax requirements were declared mandatory for Black women, and the minimum tax receipt was set at 300 dollars' worth of property . . . If the women could prove they had paid the required taxes, the next test was to require Blacks to read from the state or federal constitution and to interpret the documents. None of these tests was required of white women. Furthermore, white lawyers were on hand to quiz and harass Black women.[17]

At the end of the registration period, "thirty-two women hired a lawyer in Columbia to appeal the discriminatory actions of the registrars, and the suit was filed with the attorney general of the state.[18] But that legal action was not successful. "Black support of woman suffrage in South Carolina was not enough to prevent the disfranchisement of the large majority of African American women by the early 1920s."[19]

Before and after ratification of the Nineteenth Amendment, the NAACP played a significant role in resisting efforts to disenfranchise women:

> [A]ttempts to disfranchise Black female voters failed in Houston in 1918. When the women attempted to register, they were informed that the law specifically stated that only white women were eligible to register. The local branch of the NAACP had a legal document drawn that quoted the Texas bill granting woman suffrage in the state. The bill said "any" woman, and it provided for the elective franchise at any and all primaries, nominating conventions, and general elections. Following the NAACP threat to sue, Black women were allowed to register.[20]

As noted earlier, legislation had been enacted pursuant to the Fourteenth and Fifteenth Amendments, when election officials in the southern states refused to allow African American men to vote. Yet no similar legislation was to come out of Congress pursuant to the Nineteenth Amendment, although its text was exactly the same as the Fifteenth Amendment. Both had precisely the same section two, authorizing Congress to enact enforcement legislation. White southern politicians, fearing a "second reconstruction" resisted the specter of such legislation.[21] But splits among the suffragists themselves post-ratification were also salient. Those divisions—most significantly over the equal rights amendment (ERA)—resulted in a lack of unified pressure on Congress to enact legislation enforcing the Nineteenth Amendment. The NWP, in particular, perceived the need to court white southern congressmen to support its new amendment, as well as southern state legislators for its campaign to overturn state laws that perpetuated the legal disabilities of women.

As noted in the previous chapter, Florence Kelley, NWP National Advisory Council member and general secretary of the NCL, had been a significant force in bringing test case litigation in the context of protective labor laws for women. Not only was Kelley was an experienced lawyer, well versed in test case litigation like *Muller v. Oregon* in 1908, she was also one of the white co-founders of the NAACP in 1909. Her connection to all three groups could have laid the groundwork for the NWP to join with the NCL, the NAACP, the NACW, and the NLWV, to work together to challenge devices like the poll tax, literacy tests, and intimidation used to deny African American women the vote.[22] The NAACP itself had developed a series of test cases under the Fifteenth Amendment to challenge such devices, including "grandfather clauses," used to prevent African American men from voting:

> Many southern and border states devised legal barriers to circumvent the Fifteenth Amendment and prohibit black voting. These barriers included poll taxes, literacy tests, "grandfather clauses," and the "white primary." In 1910 Oklahoma passed a constitutional amendment, which held that only residents whose grandfathers had voted in 1865 could vote, thus disqualifying the descendants of slaves. The NAACP persuaded the U.S. attorney general to challenge the constitutionality of the "grandfather clause," encouraged by a Maryland Circuit Court decision in 1913. Oklahoma appealed the case to the Supreme Court . . . In June 1915, the Supreme Court ruled unanimously in *Guinn v. United States* that the "grandfather clause" was in violation of the Fifteenth Amendment.[23]

Even prior to ratification of the Nineteenth Amendment, supporters seemed to anticipate that enforcement legislation might be necessary to protect women voters who tried to register and might be turned away.[24] Senator James Watson (R-IN), chairman of the Senate Suffrage Committee, introduced a bill in May 1920, before ratification. While it was referred to the Senate Judiciary Committee, no further action was taken because Congress did not have the power to consider it until ratification was complete.[25] In an editorial in its newspaper, *The Suffragist*, the NWP editorial board announced that "[a] legislative campaign for immediate action on the enforcement bill will be begun with the opening of Congress on December 6 . . . " It identified Maud Younger, legislative chairman of the NWP, as the member who would be leading the effort.[26]

The editorial suggested that such enforcement legislation was "in line" with legislation enacted pursuant to what it called "the Civil War amendments" and the income tax and prohibition amendments. And it noted that the proposed Nineteenth Amendment enforcement legislation was "modelled upon the one applying to the amendment enfranchising the negro men of this country." The editorial identified the fact that women in Georgia had not been able to vote in the November 1920 presidential elections as a glaring example of the need for enforcement legislation.[27] Without it, women denied the right to vote would have "to bring damage suits personally against the local officials" who denied them the right. The editorial argued that, without such legislation, states had no power to make sure "that the provisions of the amendment are carried out."[28]

Notably, the NWP editorial board did not identify the suppression of African American women's votes as a basis for their strong support for enforcement legislation.[29] Clearly, the idea of enforcement legislation had been resisted by those southern politicians concerned about a "Second Reconstruction."[30] That is evident in the editorial board's description of the inclusion of section two of the Nineteenth Amendment, "about which so much controversy arose while the amendment was before Congress. Repeated attempts were made to induce suffragists to accept a compromise measure leaving out the enforcement sections of the amendment, but they always insisted, upon the advice of their lawyers, on the inclusion of the enforcement provisions as a necessary protection." The editorial board concluded by declaring that the work for the federal suffrage amendment could not be considered complete "until this enforcement measure is passed."[31]

The NWP, in particular, was publicly identified with the enforcement legislation. While there is slim, if any, record of floor debate on the legislation, since it never came out of committee, it is clear from the floor debate about section two of the Nineteenth Amendment itself, what the editorial meant by the "controversy" around enforcement legislation. Southern congressmen warned that if the enforcement clause were included in the Nineteenth Amendment, they would "find Federal supervisors and inspectors attending all our elections, and perhaps Federal Appointees holding all elections under this provision."[32] Most importantly, alternative language was considered, though not adopted, which would have put state sovereignty at the forefront of any enforcement legislation. It provided, "that the several States shall have the authority to enforce this article by necessary legislation, but if any State shall enforce or enact any legislation in conflict therewith, then Congress shall not be excluded from enacting appropriate legislation to enforce it." The Senate also, "tabled a proposed amendment which would have removed the words 'or any State' from the text of the joint resolution." Finally, "when a member proposed removing the enforcement clause from the joint resolution, the House took no action to overturn a point of order striking the proposal."[33] The nature of the enforcement legislation introduced, with its specific application to state and local elections, supports the view that Congress had a broad sense of its power to enforce the Nineteenth Amendment.[34]

In a *New York Times* article headlined "Wants New Suffrage Act: Woman's Party Will Urge the Passage of Enforcement Measures," the *Times* wrote that the NWP would pursue such legislation, "as soon as Congress reconvened in December [1920]."[35] And, indeed, H.R. 15018 was introduced in the House by Rep. Simeon Davison Fess (R-Ohio) on December 13, 1920, and referred to the House Committee on Woman Suffrage. Similarly, S. 4739 was introduced in the Senate by Senator Wesley Livsey Jones (R-Wash.) on December 30, 1920, and referred to the Senate Committee on Woman Suffrage.[36] The text of the Senate bill was exactly the same as the House bill. It was also similar to some of the provisions in the Enforcement Acts, enacted pursuant to the Fourteenth and Fifteenth Amendments. However, it was not quite as broad and did not mention jury service or holding public office. The bills provided as follows:

> Be it enacted by the Senate and House of Representatives of the United States of America in Congress assembled, That all citizens of the United States who are otherwise qualified by law to vote at any election by the people in any State, Territory, district, county, city, parish, township, school district, municipality, or other territorial subdivision, shall be entitled and allowed to vote at all such elections, without distinction of sex; any constitution, law, custom, usage, or regulation of any State or Territory, or by or under its authority, to the contrary notwithstanding.
>
> SEC. 2. That every person who shall be required by law to assess, enroll, or register citizens of the United States or to perform any other duty in order that such citizens may be qualified to vote; and every person who shall be required by law to receive or count the ballots of voters or to perform any other duty as an officer of any election or to certify the result of any election, shall perform the said duties without discrimination against any citizen of the United States on account of sex.
>
> SEC. 3. That any such person who shall refuse to perform any of the said duties without discrimination against any citizen of the United States on account of sex, may be compelled to perform such duty by mandamus issued by a district court of the United States upon relation of the Attorney General or of the United States district attorney, or by a State court upon petition of the citizen aggrieved.

SEC. 4. That any such person who shall violate the provisions of this Act shall be guilty of a misdemeanor and shall be subject to a fine of not more than $500 and to imprisonment for not more than one year, or to both, in the discretion of the court. The courts of the United States and of the several States shall concurrently have cognizance of such misdemeanors.

SEC. 5. That all laws or parts of laws in conflict with this Act are hereby repealed, and if any part of this Act is held invalid for any reason it shall not affect the remainder of said Act.

In *Fairchild v. Hughes*, the plaintiff tried to prevent the implementation of any pending enforcement legislation under section two of the Nineteenth Amendment, if it were to pass.[37] *Fairchild* was a companion case to *Leser v. Garnett*.[38] And like *Leser*, the plaintiff in *Fairchild* was represented by Baltimore lawyer William L. Marbury Jr. In *Fairchild*, Marbury argued that the secretary of state should be enjoined from issuing an official proclamation that the Nineteenth Amendment had been properly ratified. He also argued that the attorney general should be enjoined from enforcing the amendment since it would cause significant harm. Marbury described the potential harm as follows: "The alleged wrongful act of the Attorney General, said to be threatening, is the enforcement, as against election officers, of the penalties to be imposed by a contemplated act of Congress which plaintiff asserts would be unconstitutional."[39] The court rejected Marbury's arguments and refused to allow a private citizen to challenge the constitutionality of the Nineteenth Amendment or any pending enforcement legislation. It affirmed the lower court's refusal to allow the suit to proceed. But, in the end, the plaintiffs got the result they sought. Congress failed to take action on H.R. 15018, S. 4739, and H.R. 24 introduced pursuant to section two of the Nineteenth Amendment, and the legislation never came out of committee. If it had been enacted, the legislation would have provided for concurrent jurisdiction, so that state and local violations by election officials could have been brought in federal court. That, in turn, would have provided a forum for federal judges to opine as to their broader views about the scope of the Nineteenth Amendment. While these specific bills did not address jury service or officeholding, much like the multiple, sequential Reconstruction era Force Acts, there could have been additional enforcement legislation enacted. Such legislation might have provided some more specificity about congressional intent about the scope of the Nineteenth Amendment. For example, was it to include not only voting, but arguably lesser political rights like jury service and officeholding? Such legislation might well have met with attitudinal and institutional pushback about proper spheres and fears about extending too much political power to women. And it is likely that federal courts would have cabined its scope and impact, much as they did that of the Force Acts. However, like their deliberations around those acts in cases like *Strauder* and *Neal*, federal cases triggered by enforcement legislation would have provided a forum for courts to opine in a more fulsome way about how they saw connections among the Fourteenth, the Fifteenth, and the Nineteenth Amendments and their view of the scope of Congress's role in enforcing the Nineteenth Amendment.

The relationship between the woman suffrage movement and race in the United States had always been fraught.[40] As the Fourteenth Amendment was debated in the Thirty-Ninth Congress, "the issue of women's voting rights in particular, and gender more broadly, was never far from Congress's collective consciousness."[41] The debates about former slaves and suffrage were gendered. In adopting the Fourteenth Amendment, Congress:

> [D]efined the newly reforming American political community as a male family consisting solely of fathers, sons, and brothers. They deemed political actions they approved of as manly acts, those they opposed as unmanly. They argued that African American men's wartime military service, their newly acquired roles as household heads in the South, and their fundamental personal identity as independent men—all duties or rights of men—entitled them to the ballot. And they articulated deep disapproval of the woman suffrage petitions they received. The Fourteenth Amendment's language reflected all of this, demonstrating that the members of Congress believed that manhood and voting were, and should be, synonymous. In this way, members of Congress definitively declared that gender, and not race, would be the central criterion for membership in the postbellum body politic.[42]

After its ratification, the suffragists continued their fight to have the Fourteenth Amendment interpreted to include women's right to vote through its privileges or immunities clause.[43] They lost that battle in 1875 in *Minor v. Happersett* when the court refused to interpret that clause to mean that voting was a privilege of national rather than state citizenship.[44] Suffrage leaders Susan B. Anthony and Elizabeth Cady Stanton then moved on to a federal constitutional amendment in 1878, with Anthony testifying in Congress for the first time in 1884, urging support for such an amendment.

As described in Chapter 1, "Ratification," after enactment of the Fifteenth Amendment, there had been a split in the original suffrage movement between Lucy Stone and her AWSA and Stanton and Anthony's NWSA. And there were years of wrangling before the two groups joined forces to form NAWSA in 1890. Like the later split between NAWSA and Paul's Congressional Union in 1914, the Stone versus Stanton and Anthony split reflected the spectrum of thought about what the vote meant, who should have it, and what tactics should be deployed to achieve that goal.

Many of the early suffragists like Stone and her husband, Henry Blackwell, were abolitionists. The sharp appeal to racial divides by some like Stanton around the passage of the Reconstruction Amendments, and in state suffrage campaigns, were anathema to many suffragists. But Stanton exploited fears about black men and other poorly educated immigrants as a way to mobilize white male politicians to support her cause. Racist politics were deeply embedded in the suffrage movement from the late nineteenth century on, after the AWSA and NWSA were merged into NAWSA in 1890:

> Under the guiding hand of Susan B. Anthony and Elizabeth Cady Stanton, NAWSA adopted a strategy of "expediency." The aim of this strategy was to prove that the enfranchisement of White women would further, rather than impede, the power of a White ruling class that was fearful of Black and immigrant domination . . . "The government is menaced with great danger," observed Carrie Chapman Catt in 1894. "That danger lies in the votes possessed by the males in the slums of the cities, and the ignorant foreign vote."[45]

By resolution, NAWSA endorsed educational requirements "to ensure permanent supremacy for the native-born White portion of the population." Black women pushed back. Francis Ellen Harper "struck the familiar Black theme that it was character, and not color, class or education, that should be the criterion for the vote." And while leaders like Anthony had previously listened carefully to black suffragists like Ida B. Wells-Barnett, things changed when Catt took over as the leader of NAWSA. A wave of "southern white women and others who had not been weaned in the abolitionist or natural rights tradition" came in too.[46] By 1903, with Catt in the leadership, NAWSA adopted a policy whereby state affiliates could determine their own qualifications for membership. This "states' rights" approach attracted

"White women who could practice racist principles without censure from other suffragists."[47]

NAWSA became identified as an organization where southern suffragists could feel comfortable. In 1899, Anthony's decision not to support a resolution against segregated seating on trains resulted in, "NAWSA [being put] on record as saying that woman suffrage and the Black question were completely separate causes."[48] Despite her decision not to support the 1899 resolution on desegregation, some have argued that:

> [Anthony] would have probably objected to the use of her name to continue to drive a wedge between the struggles for racial and gender justice. African-American women had good reason when they appealed to her memory for historical inspiration. In 1921, when a group of African-American suffragists wanted to call attention to the mounting obstacles they faced in enjoying de facto the right to vote that they just been granted de jure, they named themselves the Women's Anthony League in her honor.[49]

NAWSA leaders like vice president Kate Gordon of Louisiana and Laura Clay of Kentucky began the Southern States Woman Suffrage Conference (SSWSC) with the goal of persuading the southern states to adopt women's suffrage. They argued that if states did not extend the franchise to white women, there would be a push for a federal amendment that would enfranchise black as well as white women. When NAWSA endorsed a federal amendment in 1916, the SSWSC split from NAWSA, although many remaining NAWSA members shared the states' rights views of SSWSC members like Clay and Gordon.[50]

NAWSA leaders actively sought to appease white southern politicians. In March 1919, Mary Church Terrell was approached by Catt, via Ida Husted Harper. Catt's goal was to get Terrell, "to persuade the Northeastern Federation of Colored Women's Clubs, an organization of 6000 black women, to withdraw a request for cooperative membership in the NAWSA." The application was "inexpedient for NAWSA because the association was calling upon white southern support for the national amendment." The opposition to the Nineteenth Amendment by white southerners was driven by the "perception of many whites that Black women were eager to win the right to vote in the entire region." And, in fact, the "overwhelming majority of negative votes in Congress against the amendment in 1919 came from Mississippi, South Carolina, Alabama, Georgia, Louisiana, and North Carolina."[51]

The move to separate woman suffrage from race was similarly embraced by Alice Paul and the NWP. While Catt was Paul's archrival, in terms of having supported a state-by-state approach to suffrage rather than a federal amendment, Paul and Catt were aligned in terms of the racial issue. They both deployed the same tactical move—separating the issues of sex and race—in order to avoid antagonizing white southerners who could be allies in achieving female suffrage. When organizing the 1913 suffrage march, Paul signaled her acquiescence to the NAWSA tactic by segregating the march. Ida B. Wells-Barnett's Alpha Suffrage Club was the first black women's suffrage club in Illinois; and Terrell, an NWP member, was the first president of the NACW. Wells-Barnett and Terrell planned to lead the Alpha Suffrage Club and Howard University's Delta Sigma Theta Sorority chapter in the 1913 march, but they were told by Paul and the organizers that they would have to march at the end of the column. Nevertheless, Wells-Barnett confounded them by slipping into the middle of the column "between two white women, and marched as she pleased."[52] African American women's clubs had special suffrage departments and "by the 1900's, Black suffrage clubs were to be found all over the country . . . and a number of women from the club movement worked in the recently created suffrage department of the NAACP."[53]

After ratification, in the months leading up to the NWP's first post-ratification national convention in February 1921, Paul was confronted by white women, like white NAACP co-founders, Mary White Ovington and Florence Kelley; and black women, like NAACP field secretary, Addie Hunton; and NACW founder, Terrell.[54] As the NWP's leadership continued to meet in the months before the February 1921 convention, these women raised the continuing barriers to African American women voting in the southern states:

> [Ovington] [w]rote to all members of the NWP National Advisory Council whom she knew personally, urging them to arrange for a black woman to address the group. Describing how prospective black voters in the South were being terrorized, Ovington stressed that black women would never vote unless their rights were upheld by all other women. She urged that the convention appoint a committee to investigate and take action on this issue. Although several National Advisory Council members endorsed

Ovington's proposal, the response from the NWP headquarters was negative. Headquarters secretary Emma Wold, writing for Paul, explained that the convention could give the podium only to groups with legislative programs for women or with feminist aims. The point was to ensure that the NWP, in choosing its goals, did not duplicate another group's work. Since Mary C. Talbert of the National Association of Colored Women's Clubs, the speaker whom Ovington recommended, represented a group with a "racial," not "feminist," intent, she could not be featured.[55]

Despite the NWP's playing a very public role in supporting the enforcement legislation introduced in Congress in December 1920, calls to put the full force of the NWP behind actually passing such legislation went unheeded and, one might argue, were actively suppressed.[56] As discussed in the previous chapter, in response to Mary White Ovington's call for action, NWP national advisory council member Ella Rush Murray introduced a resolution at the council's meeting on January 28, 1921, less than a month before the convention. Murray asked the NWP to form a committee for the specific purpose of bringing "pressure to bear on Congress for a special Congressional Committee to investigate the violation of the . . . 19th Amendment."[57] That resolution "was left out of that meeting's minutes and did not appear in the convention issue of the NWP's newspaper, the Suffragist."[58] As Mary Church Terrell recalled the events surrounding the 1921 convention:

> The only disappointment I suffered was at the time a colored deputation visited Miss Paul on the question of the passage of a resolution affecting the vote of colored women. I was the spokesman of that deputation and I will confess that I was grievously disappointed that the Woman's Party could not see its way to do what we asked, which was that they take up as their next work after the winning of the suffrage a campaign to see that no colored women were debarred from voting on account of their race.[59]

Hunton, Terrell, and sixty other women met with Alice Paul, who was "thoroughly hostile to the delegation" but who "said it was the most intelligent group of women who ever attacked her."[60] The delegation succeeded in getting their resolution heard on the floor of the convention although it was voted down.[61] The resolution was presented by Terrell before the Resolutions Committee[62] but it was presented by white NWP member

Murray on the floor of the convention. It stated, in part, that "We have come here as members of various organizations and from different sections representing five million colored women of this country. [Black women] have also come today to call your attention to the flagrant violations of the Susan B. Anthony Amendment in the elections of 1920 . . . " The resolution called for the NWP to lobby for a Special Committee in Congress to launch a federal investigation of that voter suppression. The resolution added, "We cannot . . . believe that you will permit this Amendment to be so distorted in its interpretation *that it shall lose its full power and effectiveness* [emphasis added.] Five million women in the United States cannot be denied their rights without all the women of the United States feeling the effect of that denial. No women are free until all women are free."[63] The prediction that the Nineteenth Amendment might "lose its full power and effectiveness" was haunting and accurate. As described in this chapter, the NWP's refusal to engage with voter suppression in the South was a factor in the thin conception of the Nineteenth Amendment that emerged by the end of the 1920s.

When asked about the issue of race in an oral history interview by Amelia Fry in 1973, Paul asserted that white southern members were not concerned about African American women voting in the South; rather they did not want to be "associated" with black women. But Paul's concern about cultivating continued support among southerners was clear in her acknowledgment that she wrote an editorial trying to assuage white southerners that the African American vote was not a threat.[64]

The correspondence surrounding the plans for the February 1921 convention demonstrates that Paul was, in fact, deeply concerned with placating white southern NWP members and politicians, both before and after ratification of the Nineteenth Amendment. The letters provide a picture of Paul as a tactician still very concerned with "inflaming" southerners, even after she no longer needed their support for the suffrage amendment. As noted above, Ovington lobbied the NWP's Advisory Council members to push Paul to allow prominent African American suffragist, Mary Talbert, a speaking role at the February 1921 convention. Talbert was a leader of the NACW, and she had been an American delegate to the International Council of Women Convention in Paris in 1920. Seeking to have Talbert invited as a speaker at the convention, Ovington wrote first to NWP advisory council members she knew, including Florence Kelley and Harriet Stanton Blatch. She then wrote directly to Paul. Citing the egregious behavior of many southern election boards in denying African American women the vote in the November 1920 election, post-ratification, Ovington wrote:

> May I point out, that Mrs. Talbert does represent the colored women of the United States and that no white woman can today represent the colored women of this country. Owing to our caste system, these women are little known by white women and carry out their organization largely distinct from the organizations of your and my race. This being the case, it is surely eminently proper that a meeting which has as one of its objects the honoring of the great feminists of the nineteenth century should have on its program a representative colored woman. Indeed, I think when your statue of Lucretia Mott, Susan B. Anthony and Elizabeth Cady Stanton is unveiled and it is realized that no colored woman has been given any part in your great session, the omission will be keenly felt by thousands of people throughout the country. Believe me.[65]

Florence Kelley had communicated Ovington's plea to Paul. But Kelley later wrote back to Ovington that Paul had made her usual tactical objection to the fact that Talbert's issues were around race, and not sex. In addition:

> Miss Paul advanced another difficulty . . . the Woman's Party, if it continues in existence, will have as its first job the passage of an enforcement bill prescribed in the second paragraph of the Woman Suffrage Amendment. This would take great care, so far as a Congressional law can do it, of the suppression of Negro women voters anywhere. *She considers this by far the most important item of their immediate program, in fact the only one on which all their efforts should be centered until the task is accomplished* [emphasis added]. She was of the opinion that the appearance of Mrs. Talbert on our program talking about lynching would inflame the Southerners, both in and out of her organization, as soon as it became known that this enforcement bill is to be pushed with the same vigor now that the Suffrage Amendment was pushed until its passage, and for the colored women voters, it might be bad tactics to have Mrs. Talbert speak on this particular occasion. Miss Paul, as a Quaker woman, is of course entirely in sympathy with Mrs. Talbert and her work. As a tactician, however, her judgment was against granting my request.[66]

Paul must have responded similarly to NWP advisory council member Mary Winsor, who wrote to Ovington:

> I suppose you don't realize that the National Woman's Party is doing the most effective work possible to protect the colored woman voter when they urge the passage of an act by Congress providing penalties for election officials who disregard the 19th Amendment. Without such a law nothing at all can be done to help the colored women get their right at the polls.[67]

Paul apparently arranged for Emma Wold, NWP headquarters secretary, to respond to prominent suffragist and council member Harriet Stanton Blatch on the subject. The response made the usual arguments about keeping speakers to those who represented women's issues, not racial issues, hewing to the fiction that African American women engaged in organizations like the NAACP or the NACW were not representing a feminist agenda, but only a racial one. Wold's response (clearly channeling Paul) again threw up the NWP's "support" of the Enforcement Bill as a dodge to Blatch's request to include Talbert as a speaker:

> I'm sure you will realize that it is not indifference to the cause of colored people, but rather a recognition of the limitations of our program, that makes it unwise to extend to Mrs. Talbert a special invitation to speak at the convention. Of course, you recognize the work we are doing in securing the adoption of the Enforcement measure by Congress is one way of helping to meet the problem of the colored woman's right to register and to vote. This measure we hope to get through the present session of Congress so that the right of women to an unhampered vote will be established, so far as the Federal authorities can establish it.[68]

Blatch responded to Ovington by writing a note, in her own handwriting, at the bottom of a copy of this letter. In that response, Blatch noted that Wold's letter to her, "evades the point obviously. Whenever Miss Paul does not wish to face an issue, she always manages to be so busy or absent, so that she delegates the answer to a subordinate. H.S.B."[69]

The NWP had a legendary lobbying infrastructure. As NWP member Florence Bayard Hilles said after ratification: "What we have done has been, of course, to get national action on the great federal amendment and in order to do that we had to get the folks back home to prod their representatives in Congress, and that has been done."[70]

A large part of Paul's leadership ability lay in her ability to organize and set strategy.[71] During the battle for the Nineteenth Amendment, the NWP had developed a unique and comprehensive political infrastructure, built for lobbying on behalf of the Nineteenth Amendment. That lobbying expertise was presumably behind Paul's promise, repeated by Kelley when she wrote to Ovington on December 22, 1920, "She [Alice Paul] considers this by far the most important item [enactment of enforcement legislation] of their immediate program, in fact the only one on which all their efforts should be centered until the task is accomplished [emphasis added.]" The Legislative Department of the NWP was particularly known for its unique "card-indexing" work, which "had received praise from newspapers and magazines."[72] Connecting lobbying with nonviolent protest as a social movement tactic, some scholars have linked Paul's use of civil disobedience to similar tactics in later social movements:[73]

> Although lobbying can be part of any political effort, Paul believed it had a special role in a nonviolent campaign. She wanted to influence legislators but she also wanted to further extend women's physical presence. Whereas paid lobbyists often try to remain anonymous, working behind the scene, Paul wanted hers to be known, by legislators and the press, to prove the determination and organization of suffrage workers and their ability to work within the political arena, just as women would when they began voting.[74]

Maud Younger and Alice Paul devised a carefully controlled approach to congressional visits:

> Whenever lobbyists went out, they did so with detailed instructions concerning the information they should secure, relying on a card system that allowed women who might never meet each other to build the group's power over the years. When a lobbyist started out for the Capitol, she was given a set of twenty-two cards, with checks by those items on which Younger wanted her to concentrate. Each one covered an influence that might determine a legislator's opinion on suffrage, such as his ancestry birthplace, education, family (especially the opinions of his mother, wife, and daughters), religion, military service, occupation, offices, hobbies and clubs, the newspapers he read, his greatest achievements, those people who had the most influence on him, previous votes and opinions on federal and

state suffrage, and strengths and weaknesses of his state. Even daily habits rated a card and careful attention.[75]

The "card-indexing" work was seen by some as "blackmail," seeking out the details about men and then threatening to expose those details to their constituents."[76] But it proved powerfully effective in taking the federal suffrage amendment over the finish line. However, the promised lobbying for the related enforcement legislation never seemed to materialize. And the NWP apparatus was turned toward drafting the ERA, and lobbying for equal rights legislation in the states:

> Soon it became obvious why Alice believed she needed a legal education. Over the next two decades, the Woman's Party drafted 600 pieces of legislation and saw 300 passed. Alice wrote the original version of the Equal Rights Amendment (ERA) in 1923 and revised it in 1943. The narrow legal reforms, however, did not tap the springs of emotion unloosed by the suffrage struggle, nor did they lend themselves to pageantry of demonstrations.[77]

So Paul and other suffragists turned to other goals that improved the lives of American women. Those three hundred enacted bills, and the eighty-six bills supported by the NLWV, ameliorated discrimination against women. Thus, suffragist advocacy by national organizations continued in an important way post-ratification. But it did not continue to be focused on developing the Nineteenth Amendment as a matter of law.

As the NWP gathered at its February 1921 convention, the organization claimed fifty thousand NWP members across the country.[78] At the convention, the old party disbanded, and the new party moved away from woman suffrage as its mission, and toward the elimination of all legal disabilities based on sex. This sharp pivot in February 1921 brought a drop in membership numbers. By 1925, the NWP claimed only twenty thousand members. Paul had used political boycotts of Democratic candidates in 1914 and 1916 to move the Democrats, as the party in power, to support a federal amendment.[79] Similar boycotts could have been deployed in the southern states.

If the forty-eight state branches had continued to focus on the Nineteenth Amendment, by pressuring their representatives in Congress to pass enforcement legislation, the Nineteenth Amendment might have taken deeper root through federal litigation around such legislation. It is puzzling that a lobbying effort identified by Paul as so important, as late at December 1920, never materialized. The failure by states like Georgia to allow women to register in the November 1920 presidential election was a legitimate motivation for the NWP to support such legislation. But it appears that the NWP's publicly announced support for the pending enforcement legislation, in December 1920, was also used as a tactic to deflect the requests by members, like Kelley and Ovington. Both women, and other NWP members, pushed for the NWP to deploy resources in the southern states to fight literacy tests, poll taxes, and outright refusals to register African American female voters. The correspondence described earlier illustrates how Paul used the pending enforcement legislation to deflect calls for such advocacy, and for African American suffragists to be allowed to speak about conditions on the ground at the pivotal February 1921 convention.

So from December 1920 through the February 1921 convention, Paul continued to articulate the NWP's support for the legislation. But after the convention, she stepped away from a formal leadership role. And the NWP moved away from the Nineteenth Amendment as its mission, adopting the ERA and similar state legislation as its new goal. Three months after that convention, in May 1921, the new NWP executive committee met in Washington, DC, and failed to vote to support putting NWP resources behind the pending enforcement legislation. "After the convention the issue of the enforcement bill slipped from sight and was dropped entirely at a meeting of the National Executive Committee in May 1921 attended only by Hill and three southerners."[80] A close reading of the minutes of that meeting indicate that it was held at NWP Headquarters in the Bond Building at 10:30 a.m. on May 16, that it was chaired by Elsie Hill of Connecticut, and attended by Mrs. Townsend Scott of Baltimore, Maryland; Mrs. Sophie Meredith of Richmond, Virginia; and Miss Sheldon Jackson of Washington, DC. And Maud Younger of California came late, although before the close of the meeting. The minutes described the part of the meeting where the "Enforcement Bill" was discussed as follows:

> The Chair then asked what was the will of the members present regarding the suffrage amendment Enforcement Bill which had been prepared and introduced under the direction of the Woman's Party in the last session of Congress. In the discussion that followed, those present were unfavorable to taking action upon the measure at all. No vote upon this was taken.[81]

While Maryland was actually a border state and part of the Union, Mrs. Townsend Scott was a self-described "southern woman." In the transcript of a congressional hearing three years before the 1921 Executive Committee meeting, Scott was closely questioned by the House members on whether white southern women were afraid of "colored women" having the vote. While noting that the states would reserve the right to impose checks on "negro" voting like literacy tests, she repeatedly took the position that white southern women were not afraid of giving African American women the vote:

> From the southern woman's point of view, I am quite sure I express the sentiment of all southern women when I say they are not afraid of the southern woman's vote. This is a bugaboo that the South has held over her long enough, and I think it is nothing more than an excuse. Every other argument has been settled, and this is just one remaining thing our opponents are trying to hold over us, and in their hearts I really do not believe they are afraid; they just pretend to be afraid. I think. We free women are going to teach them we are not afraid.[82]

So it would appear that, while Scott identified as a southern woman, she was from Maryland. Therefore, she may have been less concerned than women from states like Mississippi, where there were potentially more African American voters than white voters. In addition, the new NWP's mission shift away from suffrage and toward an equal rights amendment may help explain why she, and the others in attendance, took the position that the new NWP should do nothing to support the Enforcement Bill. While there is no discussion in the minutes about *why* the three executive committee members were not in favor of providing any further support for the enforcement legislation, it is plausible that they felt that way because the NWP had a new mission. Yes, two of the three members were white southerners. So racism could well have played a part in their decisions. But they were also the Executive Committee of the new NWP. The old NWP and its mandate to support a federal suffrage amendment were behind them. The new NWP no longer had as its goal supporting the Nineteenth Amendment. Rather it had the ERA and equal rights legislation as its primary mission. And the NWP perceived the need for white southern congressmen's votes for that new amendment. Similarly, it needed southern state legislators to support its state campaign to remove the legal disabilities of women.

Both the House and Senate enforcement bills eventually died in committee.[83] Given Paul's extensive NWP network around the country, with chapters in all forty-eight states and a significant lobbying presence in Washington, DC, presumably more could have been done to help try to push the legislation out of committee and to the floor for a vote. But the decision to disband the old NWP and its focus on the Nineteenth Amendment was arguably instrumental in the NWP's position to do nothing further in May 1921, after its initial efforts to have such legislation introduced. The new NWP had as its goal, a new amendment. It had little time, or inclination, to go backward. But concern about white southern congressional support for the proposed ERA, and the NWP's state legislative campaign, presumably played a significant role. The enforcement legislation had been introduced in 1920, during the rise of Jim Crow and the use of lynching and violence as a mechanism of terror and intimidation. White southern politicians saw any enforcement legislation that interfered with state sovereignty as anathema. Their fear of a Second Reconstruction, with robust voting rights enforcement, presumably explains, in part, why the enforcement legislation never made it out of committee. But the lack of resistance from Paul's NWP certainly made that outcome more likely. The former suffrage organizations had succeeded in helping to move the Nineteenth Amendment, with an enforcement clause, through a Congress where there was strong pushback on including that clause. So it is plausible to suggest that they might have been successful in pushing enforcement legislation through to enactment, despite likely pushback from the same southern congressmen who had resisted, but who had lost the battle on including section two in the Nineteenth Amendment.

Paul had been deeply concerned with maintaining the support of southern women and politicians during her campaign for ratification of a federal suffrage amendment. Once the Nineteenth Amendment has been ratified, she should have been free to answer the call of white and black suffragists to push for passage of the enforcement bill in Congress without further fear of alienating white southerners. But her immediate pivot to the ERA kept her tethered to those white southerners and vulnerable in this regard. Paul wanted to avoid "inflaming" white southern politicians, so she kept her distance from those calling for the NWP's powerful lobbying resources to be deployed in support of federal enforcement legislation. Not only would that have been the moral move, but strategically it would have given the Nineteenth Amendment a chance to be debated and fleshed out in federal courts.[84]

Contemporary scholars have suggested innovative and exciting ways in which, by reading the Nineteenth Amendment in para materia with the Fifteenth Amendment, fairly broad enforcement legislation could be enacted and sustained today to expand voting rights.[85] Had any enforcement legislation been enacted pursuant to the second section of the Nineteenth Amendment in the 1920s, it would likely have been construed narrowly. But it would have given federal courts a forum to parse and debate the text of the Nineteenth Amendment, in the context of more specific direction from Congress about its meaning and scope. However, after December 1920, no discernable effort was made by Paul and the NWP to put much muscle behind passage of the enforcement legislation. She certainly did not signal to the new leaders of the NWP, like Chairman Elsie Hill, that she wanted them to put party resources behind that effort. Such a signal would have been reflected in the minutes of the May 16, 1921, Executive Committee meeting. Paul was focused on a different piece of legislation. Highlighting the racist policies of southern election authorities who refused to register African American women would likely alienate southern congressmen that Paul felt she needed to support her new amendment. It would also alienate state legislators in the South that might be needed to ratify that amendment, and enact state reform legislation.

Were there other groups that could have pushed for enforcement legislation? NAWSA had had a similar, extraordinary legislative network and system for lobbying in the states and in Washington, DC. Either NAWSA or its successor, the NLWV, could have used that legislative and lobbying clout to push for enforcement legislation to be voted out of committee, and onto the floor of both houses of Congress for a vote. But Carrie Chapman Catt and the NAWSA leaders, many of whom became leaders of the NLWV, had long excluded African American suffragists, too:

> The inability of Congress and the NAACP to protect the rights of Black women voters led the women to seek help from national white woman suffrage leaders. Not surprisingly, these attempts also failed. In 1920 NAWSA had changed its name to the National League of Women Voters (NLWV), a nonpartisan organization designed to maintain women's political participation on national and local levels. At the 1921 national convention held in Cleveland, African American women brought their complaints about disenfranchisement before the NLWV. Although some of the white southern suffrage leaders had refused to join the NLWV, those southern delegates

at the convention threatened to walk out if the "negro problem" was debated. In typical League fashion, a compromise resulted wherein African American women were allowed to speak before the body, but no action was taken by the organization.[86]

Like the NWP, the NLWV turned to new legislation. The NLWV turned toward an education and social welfare agenda. And it opposed the ERA for many years.[87] Even within the NWP, former colleagues, like lawyer and social feminist Florence Kelley, strongly opposed the ERA, as they became the architects of a new social welfare state:

> It is not an exaggeration to say that organized women were responsible for carrying the social welfare agenda of the Progressive Era into state government in the 1920s. Restricting child labor and improving working conditions of women were among the most frequent issues that engaged women's energies, but there were many others. The earliest national achievement directly attributable to women voters was the Sheppard-Towner Act of 1921 . . . establishing a federal-state program [to reduce maternal and infant mortality] one of the first national programs for social welfare.[88]

As a social feminist and legal progressive, Florence Kelley took the position that Paul's ERA was a threat to the protective legislation for women, which legal progressives had been successful in achieving. If Paul had not shifted so quickly to an equal rights amendment, she and Kelley might not have had the acrimonious parting of the ways described in Chapter 7, "Defining Equality." And Kelley might well have continued to work within the NWP to push for enforcement legislation in Congress. She pushed hard for the issue to be raised at the February 1921 convention. But when she sensed that Paul had another agenda that put protective legislation at legal risk, Kelley felt compelled to push back on the ERA, rather than continuing to collaborate with Paul.

One is left to imagine the collaboration that the NWP, the NCL, the NLWV, the NAACP, and the NACW could have achieved if Paul had not been so focused on continuing to placate southern legislators for possible support of an equal rights amendment. Kelley was a leading figure in both the NWP and the NAACP. As one who had pushed Paul to support efforts against voter suppression in the South, Kelley could have brought together NWP and NAACP resources, to more effectively push for an enforcement bill. If the legislation had been enacted, that would have provided the opportunity to revisit the scope of congressional power to enact such legislation. Such federal litigation could have been part of a test case litigation strategy similar to that developed by Kelley, Louis Brandeis, and others, in cases like *Muller v. Oregon*. Such federal test cases would have focused on an amendment that enfranchised half the adult population, a much larger segment than that enfranchised by the Fifteenth Amendment. In this way, the Nineteenth Amendment was deprived of that forum for its constitutional development. And, in the absence of federal enforcement legislation under section two of the Nineteenth Amendment, state courts were left as the primary site for any constitutional development of the amendment.

While not the subject of extensive federal litigation, the Nineteenth Amendment was the subject of substantial state litigation in the decade after its ratification. That litigation implicated big constitutional questions like federalism, citizenship, and equality, as those issues intersected with race, gender, and class. The following chapters trace those cases and their impact on questions like where to draw the elusive line between state and federal sovereignty, the scope of women's citizenship beyond voting, and the definition of gender equality as a constitutional matter.

4

A Self-Executing Amendment

The Nineteenth Amendment to the Constitution of the United States is self-executing, and immediately upon its becoming operative all females were entitled to vote, provided they complied with the regulations surrounding voter's qualifications in the state of their residence.

—*Hawthorne v. Turkey Creek School District*
(Supreme Court of Georgia 1926)

While the NWP and NAWSA did attend to the early litigation around the validity of the Nineteenth Amendment's ratification, they were less visible in the state court litigation that ensued during the 1920s. Soon after ratification, the constitutional effect of the Nineteenth Amendment on state law was contested in state courts—without the benefit of any federal enforcement legislation to guide those courts as to Congress's understanding of the scope of the Nineteenth Amendment. A steady stream of cases raised questions about whether the federal amendment was "self-executing"; in other words, did it require further state legislation for its implementation?[1]

In one line of cases, petitioners challenged the validity of local elections in which women had voted. Another line involved whether poll tax statutes that applied to men should be extended to women. In examining the doctrinal question of whether the amendment was self-executing, courts considered whether and how the federal amendment affected state law governing voter eligibility criteria. In the decade after ratification of the Nineteenth Amendment, state courts were thus engaged in broad questions of federalism, in an environment characterized by deep divisions over state versus national government power, in a federal republic. These political philosophies had been in tension since the nation's founding. And, as noted in previous chapters, they remained driving forces in shaping the country's

Constitutional Orphan. Paula A. Monopoli, Oxford University Press (2020). © Paula A. Monopoli.
DOI: 10.1093/oso/9780190092795.001.0001

political and constitutional development during the ten years that followed the Nineteenth Amendment's ratification.

Article I, Section 2 of the federal Constitution provides that "[t]he Times, Places and Manner of holding Elections for Senators and Representatives, shall be prescribed in each State by the Legislature thereof; but the Congress may at any time by Law make or alter such Regulations . . ."[2] Thus, the original Constitution conferred on the states almost, "complete control over the voter qualification for both state and federal elections."[3] This constitutional framework gave states broad authority to establish voter eligibility criteria, subject only to specific override by Congress. Ratified in 1868 and 1870, the Fourteenth and Fifteenth Amendments constituted such an override. Read together, they nullified any state law that prevented citizens from voting based solely on their race, color, or previous condition of servitude. They also provided for reduced congressional representation and other enforcement actions against states that abridged voting rights on such a basis.

The United States Supreme Court had reiterated this state-centered paradigm in *Minor v. Happersett* in 1875.[4] In that case, Virginia Minor argued that she had the right to vote as a national citizen under the Fourteenth Amendment's privilege or immunities clause. The court held that the elective franchise was not a privilege of national citizenship under the Fourteenth Amendment, but, instead, was within the purview of the states. As a result, while states could not abridge a male citizen's right to vote based on his race, color, and previous condition of servitude, they were still free to exclude citizens from voting based on their sex.

In 1920, ratification of the Nineteenth Amendment added sex to the list of voter eligibility criteria that states were expressly forbidden from using, in determining who could vote. But the text of the Nineteenth Amendment, simple in theory, proved more difficult in its implementation. There were immediate challenges to women's eligibility to vote on state constitutional amendments and to validly sign petitions calling for an election. Three Georgia cases (decided in close sequence in 1921, 1922, and 1923), a 1930 Missouri case, and an Illinois case decided in 1930, indicated consensus about the threshold question—whether the Nineteenth Amendment was a self-executing constitutional amendment.[5] Finding that an amendment was self-executing allowed courts to read state statutes as if words in those statutes had been struck. It gave courts significant power. They did not have to wait for state legislatures to act. Rather they could essentially enforce state law—not as it was actually written—but as it had been revised by a federal amendment.

In 1921, the Supreme Court of Georgia considered the legality of an amendment to the Georgia Constitution that authorized any municipality to "incur a bonded debt or debts for . . . public purposes. . . ."[6] State constitutional amendments in Georgia required ratification by two-thirds of the qualified voters who voted in an election.[7] In *Brown v. City of Atlanta*, the plaintiff argued that the ten thousand women who voted in such an election in Atlanta were not qualified, thereby invalidating the passage of the amendment.[8]

The *Brown* court invoked the constitutional meaning and effect of the Fifteenth Amendment, as interpreted by the US Supreme Court in *Neal v. Delaware*. It held that no further legislation was needed, beyond the amendment itself, to implement the amendment's mandate that states could not withhold the vote from women, based on sex alone:

> The Nineteenth Amendment to the Constitution of the United States provides that the right of suffrage shall not be denied on account of sex. The Constitution of the United States is the supreme law of operation in this state. The Nineteenth Amendment became automatically operative on August 26, 1920. We are of the opinion that that amendment is self-executing, and that under it females are not now disqualified on account of their sex to register and to vote, but on the contrary they are qualified. In Neal v. Delaware, the question was what effect the Fifteenth Amendment to the Constitution of the United States had upon the laws of Delaware, which were to the effect that all jurors should be "white male electors." It was held that the Fifteenth Amendment had the effect . . . of striking from the laws of Delaware the word "white," and left the remainder of the law intact. So we think in the present case, where the Nineteenth Amendment strikes the word "male," as used in defining who may become qualified voters.[9]

Because it determined the Nineteenth Amendment to be self-executing, the *Brown* court held that the women voters were prima facie qualified to vote.[10] The court thus placed on the plaintiffs the burden to prove that the women voters were unqualified. And the plaintiffs failed to provide any evidence that the women were registered illegally.[11]

In 1922, the Supreme Court of Georgia once again addressed the self-executing nature of the Nineteenth Amendment. In *Stephens v. Ball Ground School District*, it addressed the legality of woman suffrage, in the context of a school district election.[12] The *Stephens* court was asked to address the validity of an election that gave voters the opportunity to authorize the issuance of bonds to finance a new schoolhouse.[13] The plaintiffs argued that 157 women voted in favor of the bond issuance, and their votes were illegal on the grounds that "females are not qualified voters in the state of Georgia."[14] The *Stephens* court noted that the election took place on October 9, 1920, more than a month after the Nineteenth Amendment was certified by the US Secretary of State on August 26, 1920.[15] The court summarily concluded that "[s]uch amendment to the Constitution removed all disqualifications of females to vote in this state, theretofore existing on account of their sex," citing *Brown v. Atlanta* and reversing the lower court decision.[16]

And in 1923, the Supreme Court of Georgia was presented with yet a third election dispute, in which it discussed the impact of the Nineteenth Amendment on the state constitution. In *Stewart v. Cartwright*, the court noted that the state's constitutional voting provisions were "modified by the Nineteenth Amendment" to exclude "male" as a qualifier.[17] "The words 'shall be an elector and entitled to register and vote at any election by the people' are unequivocal, and the entire provision amounts to a constitutional guaranty of the right of suffrage, which, though subject to reasonable regulation, cannot be absolutely denied or taken away by legislative enactment."[18]

In 1930, the Supreme Court of Missouri interpreted a pre-suffrage statute, in light of the somewhat dramatic facts in *In re Graves*. Graves was a member of the board of election commissioners of Kansas City, and thus, by statute, had the duty "to have printed and furnish to the judges of election in said city ballots in the form and manner provided by law for the use and benefit of persons entitled to vote under and by virtue of the provisions of this act."[19] In this 1919 statute, Missouri had granted partial suffrage to women, permitting them to vote for president and vice president.[20] The statute required the election commissioners to print on separate ballots, in a different color, only the names of the candidates for president and vice president.[21] Graves failed to do so and printed the names of the presidential and vice presidential candidate, along with all other candidates. He was arrested for the misdemeanor of violating election law.[22] Graves filed a habeas corpus petition, arguing his detention was unlawful because the ballot provision was no longer valid.[23]

The *Graves* court first observed that the separate ballots needed only be printed for the benefit of people "entitled to vote under and by virtue of the provisions of this act."[24] The court reasoned that women, not men, were given partial suffrage under that act.[25] The court then noted that by virtue of the Nineteenth Amendment, women were granted full voting rights, thus superseding the partial voting rights granted to them by the state statute.[26] The *Graves* court reiterated the impact of the Nineteenth Amendment on state law, which was to strike the word "male" from state constitutions and statutes, where that word limited the right to vote. It also made clear its view, that further legislation was not required. In other words, the amendment was self-executing as to the right to vote: "Its adoption struck from the Constitutions and statutes of the several states the word 'male' wherever it occurred as a limitation upon the right of the citizen to vote. From that date female persons were entitled to vote the same as male persons *without the aid of state legislation* (emphasis added). . . ."[27]

So the Nineteenth Amendment did not simply strike out the word "male" going forward, in state statutes that had previously limited the class of citizens eligible to vote. As interpreted by the *Graves* court, the Georgia statute must be read with the understanding that state legislators knew a federal suffrage amendment was on the horizon. Thus, the state statute must be interpreted as accommodating such a subsequent change in federal law. The *Graves* court described this effect that the Nineteenth Amendment had on this state law regarding partial suffrage:

> At the time the [Missouri partial suffrage] act was passed, it was a matter of common knowledge that a proposed amendment of the Constitution of the United States extending the right of suffrage to women was in process of ratification by the states . . . We cannot assume that it was [the Legislature's] intention to entitle women under and by virtue of this act to only a limited right of suffrage in case a constitutional amendment either state or national became effective entitling women to full right of suffrage, because to do so would be to ascribe to them an intention to pass an unconstitutional act.[28]

Thus, the *Graves* court found that ratification of the Nineteenth Amendment altered the meaning of the state law regarding partial suffrage, without any further action by the Missouri legislature. And it concluded that "the requirement of the act that [women] be furnished with separate ballots having printed thereon only the names of candidates for electors for President and Vice President of the United States was thereafter inoperative."[29] As the law was inoperative, the court held that Graves was wrongly detained and ordered that he be discharged.[30]

As previously noted, even after ratification of the Fourteenth and Fifteenth Amendments, states were left with tremendous latitude to create voter eligibility requirements, other than race, color, or previous condition of servitude. And those eligibility requirements were often used as a mechanism to cabin the nature of citizenship, limiting the extension of political rights to a select few. A number of states employed "poll taxes," authorized by state constitutions and statutes to accomplish this end. The poll tax had been used from colonial times to "means-test" potential voters. These taxes were justified by the "well-accepted political principle . . . that a potential voter ought to be able to demonstrate a sufficient degree of financial independence in order to prove his or her political independence and thus qualifications to vote."[31] The tax was based on property ownership, and had to be paid at every election, "whether or not one voted. Typically, the tax had to be paid months in advance, and proof of payment of the current tax, as well as payment of poll taxes for the past two years, was required to vote."[32]

Southern states continued to use poll taxes well into the twentieth century. Such taxes clearly suppressed African American voting in particular, and in the early twentieth century, "[v]oter participation often was less than 5% among African Americans in states with a poll tax."[33] In the aftermath of ratification of the Nineteenth Amendment in 1920, state courts took up the question of how and when the new federal amendment altered not just who could vote, but under what conditions they were eligible to vote. A number of these cases centered on the poll tax and most arose in the southern states, including Texas, Alabama, Georgia, and Arkansas. The poll tax cases described in this chapter became a vehicle for testing the impact of the Nineteenth Amendment on state constitutional and statutory doctrines other than voting, for example, the state's general taxing power.

Like the election cases just described, much of the poll tax litigation revolved around whether the Nineteenth Amendment was self-executing.[34] A 1921 Alabama case, two Georgia cases (decided in 1923 and 1926), a 1923 Texas case, and a 1927 Arkansas case all indicated consensus about the threshold question—whether the Nineteenth Amendment was a self-executing constitutional amendment. The cases generally held that it was, even when it came to the poll tax. That tax implicated not just voting per se, but the general taxing power of the state, a related but arguably separate constitutional doctrine. The 1923 Georgia Supreme Court case was the only case that did not apply the self-executing doctrine beyond voting statutes to the state's poll tax statute. But the court did so in such a way as to validate women's votes, rather than nullify them.

The first southern court to address this issue was the Supreme Court of Alabama in 1921 in *Graves v. Eubank*.[35] In *Eubank*, the court considered a tax collector's refusal to collect the poll tax of a female voter. In October 1920, the petitioner had tendered the poll tax due to the tax collector, which the tax collector refused. He also refused to issue an official poll tax receipt to the female voter.[36] The payment was thus delinquent in February 1921.[37] The government took the position that, by its terms, the Alabama Constitution only levied a poll tax on men.[38] The *Eubank* court reasoned that the Nineteenth Amendment effectively struck any sex discrimination in voting from state laws and constitutional provisions. The court's analysis focused on the "self-executing" nature of the Nineteenth Amendment.[39] The *Eubank* court began by reiterating the text of the amendment. It observed:

> This amendment automatically strikes from the state laws, organic and statutory, all discriminatory features authorizing one sex to vote and excluding the other, or placing conditions or burdens upon one not placed upon the other as a condition precedent to the right to vote, but in no wise interferes with, changes, or alters state laws with reference to elections that cannot and do not amount to a discrimination in favor of one sex against the other. It protects the man and woman alike, and a burden cannot be placed upon one sex that is not put upon the other, nor can a privilege, benefit, or exemption be given one to the exclusion of the other.[40]

The *Eubank* court reinforced the idea that the Nineteenth Amendment had the power to affect how other statutes were to be construed, albeit within the limited ambit of voting and sex. But that left open the question of where a law stopped affecting voting or sex?[41] That line drawing and issue framing, which was often outcome determinative, was left up to the state courts.

> The said amendment, by its own force and effect, strikes from section 177 of our state Constitution the word "male," as used in defining who are or may become electors, as well as where used in other parts of our organic or statutory laws when used in connection with the right and qualification to vote, and also strikes therefrom the use of the masculine pronoun wherever it appears, so as to make the same include and applicable to both sexes.[42]

In finding that the Nineteenth Amendment was self-executing, and defining what that meant for Alabama law, the *Eubank* court looked to *Guinn v. United States,* which had delineated the impact of the Nineteenth Amendment's mirror image, the Fifteenth Amendment, on contrary state law. The court quotes extensively from the US Supreme Court's decision in *Guinn*:[43]

> While in the true sense, therefore, the amendment gives no right of suffrage, it was long ago recognized that in operation its prohibition might measurably have that effect; that is to say, that as the command of the amendment was self-executing and reached without legislative action the conditions of discrimination against which it was aimed, the result might arise that as a consequence of the striking down of a discriminating clause a right of suffrage would be enjoyed by reason of the generic character of the provision which would remain after the discrimination was stricken out . . . A familiar illustration of this doctrine resulted from the effect of the adoption of the amendment on state Constitutions in which at the time of the adoption of the amendment the right of suffrage was conferred on all white male citizens, since by the inherent power of the amendment the word 'white' disappeared and therefore all male citizens without discrimination on account of race, color, or previous condition of servitude came under the generic grant of suffrage made by the state.[44]

In addition to defining the self-executing nature of the Fifteenth Amendment, the *Guinn* court made it clear that the federal Constitution does not explicitly grant citizens a "right to vote." But even though it is not an enumerated right, the decision in *Guinn* suggests that a federal constitutional amendment, which prohibits state voting eligibility criteria based on race, color, or previous condition of servitude, creates such a de facto right to vote, by implication. And that de facto right was extended to those citizens who had previously fallen outside the ambit of eligible voters, by reason of those characteristics. *Guinn* also illustrates how the doctrine of self-execution, in the case of federal constitutional amendments, transforms state law. Such provisions, in effect, "amend" state constitutional and statutory provisions that conflict with them.

As a result of its conclusion that the Nineteenth Amendment was "self-executing," the Alabama Supreme Court in *Eubank* went on to find that the Nineteenth Amendment had an effect, not only on the state law governing *who* could vote, but also on whether a corollary state statute, like the poll tax, was altered by ratification of the federal amendment. In so doing, the *Eubank* court acknowledged that the impact of the Nineteenth Amendment extended to state constitutional and statutory law, beyond voting. In this case, it altered how state law, promulgated under the general taxing power, should be interpreted:

> Since the fixation of a poll tax, the time of the accrual of same and for the payment thereof as a condition to vote, as well as all exemptions therefrom, are provided for and regulated by our state Constitution, as amended by the Nineteenth Amendment . . . [t]he result is that, the Nineteenth Amendment becoming operative prior to the 1st day of October, 1920, all women who were over 21 years of age and under 45 on said date became liable to the payment of the poll tax due on said date and which would become delinquent the 1st of the following February as a condition to vote in succeeding elections.[45]

The court concluded that the female petitioner was entitled to a writ of mandamus forcing the tax collector to let the petitioner pay the tax and receive a receipt. One justice dissented, arguing that the Nineteenth Amendment only barred discriminatory laws, and should not be construed as mandating that women pay the poll tax.[46] That dissenting justice took an extremely narrow view of the nexus between voting and the mechanism by which the government conditioned that right, that is, payment of the poll tax. The majority's view of the nexus was much more capacious. This demonstrates that the power of state court judges to construe the scope of just what "voting" encompassed, was outcome determinative. It could imbue the Nineteenth Amendment with more, or less, power to have an impact on state constitutional and statutory law, other than voting.

As the dissent in *Eubank* suggested, the Nineteenth Amendment implicated not only *who* poll taxes were due from but whether the payment of such taxes was mandatory, even if newly enfranchised women did not want to vote. In 1923, the Court of Civil Appeals of Texas, Fort Worth, in *Stuard v. Thompson*,[47] considered the protest of a married woman assessed a poll tax, even though she had no intention of exercising her right to vote. Fannie Stuard owned property in Parker County, Texas, and was assessed a state poll tax of $1.50 and a county poll tax of 25 cents as part of her property taxes.[48] Mrs. Stuard "did not desire to vote or in any manner exercise the right to suffrage in any primary or general election in the state of Texas, and so informed the said assessor at the time."[49] Mrs. Stuard's husband paid the tax collector $59.47 of the $61.22 assessed, the $1.75 discrepancy being the amount of Mrs. Stuard's poll tax.[50] The tax collector refused to receive the incomplete property tax payment.[51]

Mrs. Stuard argued that the right to pay a poll tax was "optional with her and [was] only prescribed by the law as a prerequisite to vote." Since Mrs. Stuard had no intention of voting, "the payment of the poll tax [was] not compulsory."[52] The *Stuard* court began its analysis by laying out the constitutional foundation for the poll tax in Texas. The Texas State Constitution gave specific authority to raise revenue through a poll tax, and the state's legislature acted under that power to fix the amount, and the persons, who would be subject to that tax.

The *Stuard* court described its view of the Nineteenth Amendment's impact: the amendment extended the privilege of voting to women but it did not mandate that they must vote. Indeed, voting was not a right but a privilege conferred by the legislature on those citizens it considered properly equipped to exercise it. Citing *Solon v. State*, the court quoted the late Justice Ramsey:

> The right to vote is not a necessary or fixed incident to citizenship, or inherent in each and every individual, but that voting is the exercise of political power, and no one is entitled to vote, unless the people in their sovereign capacity have conferred on him the right to do so. It may be laid down as a general proposition that the right of suffrage may be regulated and modified or withdrawn by the authority which conferred it.[53]

The *Stuard* court went on to note that the legislature had the power to require women to pay a poll tax, whether or not they chose to vote. The power to limit the privilege of voting included the exercise of the state's general taxing power, to require that citizens pay a poll tax as a condition of voting. The court described the general power of the state to tax and its source:

> The power of taxation is inherent in a sovereign state. The right to tax is not granted by the Constitution but of necessity underlies it, because government could not exist or perform its functions without it. While it may be regulated and limited by the Constitution, it exists without express authority in the fundamental law as a necessary attribute of sovereignty. The provisions of the Constitution which relate to the power of taxation do not

operate as grants of the power of taxation to the government thus set up, but constitute limitations upon a power which would otherwise be without limit.[54]

The *Stuard* court concluded that the state could require payment of the poll tax, even if a citizen chose not to exercise the privilege of voting.[55] It found that the law mandating payment, whether or not one intended to vote, was a "reasonable and an effective means of forcing the payment of the poll tax levied by the Constitution and Legislature, similar in purpose to the legislative provision denying the privilege to vote without payment of such tax."[56] Thus, the court affirmed the judgment below. And it refused to issue a writ of mandamus, a court order that would have forced the tax collector to accept Mr. Stuard's poll tax, without Mrs. Stuard's poll tax, as payment in full.[57]

In 1923, in *Davis v. Warde*, the Supreme Court of Georgia also considered the effect of the Nineteenth Amendment on *when* women became liable for a poll tax.[58] On December 4, 1922, the city of Albany held an election, focused on changing the structure of local government.[59] In that election, 257 women had voted without paying a poll tax.[60] The mayor, who was unhappy with the electoral outcome, ordered the voter registration lists purged of anyone who was not eligible to vote "in accordance with law." This would include anyone who had not paid his or her poll taxes. If the 257 votes by women were excluded, the result of the election would be overturned. Those challenging the validity of the 257 female votes argued that a new act, passed by the Georgia legislature in 1921, required that women pay the tax *prior* to voting. The challengers argued that the only exemption from payment of the tax, under that act, was being blind or having lost limbs fighting for the Confederacy.[61]

The challengers asserted that the 257 women voters had not paid their poll tax in 1921 and 1922. Therefore, they were not eligible voters and should not have been allowed to register to vote in 1921. Nor should they have been allowed to actually vote in the December 4, 1922, election about the city charter. The *Davis* court examined the impact of the Nineteenth Amendment on the question of whether and when those women had to pay the poll tax, in order to be eligible to vote in the 1922 election:

> The plaintiffs insist that upon the Nineteenth Amendment becoming effective women were subject to the payment of poll tax the same as men, from that date, and that they were liable for the payment of such tax from

the date on which such amendment became effective; and it is argued that from that date no state could require a poll tax from men as a condition precedent to their right to vote, unless it also required the same poll tax from all women as a condition precedent to their right to register and vote, for otherwise, it is argued, the state would be abridging the right of a man to vote by requiring of him the payment of a poll tax, while it did not require the payment of such poll tax from a woman as a condition precedent to her right to vote.[62]

The *Davis* court went on to note that those challenging the women's votes relied on the *Graves v. Eubank* decision in Alabama. The Georgia Supreme Court had previously viewed that decision favorably in *Brown v. Atlanta*.[63] In *Brown*, the court had said, "The Constitution of the United States is the supreme law of operation in this state . . . We are of the opinion that [the Nineteenth] amendment is self-executing and that under it females are not now disqualified on account of their sex to register and to vote, but on the contrary they are qualified." The *Brown* court ruled that women could vote even though they had not paid a poll tax, since there was no state legislation *requiring* them to do so at the time the Nineteenth Amendment was ratified. The Georgia statute was finally amended to include women, as well as men, in the poll tax requirement. But that law did not go into effect until January 1, 1922.[64]

The *Davis* court noted that the new law requiring women to pay the poll tax was exactly the same as the prior law, except that it no longer included the word "male" to modify "inhabitant." Therefore, the court found that the purpose of the 1921 legislation was to add a poll tax on women *and, by implication, provide that none had been due prior to January 1, 1922*. Affirming the judgment of the lower court that the 257 votes by women were valid, despite their not having paid the poll tax prior to voting, the *Davis* court explained that "No poll tax was required to be paid by women in this state until January 1, 1922, and the expiration of the time fixed by law for the payment of taxes for that year was December 20. The election was held on December 4, 1922, prior to the expiration of the time for the payment of taxes for that year, and therefore, under the constitutional provision above quoted, if their names appeared on the registration list for 1921 they were legally qualified voters, so far as not having paid a poll tax for the year 1922 is concerned."[65]

Thus, the *Davis* court construed the absence of a law requiring women to pay a poll tax to mean that no tax was required, and therefore their votes were still valid. The court was applying rules of construction to determine the meaning of the absence of a statutory mandate to pay tax. It decided that the absence of such a statute, impliedly allowed women to meet a different precondition prior to voting than men, at least until the state stepped in, and enacted a statute requiring women to pay such a tax, too. The court could have construed the absence of a statutory provision the opposite way, to mean that the existing statute requiring men to pay a tax should be automatically extended to apply to women, back to the date of ratification.

But the construction the court chose actually facilitated the counting of women's ballots, even though, in this case, it did not result from an extension of the doctrine of self-execution to the state poll tax statute. The *Davis* court's decision allowed the 257 female votes to count and, in fact, those votes made the difference in the election that resulted in a change in the form of city government. The challengers' efforts to nullify the female votes failed, as a result of the court's use of statutory construction, finding that the legislature implicitly required no poll tax prior to January 1, 1922. It refused to endorse the view that the self-executing nature of the Nineteenth Amendment meant that a poll tax implicitly applied retroactively, back to the date of ratification. The challengers argued that such a reading discriminated against male voters, violating the terms of the Nineteenth Amendment itself prohibiting a state from denying or abridging the right of citizens to vote on account of sex. But the court rejected their argument that the Nineteenth Amendment itself should be read to prohibit a state from having any period after ratification where men, but not women, were liable for the poll tax.

In 1926, the Supreme Court of Georgia again addressed the question of women paying the required poll tax, after the ratification of the Nineteenth Amendment, in *Hawthorne v. Turkey Creek School District*.[66] The case, a follow-up to *Davis v. Warde*, concerned a school district election in which thirteen women voted without having paid a poll tax; these thirteen voters would have made the difference in the outcome of the election.[67] The women registered and actually voted in 1925, and they had not paid the poll tax in 1922, 1923, or 1924.[68] As noted before, the Georgia state legislature had passed a tax law in 1921, requiring women to pay poll taxes to be eligible to vote, beginning on January 1, 1922.[69] The question the *Hawthorne* court considered was whether, under the tax law, women were required to pay all "back" poll taxes due before being eligible to vote.[70]

The *Hawthorne* court first noted that there was no law requiring women to pay poll taxes between 1920 and 1922.[71] There was some inconsistency in the history of the poll tax legislation that was enacted as of January 1, 1922—the title of one version of the act described it as a law, "[requiring] all females to pay all back poll taxes due from the time they shall become eligible to vote to the date of their registration," but the text of the act did not contain such a clause.[72] A later amendment of the act, which the court noted superseded all previous versions, provided that the tax "shall not be required or demanded of female inhabitants of the state who do not register for voting."[73] This is the clause the *Hawthorne* court eventually found dispositive. Since the women were not registered to vote until 1925, they were not required to pay the poll taxes for 1922–1924 before voting.[74] Their votes were therefore correctly counted and the election was fairly decided.[75]

In deciding the case, the *Hawthorne* court reiterated the self-executing nature of the Nineteenth Amendment, invoking *Brown* and *Davis*, "The Nineteenth Amendment to the Constitution of the United States is self-executing, and immediately upon its becoming operative all females were entitled to vote, provided they complied with the regulations surrounding voter's qualifications in the state of their residence."[76]

Seven years after ratification, state courts were still addressing the impact of the Nineteenth Amendment on the general taxing power of the state. In 1927, in *Taaffe v. Sanderson*,[77] the Supreme Court of Arkansas considered the requirement of a poll tax for married women, whose husbands had paid the tax. It was the practice of the local sheriff to issue, "poll tax receipts to voters favorable to them," by simply adding the words "and Mrs.," to the voting list, without actually assessing those wives any tax due.[78] The trial court below held that the challenge to the election at issue had been wrongly dismissed.[79]

The statute required that "[e]very citizen" shall pay the poll tax prior to voting in any election.[80] The *Taaffe* court concluded that, although masculine pronouns were used throughout the section, the language was "broad enough to include women."[81] The court explained that there was a long-standing principle, which applied both to the construction of Constitutions and statutes, providing that "a statute extends by inference to cases not originally contemplated when it deals with a class within which a new class is brought by later statutes."[82] It based its interpretation that the masculine pronouns should be read to include women on, "the principle [of statutory construction] that, where a privilege is extended to one class of citizens upon certain conditions, and that subsequent thereto a like privilege is conferred upon another class, the conditions attached to the exercise of such privilege by the former class necessarily attaches in like manner to the subsequent class."[83]

A minority of justices were of the opinion that women were not required to pay a poll tax, because that section of the voting statute did not apply to women.[84] That minority argued, "a study of the constitutional provisions relating to the assessment and collection of a poll tax, and the provisions of the statutes enacted pursuant thereto, leads inevitably, in the opinion of the minority, to the conclusion that, neither by constitutional nor statutory provision, a woman is not required to assess a poll tax as is required of a man." The minority described a series of amendments to the Arkansas Constitution, the most recent one having been ratified in 1927, that all imposed a poll tax on "male" inhabitants:

> The other provisions of the Constitution heretofore mentioned require *males* to assess a per capita or poll tax, but the only requirement with reference to women is that, in order to vote, they shall exhibit "a poll tax receipt or other evidence that they have paid their poll tax at the time of collecting taxes next preceding such election." The sections of the statutes, relative to the assessment and collection of such annual per capita tax, nowhere use language indicating any such requirement of women. It is, therefore, the opinion of the minority that a woman is not required to assess or pay a poll tax in any event, unless she wishes to pay same in order to vote, and that the clerk could not assess her for a penalty for failure to assess at the time required of a man, because she is not required to do so, and that the provisions of section 3738 of the Digest are not therefore applicable to women voters.[85]

The *Taaffe* court was thus split in interpreting conflicting constitutional and statutory provisions. The majority found that the women voters were obligated to pay the poll tax, despite a number of amendments, after 1920, to the constitutional taxing provisions using the word "male." The majority affirmed the lower court's decision that the women's votes should therefore not be counted in the election. But the *Taaffe* minority took the position that the legislature had to enact more specific legislation to impose the tax on women, given the continued use of the word "male" in the taxing statutes. The minority essentially would have separated the taxing statutes from the voting laws in that regard. Its view could be characterized as a narrow construction of the Nineteenth Amendment's impact on state constitutional law.[86]

Finally, in the wake of ratification of the Nineteenth Amendment, state courts not only parsed whether the doctrine of self-execution applied to alter state law; they engaged with the related question of whether a political or civil right other than voting was "coextensive" or "coterminous" with voting. Courts examined the nexus between voting and political rights, like jury service and holding public office. For example, in 1930, the Supreme Court of Illinois considered a woman's right to sign a petition calling for an election, in *People ex rel. Murray v. Holmes*. The superintendent of schools of Marion County filed a petition to organize a community high school district, which was signed by forty-seven men and eighteen women.[87] A local statute required that such a petition be signed by fifty legal voters, which the petitioners interpreted to mean fifty male voters.[88] The *Murray* court thus considered the question of whether women were legal voters in April 1921, when they signed the petition to organize the district.[89]

The *Murray* court noted that at the time the statute was passed, women were considered qualified voters for purposes of the question of organizing high school districts.[90] It could be assumed, the court reasoned, that the state's General Assembly knew of the law permitting women to participate in these elections at the time it passed the fifty-signature petition requirement.[91] The court noted that the effect of the Nineteenth Amendment's ratification was "to erase instanter . . . every provision restricting the right of women to vote."[92]

The *Murray* court addressed the federalism issue at stake, in light of the Nineteenth Amendment: "The amendment did not confer upon women the right to vote. The right of suffrage is derived from the state. The amendment to the federal Constitution merely provided that no state should discriminate concerning the right to vote between citizens on account of sex. The word 'male' was stricken from article 7 of the Constitution and from every place where it occurs in the statutes in regard to the right of suffrage."[93]

The challengers in *Murray* relied on *People ex rel. Fyfe v. Barnett*, a decision discussed in the next chapter, which refused to extend the right of jury service to women.[94] The *Murray* court distinguished *Fyfe* from the case before it. It noted that *Murray* dealt directly with the right to vote, and not jury service, a right the court described as contingent on suffrage.[95] The court asserted that the principle in *Fyfe* did not apply since all restrictions on voting had been "swept away by the Nineteenth Amendment." However, like the *Fyfe* court, the *Murray* court conceptualized jury service very differently, noting sweeping judicial change to jury service had not happened, as a result of the Nineteenth Amendment.[96] The *Murray* court stated, "The Nineteenth Amendment has nothing to do with the qualification for service as jurors. The laws of this state provide for the selection of jurors from the electors, but not all electors are eligible to be selected as jurors. The federal government has nothing to do with their selection as jurors."[97] It continued to distinguish jury service itself from voting:

> The right, the duty, or the privilege of serving as a juror, whichever it may be called, is not a natural right, privilege, or duty, but is conferred or imposed by statute. When the General Assembly granted the right or imposed the duty of jury service on certain classes of electors, no one but electors were included, though they might have been. Jury service was not an attribute or quality or privilege or duty which arose from the right of suffrage, and jury service *and the right of suffrage were, and are, neither synonymous nor conterminous* (emphasis added).

The court went on to clearly distinguish statutes defining eligibility for jury service from state laws that defined voter eligibility: "The . . . qualification of electors for voting at elections for the organization of high school districts . . . was concerned directly with the qualification of the elector as an elector. It dealt only with the right to vote—nothing else; and whatever may have been the power to restrict that right was swept away by the Nineteenth Amendment, leaving the unrestricted right to vote to men and women alike." The court went on to distinguish jury service and the different state and federal sovereignty around that issue: "On the other hand, the right of the General Assembly to restrict, abridge, deny, or enlarge the right and duty of jury service cannot be denied. . . ."[98] Because women had been given full suffrage at the time the petition was signed, the *Murray* court found that the female petitioners' signatures were deemed valid.[99]

While it was decided in 1937, long after the end of the decade that is the subject of this book, there is a final, federal poll tax case worth noting. In *Breedlove v. Suttles,* the US Supreme Court addressed the question of women paying a required poll tax, and whether exempting women discriminated against men, based on their sex.[100] The court evaluated constitutional arguments grounded in the Equal Protection and Privileges or Immunities clauses of the Fourteenth Amendment, as well as in the Nineteenth Amendment. In what has been characterized as, "the only Supreme Court case to directly decide whether a state law violated the Nineteenth Amendment, . . . The Court rejected each of these grounds for invalidating the statute, spending the most time on the equal protection argument (the only part of the *Breedlove* decision that the Supreme Court reversed in the 1966 *Harper* case)."[101]

The Georgia statute at issue in *Breedlove* required an annual poll tax on every citizen between the ages of twenty-one and sixty, with the exception of the blind and women who did not register to vote.[102] The plaintiff was a white twenty-eight-year-old male who attempted to vote despite not having paid the poll tax, and was refused by the election official.[103] He asserted, among other claims, that the poll tax exemption for women was a violation of the Nineteenth Amendment.[104] The *Breedlove* court upheld the statute, reasoning that just as minors could be exempted because of the potential burden on their parents, women could also be exempted from the poll tax, "[i]n view of burdens necessarily borne by them for the preservation of the race." The court noted that "[t]he laws of Georgia declare the husband to be the head of the family and the wife to be subject to him. To subject her to the levy would be to add to his burden."[105] The court reasoned that the Nineteenth Amendment did not serve to regulate taxes, and to interpret it as the plaintiff suggested "would make the amendment a limitation upon the power to tax."[106] The court therefore held that the poll tax did not abridge women's right to vote in violation of the Nineteenth Amendment.[107] These statements are notable, in view of state poll tax cases, like *Graves v. Eubank*, which reasoned that the Nineteenth Amendment did extend to the general taxing power of the states. *Breedlove* can thus be read as a retreat from such state court decisions' thicker reading of the Nineteenth Amendment's impact on other constitutional doctrine.

Breedlove is particularly interesting because the court lapsed into the language of coverture when it said, "the laws of Georgia declare the husband to be the head of the family." Yet, the seventy-two-year history that preceded ratification of the Nineteenth Amendment can be read as a rejection of coverture, and an endorsement of what Reva Sigel has called the democratic reconstruction of the family.[108] However, the former suffragists did not focus on the Nineteenth Amendment as a constitutional means to ending all the civil disabilities of women. And neither the NWP nor NAWSA focused on its interpretation in state courts as a means of expanding political rights. Immediately after ratification, neither the NWP's new Constitution adopted at its February 1921 convention, nor the NLWV program endorsed at its 1920 Victory Convention, explicitly included the issue of poll taxes.[109] However, both organizations did seek out the opinion of state Attorneys General about whether the lack of payment of a poll tax would hinder women registering to vote in the November 1920 elections.[110]

Poll taxes had a disproportionate impact on women voters, preventing more women than men from voting.[111] But such arguments do not appear in the state cases around the poll tax that came in the wake of ratification.[112] Those state courts were focused on constitutional doctrines like self-execution, rather than on whether such taxes deterred women from voting. That question, and the question the Supreme Court of Illinois addressed in *Murray*—whether voting was coextensive with other political or civil rights—turned out to be a hallmark of a second line of cases litigated in the decade after ratification of the Nineteenth Amendment.

In the election and the poll tax cases discussed here, there was a consensus by state courts around the self-executing nature of the Nineteenth Amendment. However, in the jury service and public office cases, there was a distinct split among state courts as to whether that self-executing nature extended to those corollary political rights. Many states had statutes that automatically made "electors" eligible to serve on a jury or hold public office. The issue of whether such statutes should be construed to automatically extend those other political rights to women became a heavily contested issue in the decade after ratification. State courts seemed able to see a close nexus between voting and voter registration, petitioning, and poll taxes. But the question of whether voting was coextensive with jury service and holding public office yielded much more division among state courts in the decade after ratification of the Nineteenth Amendment. Suffragists saw all of these political rights as essential to being full participants in governance. And many worked for state legislative change, in the areas of jury service and holding public office.[113] Yet, as the next chapter demonstrates, the partialized nature of constitutional citizenship for women continued to be upheld by state courts in the decade following ratification.

5

Voting and Jury Service

The Nineteenth Amendment to the Constitution of the United States makes no provision whatever with reference to the qualifications of jurors . . . While this amendment had the effect of nullifying every expression in the Constitution and laws of the state denying or abridging the right of suffrage to women on account of their sex, it did not purport to have any effect whatever on the subject of liability or eligibility of citizens for jury service.
—*People ex. rel. Fyfe v. Barnett* (Illinois Supreme Court 1925)

In addition to federalism, state court interpretation of the Nineteenth Amendment implicated a second significant constitutional issue, women's citizenship. The cases described in the last chapter illustrate how local elections and preconditions on voting, like poll taxes, were affected by ratification of the Nineteenth Amendment. In those cases, state courts addressed the question of whether state constitutional provisions or statutes should be interpreted to mandate such taxes on women, in the same way that men were required to fulfill that obligation prior to voting. Those cases illustrated the broader federalism issues inherent in defining the scope of the Nineteenth Amendment's impact on other state constitutional doctrine, like the general taxing power.[1] The cases described in this chapter, and the next, reflect another major constitutional question that followed quickly on the heels of ratification—What was the new scope of women's citizenship in the body politic? Would state courts simply extend the vote to women? Or would other political rights and duties of citizenship previously denied to women, like jury service or holding public office, be extended by virtue of ratification?[2]

Like the cases in the last chapter, the cases in this chapter highlight the power of the interpretive function of state courts as constitutional actors. Subsumed within the question of whether the Nineteenth Amendment was self-executing was the threshold question of whether voting was

Constitutional Orphan. Paula A. Monopoli, Oxford University Press (2020). © Paula A. Monopoli.
DOI: 10.1093/oso/9780190092795.001.0001

"coextensive" with, or closely connected enough to, other constitutional rights or statutory duties to extend them to women, without further legislative action. One of those rights, a hallmark of full citizenship for men, was jury service:

> In most states, a common qualification for jury service was the status of elector—that is, a citizen with the right to vote. This also fit with the nineteenth-century woman rights movement's conception of citizenship. As equal voting citizens, women would obtain all of the rights and privileges of other first class citizens, including the right to serve on a jury. After voting, this was the most significant right or duty that citizens commonly filled. Jury service was democracy in action—it was direct governance by the citizens. Women's exclusion from this role suggested that, even with the vote, they had yet to obtain the status of equal citizens.[3]

In case after case involving whether women who were now "electors" could also be jurors, the implicit question was whether jury service was a corollary right, with a sufficient nexus to voting, to come within the ambit of the Nineteenth Amendment.[4] The state courts were split on the issue of whether jury statutes that made all "electors" eligible for jury service automatically included women, once the Nineteenth Amendment prohibited states from using sex a criterion for voting. Some embraced a capacious statutory construction, while others adopted a narrow view of what constituted a nexus with voting, finding that it was quite separate from the right to sit on a jury. Defining that relationship between voting and jury service was central to the courts' analysis in these cases. The more expansive the view of which political rights were closely related to voting, the more likely a court was to find that women were eligible to be jurors, without further state action.

In the wake of ratification, the NWP's Research Department began to track the state cases that were bubbling up around the country. Sue Shelton White, party member and chair of the NWP's February 1921 convention, observed:

> The operation of the federal suffrage has made eligible for jury service the women of a number of states who were formerly disqualified by the use of the words "voter" or "elector" as the primary qualifying terms. In at least one of these states, Iowa, it is reported that an extremely cautious jury commission resolved to give the women a year's immunity "in which to

render themselves competent for jury service." By this subterfuge the operation of the federal suffrage amendment as it affects jury service is held in
abeyance.[5]

Shelton criticized state courts in Texas, Massachusetts, and Delaware that had
not interpreted existing state statutes to extend juror eligibility to women.
"The wrong way of thinking in regard to women is deeply rooted and by no
means to be measured by the tangible evidence of the law, the opinions which
seek to justify the decisions."[6] White's observation about state court judges,
and their decisions, highlights the role that gender and perceptions about
the proper sphere of women played in the constitutional development of the
Nineteenth Amendment. These attitudinal choices, as well as institutional
choices to reserve political power to white men, were evident in the state
cases about jury service and holding public office, from 1920 to 1930.

Jury service can be characterized as either a political right, allowing a citizen, "democratic participation in the exercise of law and justice," or it can
be described as a civil right, "a matter of individual protection against state
authority."[7] While historically, political and civil rights were seen as closely
connected, some scholars have noted that "by the early twentieth century,
rights activists began to conceive of civil and political rights more discreetly,
and the character of jury service began to be cast more narrowly as a civil
right. This shift occurred partly in response to the narrow and discrete
casting of civil rights (including jury service) by the Supreme Court in the
late nineteenth century."[8] However, most modern constitutional scholars
refer to jury service, and public officeholding, as political rights.

As noted in Chapter 3, "Enforcement Legislation," there were several sig-
nificant federal cases about jury service, in the wake of the Reconstruction
Amendments. These cases included *Strauder v. West Virginia* in 1880, and
Neal v. Delaware in 1881. Both informed the jury service cases in state courts,
which followed ratification of the Nineteenth Amendment. In *Strauder*, the
United States Supreme Court held that a state statute that prohibited African
Americans from jury service was a denial of equal protection.[9] However, the
court made clear that states could still use age or sex to limit jury service. And
the court opined that the protections of the Fourteenth Amendment were
intended to apply solely to African Americans, citing its own opinion in the
Slaughterhouse Cases: "We doubt very much whether any action of a State,
not directed by way of discrimination against the negroes, as a class, will ever
be held to come within the purview of this provision."[10]

The court decided *Neal v. Delaware* in 1881. While decided on Fourteenth Amendment grounds, the court noted:

> Beyond question the adoption of the Fifteenth Amendment had the effect, in law, to remove from the State Constitution, or render inoperative, that provision which restricts the right of suffrage to the white race. Thenceforward, the statute which prescribed the qualifications of jurors was, itself, enlarged in its operation, so as to embrace all who by the State Constitution, as modified by the supreme law of the land, were qualified to vote at a general election.[11]

In his dissent in *Neal*, Justice Field laid out the argument for why, even if one applied the equal protection clause of the Fourteenth Amendment, a state's decision to exclude African Americans would not be a denial of equal protection. Field drew a sharp line between civil rights—the right to be free from state interference—and political rights, casting jury service as a political right outside the ambit of either the privileges or immunities clause of the Fourteenth Amendment or its equal protection clause:

> Equal protection of the laws of a State is extended to persons within its jurisdiction, within the meaning of the amendment, when its courts are open to them on the same terms as to others, with like rules of evidence and modes of procedure, for the security of their persons and property, the prevention and redress of wrongs, and the enforcement of contracts; when they are subjected to no restrictions in the acquisition of property, the enjoyment of personal liberty, and the pursuit of happiness, which do not equally affect others; when they are liable to no other nor greater burdens or charges than such as are laid upon others, and when no different nor greater punishment is enforced against them for a violation of the laws.[12]

Field went on to distinguish these civil rights from political rights, noting that in his view the Fourteenth Amendment, "has no more reference to [political rights] than it has to social rights and duties, which do not rest upon any positive law, though they are more potent in controlling the intercourse of individuals. . . ."[13]

The state cases that followed ratification of the Nineteenth Amendment in 1920 often referenced prior federal cases like *Strauder* and *Neal*. And the state courts, in these cases, often cited those US Supreme Court cases, either for support for the proposition that voting and jury service were coextensive rights, or to distinguish those cases when those courts held otherwise. But, significantly, *Strauder* and *Neal* both involved not only the Reconstruction Amendments themselves, but the enforcement legislation that was enacted pursuant to section five of the Fourteenth Amendment and section two of the Fifteenth Amendment.[14] For example, in *Neal,* the court invoked the Civil Rights Act of 1875. That act expressly forbade the exclusion of citizens from jury service:

> The Reconstruction Congress added to its array of Citizenship Clause legis-
> lation by enacting the Civil Rights Act of 1875, which (among other things)
> gave blacks the same right as white citizens to serve on juries. Most states
> had excluded black citizens from jury service before the Civil War, and
> the Civil Rights Act of 1866 left this practice undisturbed. But Congress
> eventually got around to outlawing these racial exclusions in 1875, when it
> enacted a sweeping prohibition on racially discriminatory juror-selection
> practices.[15]

The 1875 act provided that "[N]o citizen possessing all other qualifications which are or may be prescribed by law shall be disqualified for service as grand or petit juror in any court of the United States, or of any State, on ac-count of race, color, or previous condition of servitude . . . ."[16] The act was sweeping, and it implicated state and federal juries.[17] But, as noted previously in Chapter 3, "Enforcement Legislation," no similar legislation was enacted pursuant to section two of the Nineteenth Amendment and that was signifi-cant in the Nineteenth Amendment's development in state courts.

The NWP and the NLWV were deeply concerned about whether women would be given full political rights after ratification, including jury service and the right to hold public office. But their efforts were focused primarily on supporting state chapters, who sought the enactment of statutes to ex-tend jury service to women, rather than on the courts. Holly McCammon notes: "Almost all of the efforts to qualify women for juries occurred at the state rather than the federal level . . . [and] the vast bulk of the advo-cacy to permit women on juries targeted state legislatures."[18] The former national suffrage organizations and their successors played a much smaller role than the state chapters. "Most commonly, the state League of Women Voters led the campaigns . . . Whereas the national League of Women Voters was in favor of women on juries, it was the state Leagues that orchestrated the campaigns . . . often working in collaboration with the other groups, including the New York branch of the National Woman's Party in the early years of the [New York] campaign."[19] In a few instances like Wisconsin, the campaign was "primarily directed by the Wisconsin branch of the National Woman's Party. State branches of the National Woman's Party—especially in the early decades of the campaigns—pressed hard for jury rights, but with mounting losses, the Party turned its focus to winning a national equal rights amendment instead of waging state-by-state campaigns for women jurors."[20] And McCammon notes that former African American suffragists, "were far more inclined to fight against lynching and their disenfranchisement than to expend efforts on jury rights" in the early years after ratification.[21]

The jury service cases that bubbled up in state courts from 1920 to 1930 can be classified by examining *who* was challenging the exclusion of women from the jury.[22] The first category of cases included challenges by a defendant, who claimed the lack of female jurors deprived him or her of a fair trial. A second, smaller category included challenges by a potential female juror, who claimed that this right had now been extended to her via the Nineteenth Amendment, despite state statutes that might indicate only male electors could serve on juries.[23] The outcomes in these cases were fairly evenly split, with five essentially holding the Nineteenth Amendment did not automatically extend jury service to women and six holding the opposite way. One of the most interesting features of this body of cases is that the judges often refer to the other state courts, deciding similar cases, during the decade after ratification. This interstate, high court dialogue indicates that divining the meaning of the Nineteenth Amendment was a significant part of state court jurisprudence, during the ten years after ratification.

I. Cases Finding That Voting Was Coextensive with Jury Service

The state court cases extending jury service to women illustrate how some judges saw ratification of the Nineteenth Amendment as a constitutional consensus about the full political and civil emancipation of women. The judges who chose to extend jury service to women interpreted jury service as coextensive with voting, and clearly *within* the self-executing ambit of the Nineteenth Amendment.

In 1920 in *People v. Barltz*, the Supreme Court of Michigan addressed the issue of whether women were allowed to serve on juries as a consequence of ratification of the Nineteenth Amendment, and the Michigan woman suffrage amendment.[24] In *Barltz*, the male defendant had been convicted by a jury of eleven men and one woman.[25] He appealed his conviction on the grounds that the juror, Miss C.M. Gitzen, was not permitted by the state constitution to sit on the jury because she was a woman.[26] The *Barltz* court began its analysis by describing the Michigan juror qualification statute, which stated that jurors must be electors and "in possession of their natural faculties," among other soundness qualifications.[27] The *Barltz* court made it clear that there was no question of the female juror's right to vote, and that she was otherwise a completely qualified juror. It then parsed the impact of the state constitutional amendment, granting women suffrage:

> What was the purpose and object of the people in adopting the constitutional amendment striking out the word 'male' from the Constitution? Was it not to do away with all distinction between men and women as to the right to vote, or as to being electors? We think there can be but one answer to this question, and that is that the purpose was to put women upon the same footing as men with reference to the elective franchise. What then was the result? Women became thereby electors. The moment a woman became an elector under the constitutional amendment she was entitled to perform jury duty, if she was possessed of the same qualifications that men possessed for that duty. In other words, she was placed in a class of citizens and electors, from which class jurors were, under the statute, to be selected.[28]

The *Barltz* court concluded that it was, "clear to us that by making a woman an elector she is thereby placed in a class which makes her eligible for jury duty," rejecting the argument that the preexisting statute should be interpreted to only include that class of persons eligible at the time the statute was enacted.[29]

Similarly, the *Barltz* court reasoned that the amendment to the Michigan Constitution, granting women suffrage, modified the constitutional provisions regarding jury service and that "the provisions should all be construed together." In other words, the phrase, "which may consist of less than twelve men" should now be read as, "which may consistent of less than twelve jurors," inclusive of women. The *Barltz* court rejected the argument that jury service should be limited to those persons eligible at common law and that, because only men were eligible at common law, the court was not free to construe the state constitution in any other way. The court noted that there was an "unbroken line of decisions in all the states" providing that the right to trial by jury should be construed as that which existed at common law, but that state legislatures controlled those qualifications. Thus, "even though such qualifications may differ from those at common law, such legislation is nevertheless a valid exercise of legislative power. So long as the essential requisites of trial by jury are preserved, it is competent for the Legislature to prescribe the necessary qualifications of jurors, and additional qualifications may from time to time be imposed by the Legislature."[30]

The *Barltz* court found that although the Michigan Constitution referred to juries as consisting of "men," by virtue of the federal and state suffrage amendments, the term "men" lost its gendered significance, and should be read to mean "jurors."[31] The court examined case law that provided rules of statutory construction that required courts to read the word "man" in its broadest sense, to include men and women. It concluded by citing dictionary definitions of "man," which defined it as including all mankind or "human being."[32] In so doing, the court invoked rules of statutory construction, drawn from prior case law, which provided that "[t]o accommodate the evident intention of the parties, words will be construed with an unusual extent of meaning, and held to be generic rather than specific; as, for instance, 'men' will be interpreted to mean mankind, and include women."[33]

The *Barltz* court's position was that Nineteenth Amendment, and the Michigan amendment, trumped the common law rule. Thus, voting and jury service were coextensive. The *Barltz* court's expansive statutory construction of the word "men" also gives a sense of how some judges saw the extension of suffrage to women as a broader emancipatory constitutional move. And they used statutory interpretation to ensure its impact on distinct, albeit related, constitutional rights and legislative privileges.

In 1921, the Supreme Court of Pennsylvania was also asked to determine whether the pool of qualified jurors was automatically expanded, as new groups became "electors."[34] In *Commonwealth v. Maxwell*, Maxwell was charged with murder and moved to quash the indictment because one of the jurors was a woman.[35] The trial court granted the motion, which the commonwealth appealed.[36]

The defendant argued that since women had not been permitted at common law to serve on juries, the Pennsylvania Constitution prohibited women from serving.[37] The *Maxwell* court noted, however, that the framers knew that the legislature, not the common law, determines who can serve as a juror.[38] The court provided a lengthy history of Pennsylvania statutory jury qualifications, beginning in 1664.[39] The court first concluded that there were no "absolute and fixed qualifications" for jurors at common law, as the qualifications were always determined by legislation.[40] Most significantly, the court concluded that "the designation 'qualified elector' embraces all electors at the time jurors are selected from the body of electors; [and] the term 'electors' embraces those who may be added to the electorate from time to time."[41]

The *Maxwell* court's opinion began by describing the impact of the Nineteenth Amendment, to give women the vote and make them electors. The court went on to detail the statutes that had governed trials by jury, prior to the enactment of Pennsylvania's first constitution. It concluded from a review of those statutes that the constitution's framers knew that "legislation determined the qualifications of jurors, not the common law . . ." It concluded that "It will thus be seen that since 1805, when the Constitution of 1790 was in force, the persons charged with the duty of jury service have been fixed, from time to time, by the Legislature, and have been 'taxable citizens,' 'white male taxable citizens,' 'male taxable citizens,' 'taxable inhabitants,' and 'qualified electors.' This follows the rule that the qualification of jurors and the manner of selecting them are usually by statute."[42]

The *Maxwell* court cited a number of cases to buttress its position that the common law trial by jury could be legislatively altered, as long at the essential features of fairness were maintained. It then relied on the Michigan Supreme Court's decision in *Barltz*, and reiterated the *Barltz* court's reliance on the proposition that "It seems to be the settled law in all the states, so far as we have been able upon examination to discover, that the qualifications of jurors are matters of legislative control, even though the qualifications laid down by the Legislature differ from those at the common law."[43]

The *Maxwell* court went on the detail the numerous changes at common law in the qualifications of jurors, including the abandonment of property holding and annual income requirements. Noting that it was difficult to say "just what was the common-law right of trial by jury," the court concluded that there were a number of modifications, from the time of King John's charter to the founding of the early English colonies in America." The *Maxwell* court cited *Hurtado v. California*, in which the US Supreme Court suggested that "It is more consonant to the true philosophy of our historical legal institutions to say that the spirit of personal liberty and individual right, which they embodied, was preserved and developed by a progressive growth and wise adaptation to new circumstances and situations of the forms and processes found fit to give, from time to time, new expression and greater effect to modern ideas of 'self-government.' "[44]

The *Maxwell* court embraced this approach to statutory interpretation. "Statutes framed in general terms apply to new cases that arise, and to new subjects that are created from time to time, and which come within their general scope and policy."[45] The court reversed the order below, which had quashed the indictment, because there had been a female juror. It reinstated the indictment, expanding the impact of its decision to all counties. While the "pending case calls for the immediate decision only of the right of women to serve as jurors in those counties which are covered by the act of 1867, [w]e entertain no doubt however that women are eligible to serve as jurors in all the commonwealth's courts."[46]

In 1926, the Indiana Supreme Court took up the issue of whether the Nineteenth Amendment extended the privilege of jury service to women. In *Palmer v. State*, the defendant was convicted of receiving a stolen automobile.[47] Palmer moved to quash the indictment on the grounds that the grand jury that returned the indictment was illegal, because a woman had acted as a forewoman.[48] As forewoman, she had participated in the investigation, voted to return the indictment, and signed the back of the document.[49]

Like the *Maxwell* court, the *Palmer* court began its analysis by observing that jury qualification was a matter for the legislature, and that historically women were not permitted to serve on juries (with the exception of all-female juries of matrons, designated to determine whether or not a woman was pregnant).[50] The court noted that the voting statute provided: "To be qualified as a juror, either grand or petit, a person must be a resident voter of the county."[51] The court concluded that, where the statute dictates jurors were to be chosen from the pool of qualified electors, "the adoption of a constitutional amendment making women electors qualifies them for jury duty."[52]

In its decision, the *Palmer* court first reiterated what many of its fellow state courts had said, "that at common law women were not qualified to serve as jurors, with only one exception. And it is now settled, beyond any controversy, that qualifications of jurors are matters of legislative control, even though the qualifications laid down by the Legislature differ from those of the common law." The court went on to describe the Indiana jury statute that required jurors to be "resident voters and a freeholder or householder." Noting that the law was in force when the defendant was indicted in 1924, the court went on to cite the Nineteenth Amendment and the subsequent amendment to the Indiana Constitution ensuring that every citizen who was otherwise qualified was entitled to vote. The court concluded that "Where, by statute, jurors are to be selected from qualified electors, the adoption of a constitutional amendment making women electors qualifies them for jury duty," citing, among others, the *Barltz* and *Maxwell* cases.[53] The court invoked the state's rules of statutory construction: "It is a rule of statutory construction that legislative enactments in general and comprehensive terms, prospective in operation, apply alike to all persons, subjects, and business within their general purview and scope coming into existence subsequent to their passage."[54]

Citing other state court decisions, including *In re Opinion of the Justices, James* and *Fyfe* discussed subsequently in this chapter, the *Palmer* court acknowledged that "In some other states, the highest courts have arrived at a different conclusion from that stated as to the effect of the Nineteenth Amendment." The *Palmer* court distinguished its decision from these other state court decisions, by invoking a 1917 statute granting women partial suffrage (later declared unconstitutional). It construed the Indiana jury statute, amended the same year, in light of that 1917 statute.[55] The *Palmer* court reasoned that, at the time the jury qualification legislation was enacted, the state legislature believed that both men and women would be voters.[56] The court therefore held that the forewoman was not disqualified from jury service. Thus, there was no reason she was incompetent to serve as forewoman, and the court denied Palmer's motion to quash the indictment.[57]

Later that same year, the Indiana Supreme Court reiterated the central holding of *Palmer v. State*, that the Nineteenth Amendment should be construed to extend jury service to women.[58] In *Wilkinson v. State*, the defendant Wilkinson had been indicted during Prohibition by a grand jury on the allegation that he, "did . . . unlawfully sell, barter, exchange, give away, and dispose of intoxicating liquor."[59] He was convicted by a jury, on which one woman served, and moved for a new trial on the grounds that women were not permitted to serve on petit juries.[60] (*Palmer* had only considered the question of grand juries.)[61]

The *Wilkinson* court noted the jury qualification statute, which applied to both grand and petit juries, required that the juror must be "a resident voter of the county."[62] It rejected the argument that, because at common law women could not be jurors, this jury was tainted, "[I]n this state the qualifications of jurors are fixed by statute. The Nineteenth Amendment to the Constitution of the United States and the amendment to section 2 of article 2 of the Constitution of Indiana guarantees to women the right of suffrage on an equality with men." The court, thus, explicitly linked its conclusion that women could serve on juries, to the Nineteenth Amendment, even though that amendment dealt on its face with the vote and not jury service.

The *Wilkinson* court concluded that "[i]t would seem from the plain wording of these constitutional and statutory provisions that any woman who is a resident voter of the county and a freeholder or householder is entitled to sit on a petit jury in the trial of a criminal case."[63]

In affirming the lower court's decision, the *Wilkinson* court cited its own decision in *Palmer* as well as *Barltz* and *Maxwell*. It found that "[t]he only objection urged in the instant case to the juror challenged was her sex, and the court did not err in overruling the challenge of said juror."

The final case, extending jury service as a result of ratification of the Nineteenth Amendment, was decided in 1929. This was toward the end of a decade of state court litigation about the meaning of the Nineteenth Amendment, in terms of its impact on jury service—a constitutional and statutory right other than voting. In *Cleveland, Cincinnati, & St. Louis Railway Company v. Wehmeier*, the Ohio Court of Appeals also addressed the issue of whether women were entitled to serve as jurors, as a consequence of the Nineteenth Amendment.[64] The railway sued Matilda Wehmeier to take certain property for railway purposes. A provision of the Ohio Constitution stated that "compensation shall be ascertained by a jury of "twelve men, in a court of record, as shall be prescribed by law."[65] The case went to trial, and the jury, on which five women sat, returned a verdict indicating the value of the land taken and damages to the residue of the property.[66] Unhappy with the lower court's ruling that the jury could include women, the Railway argued that since five women sat on the jury, it was not a legal jury under the statute.[67]

The *Wehmeier* court analyzed the state constitutional provision regarding a jury of twelve men, noting that at the time of its enactment, women were not enfranchised, and thus could not sit on juries.[68] The legislature, the court reasoned, intended merely to use "men" as shorthand for "qualified juror."[69] The court further bolstered this view by noting that "[s]ince the world began, in all writings concerning the human race, the word 'man' or 'men' has been used in a generic sense, or as representing the human race."[70] The court then reviewed the juror qualifications under the state statute, which stated that jurors were to be "electors." The court interpreted that to mean qualified women could serve on juries, and they met the relevant standard in the Ohio Constitution.[71]

Like the *Barltz* court, the *Wehmeier* court engaged in extensive statutory construction of the word "men." The court determined that the word "men" in the statute was not, "used in the generic sense, and does not mean males."[72] The court found no error in the lower court's ruling that women were proper jurors because, "[t]he Nineteenth Amendment of the Constitution of the United States enfranchised women [and] [t]he qualification of a juror, under our General Code is that such juror must be an elector. These provisions make women eligible to jury service, and come within the constitutional phrase, 'as shall be prescribed by law.'"

II. Cases Finding That Voting Was Not Coextensive with Jury Service

In 1921, the Massachusetts House of Representatives presented two questions to the Supreme Judicial Court (SJC) for guidance on the constitutionality of pending legislation that required women to serve on juries, with certain exemptions (trained nurses, hospital assistants, or mothers with children under ten years of age).[73] The House asked the SJC whether, under existing law, women could be required to serve as jurors. If they were not, the House asked the SJC to opine on whether the state legislature had the authority to enact legislation to make women liable for jury service.[74] In *In re Opinion of the Justices*, the SJC began by examining an existing statute, enacted prior to the Nineteenth Amendment, which provided that "a person qualified to vote for representatives to the general court [the Massachusetts state legislature] shall be liable to serve as a juror."[75] The SJC found that, as a matter of legislative history, the legislature did not intend by those words to mandate that women serve on juries.[76] Therefore, the SJC concluded that the answer to the first question was no, the current law did not require women to serve on juries.[77]

Turning to the second question, the SJC noted that the Massachusetts Constitution had no explicit statement regarding the qualification of jurors, but that historically jurors were selected from the pool of qualified voters.[78] The SJC further observed that when amendments to the constitution expanded suffrage to groups other than women, "there has followed a like enlargement of the class of citizens liable to jury service."[79] The SJC therefore held that the state legislature did have the authority to change juror qualifications by statute.[80] The state legislature presumably would have to affirmatively take further action to change state law, to make women eligible to be jurors. In other words, the self-executing nature of the Nineteenth Amendment did not extend beyond voting to jury service.

As it began its analysis, the SJC noted that "there exists grave question and uncertainty as to the constitutional power of the General Court to enact said bill."[81] The SJC acknowledged that the words of the statute at issue, "that 'a person qualified to vote for representatives to the general court shall be liable to serve as a juror,'" were, "broad enough as matter of mere verbal analysis . . . to include women as well as men." However, the SJC emphasized that the words of the statute were not simply to be taken literally, but were to be construed in light of, "the history of the times and the entire system of which the statute in question forms a part, in the light of the Constitution, of the common law and of previous legislation upon the same subject." In finding that current law did not require that women be allowed to serve as jurors, the SJC distinguished the US Supreme Court's decisions in both *Strauder v. West Virginia* and *Neal v. State of Delaware*:

> The decisions of Strauder v. West Virginia . . . and Neal v. Delaware were made under conditions different from those here presented. The court in those cases were considering the freedom, citizenship, civil rights and voting privileges guaranteed to the colored race by the then recent amendments to the Constitution of the United States. Those decisions recognize the powers of the states to prescribe the qualifications of jurors, and in so doing to make discriminations, and to 'confine the selection to males, to freeholders, to citizens, to persons within certain ages or to persons having educational qualifications.'[82]

The SJC suggested that the US Supreme Court's extension of jury service to African American men was distinguishable, and in no need of further explanation. The SJC determined that the Nineteenth Amendment had no similar effect on the extension of jury service to women.

Opining on the second question—whether the Massachusetts legislature could enact legislation extending jury service to women—the SJC noted that the primary qualification for jurors had been that they be selected from those who were qualified to vote. In the early years of the Commonwealth, that only included men who owned property. But the property requirement had long since been modified. The essential requirement was that "jurors be selected from the body of the electorate. The enlargement of the body of the electorate, before the adoption of the Nineteenth Amendment, so as to include substantially universal manhood suffrage, has not been treated as violating the constitutional features of trial by jury." Thus, the latest enlargement of the electorate, the addition of women under the Nineteenth Amendment, should be treated similarly, "No reason based on the Constitution is perceived why women, when they become qualified to vote under the Nineteenth Amendment to the federal Constitution, should not also be eligible to jury service, if the General Court so determines." Thus, the Nineteenth Amendment, "by its own force authorizes the General Court to make a corresponding change in the qualifications of jurors."[83]

The SJC answered the second question in the affirmative, and opined that the state legislature (referred to as "the General Court" in Massachusetts) did have the authority to enact such a statute. As noted earlier, implicit in that answer was the requirement that the legislature must take such affirmative action, in order for women to be eligible for jury service. In other words, the self-executing nature of the Nineteenth Amendment on voting did not extend to jury service.

Later in 1921, the Court of Errors and Appeals of New Jersey considered a convicted defendant's claim of error for an all-male jury in *State v. James*.[84] The defendant claimed the jury commissioners refused to select any women for the jury list (which consisted of five hundred names), despite there being over five thousand qualified women in the county.[85] James argued that the all-male jury violated his constitutional rights, because the US Constitution did not bar women from serving on juries, and the New Jersey Constitution provided for trial by an "impartial" jury.[86]

The *James* court focused on the text of the jury qualification statute to deny the defendant's motion, italicizing every time a male pronoun appeared: "reside within the county from which *he* shall be taken," "at the time of *his* selection," "on *his* own oath or affirmation," etc.[87] It noted that while the statute did not explicitly state that only men could serve on jurors, "It contains a distinct recognition of the common-law qualification that men only shall be impaneled by the use of the personal pronouns of the masculine gender 'he' and 'his.'"[88]

The *James* court observed that although the state legislature may pass legislation allowing women to serve on juries, it had not yet done so, and the Nineteenth Amendment did not by itself qualify women to serve on juries.[89]

Women still had to be qualified by legislative enactment in order to serve on juries.[90] The *James* court notes that the Nineteenth Amendment, "makes no provision whatever about jurors. It emancipates women only so far as the right of suffrage is concerned, and leaves no impediment in the way of the Legislature clothing them with capacity to become and serve as jurors ... But the amendment itself does not operate in terms or by implication to qualify women as jurors. It requires legislation to do that."[91]

So the *James* court made it very clear that the self-executing nature of the Nineteenth Amendment extended only to the act of voting, and not to the related right and duty for electors to serve on juries. The court analyzed the pronouns in the state statute to support its finding that the law remained unchanged by the Nineteenth Amendment, in terms of the right or duty to sit on a jury in New Jersey. It concluded those pronouns demonstrated, "a distinct recognition of the common-law qualification that men only shall be impaneled by the use of the personal pronouns of the masculine gender 'he' and 'his.'"[92] The court acknowledged that other state courts were grappling with the same issue—whether voting and jury service were coextensive. In that regard, it referenced the Massachusetts SJC decision earlier that year in *In re Opinion of the Justices*.[93]

As part of its analysis, the *James* court acknowledged that in 1921 (after the crime at issue in this particular case), the state legislature had amended the jury qualification statute "so as to include within the description of persons liable to be summoned as grand and petit jurors, women as well as men," but that act was "not a declaratory, but a remedial, statute" and had no impact on the case at hand.[94] It ascribed the "spirit of equality of the sexes which [the Nineteenth] breathes" as the motive behind that remedial statute's enactment. This characterization hints at a judicial acknowledgment of the potential power of the Nineteenth Amendment—at least prospectively—to drive broader state constitutional and legislative reform for women.

The following year, in 1922, the Supreme Court of South Carolina considered the effect of the Nineteenth Amendment on jury service, in *State v. Mittle*.[95] The defendant, who was convicted of manslaughter, moved to quash the verdict on the grounds that women electors were excluded from serving on the jury, in violation of the Nineteenth Amendment.[96] The *Mittle* court noted that this argument rests on two assumptions: that the Nineteenth Amendment confers the right of suffrage upon women, and that the right of jury service is implied in the granted right of suffrage.[97] The court disagreed with both contentions.[98]

Regarding the nature of the Nineteenth Amendment, the court noted that it is "a popular, but a mistaken, conception that the amendment confers upon women the right to vote."[99] The amendment, the *Mittle* court stated, only prohibits sex discrimination in voting legislation.[100] The court describes the Nineteenth Amendment as having "the precise terms of the Fifteenth." And it reiterates that the US Supreme Court has held that the Fifteenth Amendment did not confer a right to vote on African American men. Rather it simply banned discrimination in voting by the states. Thus, the court concluded that the Nineteenth Amendment must be construed in the same way, "If, therefore, the privilege of jury service can be implied from the right of suffrage, which we deny, it could not be claimed as a constitutional right unless the right from which it is derived is conferred by the Constitution."[101]

The *Mittle* court went on to analyze the nexus between voting and jury service as follows, rejecting the proposition that the "right to jury service is implied from the grant of the right of suffrage."[102]

> The right to vote and eligibility to jury service are subjects of such diverse characteristics and demanding such different regulations that it is impossible to consider the one as implied in the other. To hold that one who is a qualified elector is ipso facto entitled to jury service is to deprive the Legislature of the right to prescribe any other limitation upon the right to jury service. It could not prescribe the age limit, the sex, or the mental, moral, or physical qualifications of a juror, matters which appeal so strongly to the judgment, in prescribing the fitness for their responsible duty, with due regard to the sensibilities and delicacy of feeling of those involved.[103]

The *Mittle* court concluded that voting and jury service were not coextensive, and the Nineteenth Amendment was only self-executing as to voting.[104]

The *Mittle* court noted that the defendant at issue could not raise a Fourteenth Amendment claim, because he was "not a member of the alleged excluded class." It stated that its decision in the instant case was, "limited to a construction of the Nineteenth Amendment. The effect of the Fourteenth Amendment upon a similar contention raised by a woman upon trial is not intended to be decided."[105] A petition for certiorari was filed with the US Supreme Court but it was denied. Thus, the South Carolina Supreme Court's decision that the Nineteenth Amendment itself did not extend political rights, other than voting, to women was allowed to stand. But at the beginning of the decade following ratification, the *Mittle* court's decision left open the possibility that the Fourteenth Amendment might be interpreted to extend the political right of jury service to women. That constitutional argument, grounded in the principle of full citizenship, would be made in *Commonwealth v. Welosky* at the end of that decade, in 1931.

In 1923, the Supreme Court of Louisiana considered a challenge to women being barred from serving on juries, in *State v. Bray*.[106] The defendant was an African American woman, and she had been convicted of perjury. She moved to quash the verdict, on the ground that the jury commission omitted women from serving on the jury.[107] The jury commission argued that there was "not a woman in the parish" who met the qualifications of the Louisiana Constitution. The constitution provided that "no woman shall be drawn for jury service unless she shall have previously filed with the clerk of the district court a written declaration of her desire to be subject to such service."[108]

The *Bray* court noted that because the Nineteenth Amendment pertained only to voting, and not to juries, it should be an easy decision for the court, except for the US Supreme Court's prior decision in *Neal v. Delaware*.[109] The *Bray* court distinguished *Neal*, however, noting that *Neal* interpreted a legislative enactment barring racial discrimination on juries, and was based more on the congressional enforcement legislation enacted in 1875 pursuant to the Fourteenth, than on the Fifteenth Amendment.[110] In the absence of the enactment of similar congressional enforcement legislation pursuant to the Nineteenth Amendment, the court held that the Nineteenth Amendment had no effect on Louisiana's ban on women, who chose not to register, from serving on juries.[111] The court went so far as to say that the law is "altogether favorable to women, because it gives to each and every one of them the option of saying whether she shall be subject to jury service." However, the court acknowledged that the law did create a hurdle for women, which did not exist for men.[112]

It is notable that the court focused on the lack of enforcement legislation to guide it. In distinguishing *Neal*, the court noted the defendant's argument that the provision at issue discriminated based on sex, and was thus prohibited by the Nineteenth Amendment.[113] The *Bray* court argued that, while *Neal* seemed "at first glance contrary to the ruling in the case before us the Supreme Court's decision appears on point only because the phraseology of the Nineteenth Amendment is so similar to that of the Fifteenth." The defendant offered *Neal* for the proposition that the Fifteenth Amendment alone barred both denial of the vote, and the right of a citizen to serve on a jury. In fact, the court asserted that *Neal* did no such thing. *Neal* was inapposite because it relied as much on the Fourteenth as the Fifteenth Amendment, when it extended the reach of the latter to jury service in addition to voting. "[I]t was based upon the fourth section of the [Enforcement] Act of March 1, 1875 (18 Stat. 336 [U. S. Comp. St. § 3929]), enacted more in pursuance of the Fourteenth than of the Fifteenth Amendment, providing that 'no citizen possessing all other qualifications which are or may be prescribed by law shall be disqualified for service as grand or petit juror in any court of the United States, or of any state, on account of race, color, or previous condition of servitude . . .' "[114]

There was no similar act passed evidencing congressional intent as to whether voting should be viewed as coextensive with other political rights, pursuant to the Nineteenth Amendment. Thus, the *Bray* court was able to distinguish *Neal v. Delaware* by parsing this historical distinction. "We are not called upon to say now whether the Congress has authority to forbid the states to grant any exemption, or impose any restriction, upon women that would not be likewise applicable to men with regard to their eligibility or liability for jury service. It is sufficient to say that the Congress has not enacted any legislation on the subject of eligibility or liability of women for jury service since the Nineteenth Amendment was declared adopted . . ." The court acknowledged that the Nineteenth Amendment nullified any state law preventing women from voting based on their sex. But it did not have "any effect whatever upon any previous law on the subject of liability or eligibility of citizens for jury service.[115]

In the end, the *Bray* court affirmed the lower court and the criminal sentence it imposed on the defendant. The court rejected the idea that requiring women, but not men, to register and opt in to jury service, was discriminatory. The court relied on gender schemas about women's preferences when it noted, as quoted earlier, that the law benefitted women by giving them a choice as to whether to serve on a jury. But the court did equivocate a bit when it concluded, "It does, however, abridge the women's right to serve on juries, in that it requires them to do something that is not required of men to make them eligible for jury service."[116]

In 1928, the Supreme Court of Louisiana revisited the statute it had considered in *Bray*,[117] requiring women to opt in to jury service.[118] In *State v. Dreher*, the Louisiana Supreme Court answered the question, posed but left undecided, in *Bray*—whether the Louisiana statute requiring women, but not men, to register prior to jury service was unconstitutionally discriminatory.[119] In the context of a high-profile murder, and among over one hundred claims of error, the co-defendants (one of whom was a woman) objected that no women were chosen to serve as jurors.[120] The *Dreher* court noted the clerk had testified that no woman, residing within the parish of St. Mary, had signed the written declaration. It was therefore impossible for the jury commissioner to select a woman for jury service.[121] The court explained the rationale for the law, noting that its purpose was "avoiding compulsory service of women upon juries, contrary to their wishes to exercise such a privilege of citizenship."[122] Moreover, the court noted, defendants had the right to reject, not to select, jurors.[123] The court also found no significance in the gender of the defendant, noting that "Mrs. Le Boeuf has no more right to be tried by a mixed jury of women and men than the defendant Dr. Dreher. The Constitution of the state merely guarantees to each of these defendants 'a speedy public trial by an impartial jury.' "[124]

The *Dreher* court found that the state constitutional provision on jury service was, "reasonably permissive, as the exercise of the right to serve as jurors is not burdened with any arbitrary restriction imposed upon women because of sex or as a class, but has been incorporated into the organic law of the state solely for the purpose of avoiding compulsory service of women upon juries, contrary to their wishes to exercise such a privilege of citizenship."[125] While he dissented on other grounds, Chief Justice O'Niell concurred with the majority's ruling on the issue of women and jury service. Noting that the *Bray* court had previously distinguished the US Supreme Court's decisions in *Strauder* and *Neal*, asserting that those decisions relied more on the Fourteenth Amendment than the Fifteenth, O'Niell also challenged the idea that Congress had the right to enact legislation like section 4 of the Civil Rights Act of 1875 in the context of women. "The act of Congress [relied on in *Strauder* and *Neal*] was adopted pursuant to the Fourteenth Amendment, not the Fifteenth. *The Congress has not undertaken, and I doubt that it has authority, to enact any such legislation forbidding the states to discriminate between the qualifications or exemptions of men and those of women for jury service* [emphasis added]."[126]

In 1925, the Illinois Supreme Court addressed a case brought, not by a defendant in a criminal action, but by a woman who wanted to serve as a juror. In *People ex. rel. Fyfe v. Barnett*, in the wake of legislative defeats, the Illinois League of Women Voters chose to bring on a test case in another venue.[127] Executive secretary of the state league Edith Rockwood said, "Fortunately, in this case we had the avenue of the courts to which to turn." Hannah Fyfe was the vice president of the Oak Park League of Women Voters, and she retained attorney Elizabeth Perry to represent her. Fyfe filed a writ of mandamus against the jury commissioners for Cook County, Illinois, to compel them to include her name in the county jury lists.[128] In 1924, Fyfe had sent her jury questionnaire to the county, and answered the question of whether she knew of any reason she should not serve as a juror, "None that I know of, unless the law does not allow females that privilege."[129]

The *Fyfe* court noted that at the time the state legislature passed the act tying jury qualification to status as an elector, "the words 'voters' and electors' were not ambiguous terms."[130] The state constitution of 1870 provided that electors were to be "male citizen[s]" over the age of twenty-one who had resided in the state one year, among other qualifications.[131] The court interpreted the question of women on juries as a matter of original legislative intent, and noted that at the time the legislature enacted the law, it did not intend for women to be on the jury lists.[132] In looking to the legislature's meaning of "elector," the court noted that the term "meant male persons, only, to the legislators who used it. We must therefore hold that the word 'electors,' as used in the statute, means male persons, only, and that the petitioner was not entitled to have her name replaced upon the jury list of Cook County."[133]

In terms of the Nineteenth Amendment's impact of the Illinois law, the court clearly did not see voting and jury service as coextensive:

The Nineteenth Amendment to the Constitution of the United States makes no provision whatever with reference to the qualifications of jurors. Since the adoption of the amendment to the Constitution, the Legislature of the state of Illinois has not enacted any legislation on the subject of the eligibility or liability of women for jury service. While this amendment had the effect of nullifying every expression in the Constitution and laws of the state denying or abridging the right of suffrage to women on account of their sex, it did not purport to have any effect whatever on the subject of liability or eligibility of citizens for jury service.[134]

The *Fyfe* court also described its narrow approach to statutory construction in such a case, "The only legitimate function of the court is to declare and enforce the law as enacted by the Legislature. The office of the court is to interpret the language used by the Legislature where it requires interpretation, but not to annex new provisions or substitute different ones . . . The true rule is that statutes are to be construed as they were intended to be understood when they were passed."[135] The court went on to elucidate how it was to go about ascertaining the intent of the legislature. Citing a prior case, the *Fyfe* court made clear that "The intention of the lawmakers is the law. This intention is to be gathered from the necessity or reason of the enactment and the meaning of the words, enlarged or restricted according to their real intent."[136] While the Illinois Constitution and related legislation in existence in 1870 used the words "male citizen" in conjunction with jury service, the legislation at issue in the *Fyfe* case did not. Yet the *Fyfe* court concluded that at the time that the jury service legislation at issue was enacted in Illinois, "[T]he words 'voters' and 'electors' were not ambiguous terms. They had a well-defined and settled meaning, defining electors as "a male citizen of the United States, above the age of twenty-one years, shall be entitled to vote at such election."[137]

Applying the rules of construction that it had just described, the *Fyfe* court found that the legislature clearly, "did not intend that the name of any women should be placed on the jury list, and must be held to have intended that the list should be composed of the names of male persons, only. In interpreting a statute, the question is what the words used therein meant to those using them . . . The word 'electors,' in the statute here in question, meant male persons, only, to the legislators who used it."[138] Thus, the court held that Hannah Fyfe was not entitled to have her name put on the jury list.

In essence, the *Fyfe* court read into the legislation at issue the word "male" before the phrase "electors," when the actual text of the legislation simply said, "The said commissioners upon entering upon the duties of their office, and every four years thereafter, shall prepare a list of all electors between the ages of twenty-one and sixty years, possessing the necessary legal qualifications for jury duty, to be known as the jury list."[139] That kind of approach to statutory construction illustrates the ways in which courts, uncomfortable with constitutional reform and social change, can blunt the effects of such reform.

Fyfe v. Barnett was an outlier, in that the former suffrage organizations and their state chapters were seeking jury service reform primarily in state houses, rather than courthouses. In the immediate aftermath of ratification, the NLWV was more focused on state statutory reform as a path to jury service. Its strongly held position was that "blanket" legislation to grant women equal political and civil rights—either at the federal level or at the state level—was dangerous. The NLWV feared the effect of blanket legislation on protective labor laws for women. The NLWV's position was that legislative reform to remove the legal disabilities of women should only be done by very targeted statutory change.[140] And the national organization and its state chapters, with the exception of the Illinois chapter in the *Fyfe* case, were generally not using the courts to seek jury service reform.

However, the NWP's main objective was enacting "blanket" legislation, in the form of the ERA, at the federal level, and similar legislation at the state level. It was not afraid of blanket legislation's potential impact on protective legislation because the NWP opposed such legislation. Especially after *Adkins v. Children's Hospital* in 1923, discussed in Chapter 7 "Defining Equality," the NWP could have built on the Supreme Court's suggestion that the Nineteenth Amendment applied beyond voting, to protect civil rights like the right to contract, under the Fifth Amendment's due process clause. Since voting was the apex of political rights, they could have argued that Congress must have intended lesser political rights, like jury service or public office, to be included as well. But, as described earlier, the NWP was largely absent from the state litigation, around the relationship between the Nineteenth Amendment and jury service, in the decade following ratification. That was until *Commonwealth v. Welosky* at the beginning of the next decade in 1931.

There had been an initial increase in the number of states that either interpreted state statutes to extend, or passed laws that extended jury service, to women in the immediate aftermath of ratification.[141] But that progress was short-lived. By the end of the decade following ratification, there had only been one new state, and the District of Columbia, added to the list. Perhaps it was that lack of success using the state legislative path but, much like the Illinois state chapter of the NLWV grew frustrated with legislative defeats and brought the *Fyfe* case, in 1931 the Massachusetts chapter of the NWP got involved in bringing a test case in *Commonwealth v. Welosky.*[142] The argument in *Welosky* included a Fourteenth Amendment equal protection claim. That was significant since most of the other state cases over the decade following ratification had been limited to parsing the impact of the Nineteenth Amendment on state jury service statutes.[143] When the Massachusetts SJC held that the failure to allow women on juries did not violate the Fourteenth Amendment, Bernita Shelton Matthews of the national NWP corresponded with the local Boston attorneys to prepare to file a petition for certiorari in the US Supreme Court.[144] But the Supreme Court denied certiorari.[145] In so doing, it let stand the principle that the Fourteenth Amendment's equal protection clause did not mean that states must allow women to serve on juries.

And one does not have to wonder about the influence that the lack of any enforcement legislation, like section 4 of the Civil Rights Act of 1875, had

on the state court decisions. The *Welosky* court explicitly rejected application of that particular statute, citing its reasoning that the Reconstruction
Amendments were limited in their origins to protecting formerly enslaved
persons. "The reasons heretofore stated are conclusive, in our opinion,
against the contention that there has been a violation of the Act of Congress
approved March 1, 1875 . . . to the effect that 'no citizen possessing all other
qualifications . . . prescribed by law shall be disqualified for service . . . as
a juror in any court . . . of any State, on account of race, color or previous
condition of servitude . . ."[146] Similarly the *Bray* court had said, "We are not
called upon to say now whether the Congress has authority to forbid the
states to grant any exemption, or impose any restriction, upon women that
would not be likewise applicable to men with regard to their eligibility or
liability of women for jury service since the Nineteenth Amendment was
declared adopted . . . It is sufficient to say that Congress has not enacted
any legislation on the subject . . . of jury service . . . since the Nineteenth
Amendment was declared adopted . . . on August 26, 1920."[147] And the
dissenting judge in *Dreher* suggested Congress might not even have the
authority to enact such legislation at all, "The [Civil Rights Act of 1875]
was adopted pursuant to the Fourteenth Amendment, not the Fifteenth.
The Congress has not undertaken, and I doubt that it has authority, to
enact any such legislation forbidding the states to discriminate between
the qualifications or exemptions of men and those of women for jury
service."[148]

It would have been more difficult, if not impossible, for state courts to dis-
miss the applicability of similar congressional enforcement legislation around
jury service, enacted pursuant to section two of the Nineteenth Amendment.
In the absence of a clear signal from Congress that enforcing rights to vote
under the Nineteenth Amendment included protecting other political rights
like jury service, both the Massachusetts SJC and the US Supreme Court (by
denying certiorari) could limit the constitutional scope of the Nineteenth
Amendment in conjunction with the Fourteenth. Despite the suggestion in
Adkins in 1923, that the Nineteenth Amendment should affect how the court
interpreted that Fifth Amendment's due process clause and the scope of the
police power in regulating private employment contracts, a decade later, the
same US Supreme Court stood silent, on how the Fourteenth Amendment's
equal protection clause should be understood in light of the Nineteenth
Amendment. With its denial of certiorari in *Welosky*, the Supreme Court assured that the thin conception of the Nineteenth Amendment would be the

one that emerged at the end of the decade following ratification—a conception left mostly to state courts to develop.

The battle for the right to serve on juries went on. Feminist legal pioneers Dorothy Kenyon and Pauli Murray suggested a federal remedial legislative approach to the American Civil Liberties Union (ACLU) in 1966.[149] And, it was well into the latter half of the twentieth century before the court recognized "that equal constitutional status required equal opportunity to sit on a jury." The fundamental right to serve on a jury, in the same way as men were entitled to serve, was "finally adopted by the Supreme Court in 1975, in *Taylor v. Louisiana*, which prohibited gender discrimination in establishing the jury venire, and *J.E.B. v. Alabama* in 1994, which prohibited gender discrimination in jury selection."[150]

Why suffrage failed to transform women's citizenship remains a puzzle,[151] according to scholars like Gretchen Ritter. But a close examination of the jury cases certainly suggests, in some part, *how* that failure occurred. Gretchen Ritter characterizes the question of jury service as an indicator of the historically contingent or "partialized" nature of women's citizenship. That contingent nature was, in part, a product of state court jurisprudence on the question of just how far the self-executing nature of the Nineteenth Amendment could go. All the state courts seemed to agree that the Nineteenth Amendment itself was self-executing, as far as voting itself was concerned. No further state legislation need be enacted. But the disagreement lay in the construction of the Nineteenth Amendment, as to whether or not voting and jury service were coextensive. If they were, then the self-executing nature of the Nineteenth Amendment extended to such corollary constitutional rights or legislative privileges as jury service. Statutory construction could either amplify or dampen the impact of the Nineteenth Amendment on other constitutional or statutory doctrine.

The absence of enforcement legislation adds another piece to the puzzle Ritter poses, about why the Nineteenth Amendment failed to transform women's citizenship. In the absence of such federal legislation, state court judges were free to use statutory construction to cabin the impact of the Nineteenth Amendment. The strategic choice of the NWP to quietly withdraw support for such legislation in May 1921 was significant in that regard. The *Welosky* court's abject rejection of the Fourteenth Amendment's equal protection clause application to political rights other than voting—and the denial of certiorari by the US Supreme Court that allowed that decision to stand—meant partialized citizenship was to continue for decades to come.

6

Voting and Holding Public Office

The Nineteenth Amendment was validly adopted and has become
a part of the Constitution of the United States . . . By its own force it
struck from the Constitution of this commonwealth the word 'male'
wherever it occurred as a limitation upon the right of the citizen to
vote. That is the extent of its operation. It contains no declaration
concerning the right to hold office.

—*In re Opinion of the Justices* (Massachusetts
Supreme Judicial Court 1922)

In addition to the jury service cases described in the previous chapter, state
courts addressed other corollary political rights, like holding public office,
in the decade following ratification of the Nineteenth Amendment. And,
like jury service, holding public office was "only one of [women's rights]
reformers' myriad goals."[1] But holding public office, arguably, went beyond
voting or jury service in the challenge it posed to social norms about women's
subordination within the family, and their proper sphere.[2] Planting women
solidly in the public sphere, the right to hold public office signaled a significant shift from women remaining in the private sphere, engaged in domestic
duties. It facilitated their moving into the public sphere of state legislatures,
and even Congress. The extension of such a right meant that women would
be a consistent presence in the very public act of governing. And, like jury
service reform, the activity of the national former suffrage organizations and
their state chapters and branches, in securing the right to hold office, was
situated dominantly in the state legislative arena, not the courts.[3] This was
presumably for similar reasons. State legislatures were more susceptible to
voter pressure than were courts. And courts were interpreters of existing law
and less willing to create dramatic shifts in law, leaving that to the legislature
as the more appropriate venue.

Constitutional Orphan. Paula A. Monopoli, Oxford University Press (2020). © Paula A. Monopoli.
DOI: 10.1093/oso/9780190092795.001.0001

Like the jury service cases, the public office cases that did arise in the 1920s illustrate how courts dealt with the broader question of the impact of the Nineteenth Amendment on the nature and scope of women's citizenship, within the body politic. And like the election, poll tax, and jury service cases, the officeholding cases also implicated questions around federalism, as courts considered the impact of a federal amendment on state law. Finally, like the jury service cases, the public office cases illustrate how state courts deployed statutory construction in ways that slowed the development of women's full citizenship.

The public office cases in the 1920s were not the first cases to consider the right of women to hold public office.[4] There were cases in the nineteenth century that had determined women were not generally eligible to hold public office, as a constitutional matter. For example, in 1873, the Maine Supreme Judicial Court (SJC) had outlined the status of a woman's right to hold public office. This question of whether a woman could be a justice of the peace came before Maine's highest court, in the immediate aftermath of the Civil War, and ratification of the Fourteenth and Fifteenth Amendments.[5] In *In re Opinion of the Justices* (Me. 1873), the majority began its opinion by noting that, under the Maine Constitution, "the whole political power of the State is vested in its male citizens. Whenever in any of its provisions, reference is made to sex, it is to duties to be done and performed by male members of the community." The court suggested that neither the text of the state constitution, nor the legislative history of the debates preceding its ratification, indicated that any of the men involved in drafting it had any intention to, "*surrender . . . political power by those who had previously enjoyed it or a transfer of the same to those who had never possessed it*" (emphasis added). If the drafters had so intended, the court asserted that they would have said so. The court then reviewed the history of the common law rights of married and single women, noting that "we are led to the inevitable conclusion that it was never in the contemplation or intention of those forming our constitution, that the offices thereby created should be filled by those who could take no part in its original formation, and to whom no political power was [e]ntrusted for the organization of the government then about to be established . . ."[6]

But in his dissent, Justice Dickerson interpreted the intersection of the state constitution and common law quite differently. His introduction to the issue illustrated a surprisingly broad and progressive view of women's rights in 1873:

I am unable to find anything to prevent women from holding the office of justice of the peace, in the nature of that office, the statutes or the constitution. It is a public office with judicial functions which are clearly within the sphere of woman's capacity.

The proficiency which women, in recent times, have acquired in various departments of industry, the arts, education, literature, works of benevolence, and in some of the learned professions, vindicate and establish their capacity and fitness to discharge the simple and well defined duties of justice of the peace.

Dickerson argued that these new developments "warrant and demand" that women be given more opportunities. He relied on a common rationale of the time that "[t]he ability of women to elicit, quicken and purify the activities of humanity, is one of the most important factors in modern civilization." To support his argument, Dickerson related the history of women's subjugation, noting that "[b]y ancient usage women were regarded as inferior beings, and treated as the servants or slaves of men." He went on to give examples, including the fact that married women could be punished by their husbands, without resort to the courts; the exclusion of women from public roles in the various religions; and the indignities of coverture where a woman's "legal identity became merged in her husband, so that in fact her person, property, earnings and children belonged to him; the husband and wife were one, and the husband was the one." He added that, even in 1873, only one state granted wives equal custody rights over their children. Dickerson then noted that either "by usage or law, some of these relics of a less enlightened age, have been swept away, and women in a far greater and more just degree have come to be esteemed as the peers of men in both capacity and right."

Dickerson characterized the majority's denial of the right to hold public office as, "set[ting] back the clock of time and substitut[ing] reaction for progress." But he did not stop there. He went on to say that its denial not only stymied progress, but it implicated constitutional rights. "The exclusion of one half of the people of the State from participation in the administration of the laws, by the dominant half, however long continued, neither implies, nor confers the right to enforce such exclusion. A usage originating in contravention of the constitution, does not become obligatory by lapse of time. The constitution and not usage is the touchstone of civil and political rights."[7]

Dickerson argued that for the court to find that any impediment under the Maine Constitution to women holding public office existed, it had to find that it came from either an express provision, or by an implication derived from such an express provision. He saw no such express provision barring women from public office in the constitution. The only aspect of the constitution that he saw that might be used to deny women public office was the use of the word "male" in conjunction with the right to vote. But if that were the basis of the court's denying women the right to hold public office, it must also be used to deny women other natural rights protected by the constitution. Dickerson concluded that "[i]f women are ineligible to office for this reason, they are, also, denied the rights of enjoying and defending life, liberty and property, of religious freedom, and the right to be heard by themselves or counsel in criminal prosecutions." He found such a construction to be "unreasonable." He also found it, "contrary to the meaning of the word 'men'" that, in Dickerson's view, was used, "in a generic sense to denote the human race, including both sexes. It is only by giving the word 'men' this signification, that women have any rights under the constitution that men are bound to respect."[8]

One of the aspects of the Dickerson dissent that is particularly notable is his reference to the Fourteenth Amendment. That amendment was generally understood by courts in 1873, to extend only nonpolitical rights. It was deemed to apply only to African Americans, and not to women.[9] Dickerson would have extended the Fourteenth Amendment to women, asserting in his dissent that the amendment, "declared all persons born or naturalized to be citizens of the United States and of the state where they reside." Thus, he reasoned, "[w]omen are . . . made citizens by the supreme law of the land, and as such, are entitled to all the rights, privileges and immunities predicated of citizens, and its synonym 'people,' in the constitution which are not therein specifically denied to them; and we have seen that eligibility to office is not of that number [denied to women]. It should not be forgotten that we live under the fourteenth amendment," which Dickerson reminded the majority trumped state law.[10]

Justice Dickerson's construction of the state constitution was quite different from the majority. Rather than interpreting the Maine Constitution to bar women from holding public office, Dickerson concluded that "[t]he constitution restricts the right of suffrage to male citizens, but does not confine eligibility to office to males. In the one case words importing a sexual qualification are inserted in the constitution; in the other, they are omitted." Dickerson assigned this distinction "great significance," because it demonstrated that "the framers of the constitution placed eligibility to office upon a broader basis than suffrage, else they would have expressly restricted it within the same limits." He, therefore, criticized the majority for "disregard[ing] a plain distinction made in the constitution, and to interpolate into it a clause that would debar one half of the citizens of the State from their right to participate in the administration of the laws."[11]

Written almost fifty years before ratification of the Nineteenth Amendment, Justice Dickerson's dissent illustrates how constitutional and statutory construction could be used to either expand women's political rights, or cabin them. He argued that even though women clearly did not have the right to vote, because the state constitution explicitly limited the franchise to men, the constitution's failure to do so explicitly, with regard to officeholding, should be interpreted to mean that women *could* hold public office. In other words, Dickerson found the two rights *not* to be coextensive, while the majority linked voting and holding public office as coextensive in order to defeat a woman's right to hold public office. Thus, we see that the judicial use of statutory interpretation to find that rights were coextensive, was first used by state courts like the Maine SJC in *In re Opinion of the Justices* in the years prior to extension of suffrage to all women under the Nineteenth Amendment. At that point in time, judges were using the statutory construction move to *cabin* women's rights. As we saw in the jury service cases, in the wake of ratification of the Nineteenth Amendment, courts often used the same move to achieve the opposite result, and extend broader political rights to women.

Justice Dickerson was writing in 1873, three years after ratification of the Fifteenth Amendment, which protected voting rights from being denied or abridged by a state on the basis of race, color, or previous condition of servitude.[12] The common understanding of that amendment, at the time it was debated and ratified in 1870, was that officeholding was subsumed within voting:

> In the end, the belief that as a matter of constitutional interpretation the right to vote presumptively subsumes the right to hold office . . . contributed to Congress' deletion of the office-holding provision of the Fifteenth Amendment . . .
>
> In Georgia, for example, Governor Bullock in introducing the amendment for a ratification vote to the legislature observed that,
>
> [w]ere there any doubt . . . as to the sufficiency of this Amendment to confer equal political privileges without regard to race or color, or were

it urged that the right to vote did not necessarily include the right to hold office, it would certainly be dissipated and answered by the arguments advanced in the debates in Congress on the passage of the joint resolution proposing the Amendment, as well as by the expressed opinions of the soundest lawyers of the Nation . . . If we ratify this Amendment, to be consistent we must at once voluntarily yield to colored citizens the right to have their voices heard in your halls.[13]

And that understanding—that the right to vote subsumed the right to hold public office—was reflected in 1922 in the Supreme Court of North Carolina's interpretation of the almost textually identical Nineteenth Amendment. In a brief opinion in *Preston v. Roberts* in 1922, the North Carolina Supreme Court implicitly reasoned the Nineteenth Amendment should be interpreted to mean that voting and holding public office were coextensive.[14] The case involved the validity of a deed that had been acknowledged in front of a female notary public and probated by a female deputy clerk of the superior court. The validity of the deed was challenged on the basis that women were disqualified from serving as notaries public or deputy clerks, under North Carolina law. In interpreting the impact of the Nineteenth Amendment on state law around holding public office, the court stated, "In *Attorney General v. Knight*, it was held that the position of notary public is a public office, and that women were precluded from holding this office because they were not legally qualified voters; and in *Bank v. Redwine*, it was plainly suggested that for the same reason a woman could not hold the position of deputy clerk." But the North Carolina Supreme Court went on to find that "[t]he disqualification upon which these decisions were based has since been removed by the adoption of the Nineteenth Amendment to the federal Constitution, which became effective on August 26, 1920, and subsequent [state] legislation." The court cited the North Carolina Constitution for the proposition that "[e]very voter in North Carolina, except as in this article disqualified, shall be eligible to office." It concluded that "[t]he mere fact that the notary public and the deputy clerk who respectively took the acknowledgment and the probate of the deed were women does not invalidate the conveyance."[15]

Following ratification of the Nineteenth Amendment in 1920, the Massachusetts state legislature asked the SJC in 1922 to give its opinion as to whether the Massachusetts Constitution allowed women to hold public office. In *In re Opinion of the Justices* (Mass. 1922), the court noted that in 1871 it had previously found that women had no constitutional right to hold office.[16]

It then considered the question of whether the right to vote and the right to hold public office were coextensive. If so, the Nineteenth Amendment would be self-executing, not simply as to the vote, but as to the right to hold office.[17]

The court began its analysis by examining the nexus between voting and holding public office, stating that the Nineteenth Amendment, "makes no provision concerning the right to hold office. By its own force it struck from the Constitution of this commonwealth the word 'male' wherever it occurred as a limitation upon the right of the citizen to vote. This is the extent of its operation." It also reaffirmed that the Nineteenth Amendment was, "complete in itself. It is supreme within its sphere. The federal government possesses all incidental powers necessary to execute it." But the court took the time to point out the federalism question at issue, "under our dual system of government no implications extend the powers of the United States beyond those granted." It cited the Tenth Amendment for the proposition that "[t]he powers not delegated to the United States by the Constitution, nor prohibited by it to the states, are reserved to the states respectively, or to the people." It reiterated the power of the states with regard to eligibility to hold state office as opposed to federal office. The former, "is to be determined by the several states according to their differing needs and varying views of internal policy, subject to any controlling provisions of the federal Constitution."[18]

In the next step in its analysis, the court stated that "[t]he right to hold office is not necessarily coextensive with the right to vote." It went on to list the varying provisions governing qualifications to hold office in both the federal and the state constitutions and concluded that "it is apparent that the question whether one has a right to hold office under the Constitution is separate and distinct from the question whether one has a right to vote." The court then cautioned that its finding that voting and holding office were not coextensive did not end its inquiry. This finding was, "not decisive of the questions to be answered." It must review the state constitutional provisions themselves. The court went on to do such a review and concluded that "[n]owhere is the word 'male' found in the Constitution as qualifying the right to hold office. The only places where the word 'male' occurs in the Constitution are in chapter 1, § 2, art. 2, chapter 1, § 3, art. 4, and article 3 of the Amendments. In each of these places it is used to restrict the right of voting to 'male' citizens.'" Since the effect of the Nineteenth Amendment was to strike the word male from the state constitution, "there is now left in the Constitution no limitation of sex upon the right to vote."[19]

In cases prior to ratification of the Nineteenth Amendment, the Massachusetts court acknowledged that it had extended its interpretation of the word "male" from a limitation on who could vote, to also include a limitation on who could hold public office. It had done so on the basis of "unbroken usage" in terms of who was deemed a "citizen" under the state constitution.[20] Now that the Nineteenth Amendment had struck down that limitation, the lack of an express qualifier on the right to hold public office in the constitution should mean that "all express limitation upon eligibility for office founded upon sex created or recognized by the Constitution disappear[ed]."[21] Revisiting its pre-Nineteenth Amendment construction of the state's constitution, the Massachusetts court described its prior reasoning: "The emphasis in the Opinions of the Justices in 107 Mass. 604, and 165 Mass. 599, 43 N.E. 927, 32 L.R.A. 350, was placed upon unbroken usage. Now that the word 'male' as a limitation upon the right to vote has been eliminated from the Constitution of Massachusetts and the suffrage is thrown open to all citizens, all express limitation upon eligibility for office founded upon sex created or recognized by the Constitution disappears. The unbroken usage of the common law has been changed by the fundamental law of the Constitution." The court noted that if there had been an, "express prohibition in the Constitution against the eligibility of women for office, a quite different question would arise. There is no express prohibition." And it reasoned that "[w]hen the fundamental law is silent as to the qualifications for office, it commonly is understood that electors and electors alone are eligible."[22]

Finally, the Massachusetts court gave a poetic description of the state constitution's overarching framework, emphasizing its flexibility to adapt to changed social conditions, noting that it, "was designed to be an enduring frame of government so comprehensive and general in its terms that a free, intelligent and moral body of citizens might govern themselves under its beneficent provisions notwithstanding radical changes in social, economic and political conditions." Those changed conditions included ratification of a federal amendment with regard to voting, which had the same effect as if the state constitution had been amended. In reversing its prior decision that women were not eligible to hold office under the Massachusetts Constitution, the court explained that "The constitutional situation has become so changed by the supervention of the Nineteenth Amendment to the United States Constitution with its consequent operation upon the Constitution of Massachusetts as to render no longer of force the Opinions of the Justices in

107 Mass. 604, and 165 Mass. 599, 43 N.E. 927, 32 L.R.A. 350. The firm foundation upon which they rested has been swept away by that amendment."[23] Since there was no express prohibition in the state's constitution against women holding office, the only limitation remaining was the qualification on the right to vote, which was abolished by the Nineteenth Amendment.[24] Thus, women could now hold public office under the provisions of the Massachusetts Constitution. While the court did not specifically say so, presumably legislation authorizing women to hold office would, therefore, be constitutional.

Several years later, in 1927, the SJC of the neighboring state of New Hampshire was asked by the governor to give its opinion, as to a woman's eligibility to hold appointive office in that state. In *In re Opinion of the Justices* (N.H. 1927), the court gave its opinion on the question of whether the New Hampshire Constitution disqualified a woman from holding the appointive office of justice of the peace (as opposed to holding an elective office.)[25] The New Hampshire court first cited the Massachusetts SJC's 1922 opinion, described earlier, on the subject of women holding public office.[26] But the New Hampshire court was wary of any suggestion that the opinion in that case was, "an authority for the proposition that under their Constitution women are now eligible to appointive offices, and that enabling legislation is unnecessary," characterizing that proposition as "not well founded." The New Hampshire court went on to criticize the logic of the Massachusetts court's reasoning that, in its decisions prior to ratification of the Nineteenth Amendment, "there was an implied intent upon the part of the framers of their Constitution to exclude women from public office [which] could not be drawn after the federal amendment conferred upon women the right of suffrage." The New Hampshire court questioned how, after ratification of the Nineteenth Amendment, the Massachusetts court could argue that the previous inference it had drawn—the framers did not mean to make women eligible to hold public office—could somehow "change." The New Hampshire court found it illogical to suggest that any original intent could be "reversed or altered by any subsequent event." And, the court asserted, if the exclusion of women had been the original intent of the framers, nothing that happened later could change their actual intent. "The intent of the framers of the Constitution, in the use of certain language, was a completed fact when the words were written. Subsequent change of that intent is plainly impossible. In our opinion a present right for women to hold office cannot be based upon the grounds mentioned."[27]

The New Hampshire court went on to find that under the New Hampshire Constitution, legislation in addition to the Nineteenth Amendment was required to grant women the right to hold public office. The court suggested that this holding was aligned with the Massachusetts court's 1922 opinion, even though the Massachusetts court never explicitly stated that further legislation was required. The New Hampshire court argued that because the Massachusetts opinion was issued in the context of being asked to opine on proposed legislation, that was a reasonable inference.[28] It concluded that if no legislation had been required, the Massachusetts court "would have so advised."[29] It described the fact that, in addition to removing either express or implied constitutional limitations, "it is the conclusion in most states that legislative action, abolishing the common-law rule of disability, is also required to enable women to hold office."[30]

After discussing the 1922 Massachusetts decision, the New Hampshire court then considered the provisions of its state constitution with regard to officeholding, which provided that "[e]very person, qualified as the Constitution provides, shall be considered an inhabitant for the purpose of electing and being elected into any office." The state constitution also included several provisions limiting suffrage to men, although those provisions had been negated by the Nineteenth Amendment.[31] The court argued that while other provisions included gender limitations, the election provision did not, and that omission must have been intentional.[32] Therefore, the court concluded that women were now eligible under the state constitution to stand for election to public office on the same basis as men.[33] It reasoned that "[t]he thought expressed in article 30 is not that men are eligible to office because of their sex, but because they are qualified voters. *The right of electing and being elected are closely connected in the Bill of Rights and in Article 30. Whatever limits or enlarges the right to vote has the same effect upon eligibility to office.*"[34] Thus, the New Hampshire court found that women were eligible for elective office in the state because they, "now answer our constitutional test. They are qualified voters, and as such have the constitutional guaranty of the right 'to be elected' to office."

But the question at hand was whether a woman could hold an *appointive* office as a justice of the peace. The New Hampshire court distinguished elective from appointive positions. It argued that to suggest that the original framers of the New Hampshire Constitution thought they were creating a general, implied ban on women exercising "governmental privileges," simply because they limited some exercises, like voting, to men, was untenable. "Had they understood that a limitation of political rights and privileges to that sex was sufficiently implied throughout the Constitution, they would not have expressed it here [in the voting provision.] And, since they thought it necessary to expressly state it here, the reasonable conclusion is that its omission elsewhere is intentional, and with a purpose to let the matter remain as at common law."[35] Thus, the court concluded that, unlike elective office, which the framers of the state constitution had explicitly made available to those eligible to be "electors," the framers had been silent on appointive offices. The correct conclusion was that they had intended eligibility for appointive office to be left as it had been, at common law. At common law, women were excluded from eligibility to hold such offices. The court found that the legislature could remove that common law ban by legislation, because the state constitution was "silent as to sex qualification." But while the constitution did not, "forbid the appointment of a woman to the office of justice of the peace . . ." further legislation was required to, "remove the common-law disability."[36]

In sum, the Massachusetts court in 1922 and the New Hampshire court in 1927 did not find that the right to hold all public offices was generally coextensive with voting. Through constitutional interpretation, each found a way to argue that, without the word "male" in the state constitutions any longer as to voting, legislatures were now authorized to allow women to hold public office, although further legislation might well be necessary. In other words, while the Nineteenth Amendment was self-executing as to voting, it did not necessarily extend to holding all public offices. Further legislation was impliedly necessary to authorize women to do so, for all public offices in Massachusetts and appointive (though not elective) offices in New Hampshire. While they differed in some ways based on different constitutional provisions and inferences therefrom, it appeared that these courts were reluctant to draw a general rule that voting and all officeholding were coextensive. And that the removal of sex as a qualifier for one was automatically extended, through the doctrine of self-execution, to the other. It may be that this cautious judicial interpretation was because the right to hold public office was seen as a profound change in women's proper sphere, moving them squarely into the public realm. And that such a change should be put to the people, in the form of the state legislature. But that requirement would, of course, slow the development of women's citizenship as a constitutional matter.

Unlike Justice Dickerson's dissent in the 1873 Maine case, *In re Opinion of the Justices*, the state courts in the 1920s did not generally invoke the Fourteenth Amendment, nor did petitioners make such claims. Like the jury service cases, the public office cases were dominantly construction cases, parsing the impact of the Nineteenth Amendment on state laws and constitutional provisions governing who was eligible to hold public office. As discussed in the previous chapter, the state jury service cases also rarely included Fourteenth Amendment claims. With the exception of *Fyfe* and *Welosky*, the state jury service cases, too, were dominantly construction cases. And where the Fourteenth Amendment was invoked, those claims were rejected. It is arguable that such an approach, in conjunction with congressional legislation pursuant to section two of the Nineteenth Amendment, explicitly protecting the political right to hold public office, would have accelerated the former suffragists goal of achieving equality of political rights, beyond voting. But there is little evidence the former suffragists pursued such legislation, after the NWP's initial enthusiasm in December 1920, as discussed in Chapter 3, "Enforcement Legislation."[37] Absent such pressure from Congress, state courts were left to construe the impact of the Nineteenth Amendment on state laws around public officeholding without such constraints.[38] And the result was the same: a patchwork of state approaches to the issue, reifying women's partial citizenship for decades to come.

7

Defining Equality

> No reason is apparent why the operation of the law should be ex-
> tended to women to the exclusion of men, since women have been
> accorded full equality with men in the commercial and political
> world. Indeed, this equality in law has been sanctioned by constitu-
> tional amendment.
>
> —*Children's Hospital v. Adkins* (District of Columbia Court
> of Appeals 1922)

The women's rights movement in the United States had always been about
more than the vote. Elizabeth Cady Stanton captured that truth in her 1891
address to NAWSA, "We should sweep the whole board, demanding equality
everywhere and the reconstruction of all institutions that do not in their
present status admit of it."[1] As the nineteenth century came to a close, "the
women's suffrage organizations grew more conservative and 'narrowed in
on the single issue of suffrage.'"[2] Two major national suffrage organizations,
NAWSA and the NWP, each brought together an uneasy alliance of women
who were divided by issues of race, as discussed in Chapter 3, "Enforcement
Legislation." They were also divided by issues of class. The suffragists, in both
organizations, worked toward the same goal in the final campaign for the
federal suffrage amendment. But the divisions among former suffragists
within those groups, and between their successor organizations, split wide
open after ratification.

As Vicki Schultz has said, it is important to study, "not only the influence
of a social movement overall, but also the rise of internal divisions *within* the
movement and changes in its presence, visibility, and strength over time, in
shaping legal developments."[3] The division between the "neutrality feminists"
and the "social feminists," both within the NWP and between the NWP and
the NLWV, proved significant in the emergence of a thin conception of the
Nineteenth Amendment.[4] As a matter of constitutional development, the

Constitutional Orphan. Paula A. Monopoli, Oxford University Press (2020). © Paula A. Monopoli.
DOI: 10.1093/oso/9780190092795.001.0001

Nineteenth Amendment was affected by the different visions, among the former suffragists, as to what constituted constitutional "gender equality."[5] The neutrality feminists embraced legal formalism and an anti-classification norm, as described in this chapter. The social feminists focused on equality of outcomes, and embraced law as an instrument to achieve a leveling of the social and economic playing field, animated by an anti-subordination norm. The social feminists were afraid of the implications of a thicker conception of the Nineteenth Amendment, which had been briefly signaled by the United States Supreme Court in its opinion in *Adkins v. Children's Hospital* in 1923, in terms of its potential impact on protective legislation for women.[6] Neutrality feminists played a role in the outcome in *Adkins* by working with the lawyers challenging the minimum wage law. Yet, they failed to capitalize on the potential power of that thicker conception, as they tried to secure their goal of eliminating all legal disabilities that affected women as a class.[7] Neutrality feminists immediately pivoted to an equal rights amendment as the constitutional path to that goal, rather than persuading courts to embrace a more robust application of the Nineteenth Amendment, and advocating for enforcement legislation to that end. That pivot entangled them with their former allies among the social feminists, and it distracted them from building on the constitutional opportunity seemingly afforded by *Adkins*.[8] This chapter focuses on the story of that pivot to the ERA. It traces the impact that the resulting divisions between the neutrality feminists and social feminists had on the emergence of a thin conception of the Nineteenth Amendment.

In telling this story, it is helpful to focus on two individuals as representative of the neutrality feminists and the social feminists. Alice Paul, founder and chair of the old NWP (and vice president of the new NWP's National Advisory Council by the time of the *Adkins* case) was typical of many of the middle- and upper-class professional women, who made up the ranks of those one might identify as the neutrality feminists.[9] In contrast, Florence Kelley, lawyer and general secretary of the NCL, and NWP executive committee member, was the quintessential social feminist, who took the position that working-class women were in need of protective legislation. When ratification of the Nineteenth Amendment was being debated, both kinds of suffragists were united in a single mission, but fundamental arguments about what equality should mean drove them apart in the wake of ratification.[10] Should the Constitution be interpreted to protect "formal equality," defined as a neutral approach that simply guaranteed citizens the same opportunities by forbidding class legislation? Or should it be interpreted to ensure "substantive equality," defined as the promise of equal outcomes for all? The former view was more aligned with the laissez-faire or limited approach to the role of the state that dominated the US Supreme Court in the early 1920s. The latter was more aligned with the legal progressives' view of the scope of the inherent "police power" of the state to legislate disparate treatment that arguably produced equal outcomes. These two views of equality mapped on to the larger debate around capitalism and socialism raging in the United States, in the first decades of the twentieth century.

Anti-suffragists had long equated "suffragism" with socialism. The Nineteenth Amendment was debated and ratified as the nation was beset by the fear of anarchy, socialism, and communism.[11] The 1917 Bolshevik Revolution had raised concerns that the contagion of Marxism and Leninism would spread to the working classes in the United States. At home, the May 1921 trial of accused anarchists Niccola Sacco and Bartolomeo Vanzetti illustrated the hysteria around the threat that "Reds" posed to democratic (some would say capitalistic) values. In a murder trial that garnered international attention, the two Italian-born anarchists were accused of killing a shoe-factory paymaster and his security guard in the industrial city of Braintree, Massachusetts. Their cause was taken up by some of the most prominent legal figures of the time, including Felix Frankfurter, then a professor at Harvard Law School. In *The Atlantic Monthly*, Frankfurter wrote that the judge's decision to deny a new trial was deeply biased, and violated fundamental legal canons of fairness and due process. In Frankfurter's view, the two immigrants had been railroaded by the district attorney and the trial judge, "[b]y systematic exploitation of [their] alien blood, their imperfect knowledge of English, their unpopular social views, and their opposition to the war."[12]

Frankfurter's involvement in the Sacco and Vanzetti case was intertwined with that of US Supreme Court Justice Louis Brandeis, to whom Frankfurter owed his teaching position at Harvard.[13] An immigrant who came to New York at age twelve, Frankfurter attended City College of New York and eventually Harvard Law School. After graduating, Frankfurter held a series of government positions and came to know Brandeis, a successful Boston lawyer, twenty-six years his senior. Brandeis had become involved in a number of progressive causes over the years. He and Frankfurter shared a view of law as an instrument of social change or legal progressivism. And when Brandeis was appointed to the US Supreme Court by Woodrow Wilson in 1916, Frankfurter, "was selected to replace him as the unpaid head counsel in several maximum-hours and minimum wage legislation cases."[14] Brandeis continued to use Frankfurter as an agent for his political agenda, long after Brandeis ascended to the court.[15]

In the first two decades of the twentieth century, the national debate about capitalism versus socialism played out in the courts, in the form of labor relations cases involving challenges to state maximum-hour and minimum-wage laws. Male legal progressives, like Brandeis and Frankfurter; and social feminists, like Florence Kelley, led the effort to enact "protective" legislation limiting women's work hours. Many Americans saw this effort as socialist, given the roots of such legislation in European socialism. And business interests saw such legislation as a threat to profits, and contested it in the courts. Court challenges revolved around the scope of the police power of the state. All sides agreed that the state had inherent police power under the Constitution to regulate for the public's health, safety, and welfare. But laissez-faire capitalists did not view that power as sufficiently broad to justify legislation that regulated the private employer-employee relationship. The legal progressives' view that the Constitution allowed such regulation was anathema to those who supported very little, or no, state intervention, as the preferred approach to structuring that relationship. So laissez-faire advocates argued against such legislation. In conceptualizing the proper scope of the police power, they grounded their arguments in liberty of contract, a constitutional concept that had been contested throughout the late nineteenth century.[16]

The debate about the scope of the state's police power to protect the health, welfare, and safety of citizens in the workplace, was at the heart of the US Supreme Court's decision in *Lochner v. New York* in 1905.[17] The *Lochner* court struck down a New York state statute, which limited the working hours of bakery employees, as violative of the due process clause of the Fourteenth Amendment. The decision was grounded in what the five-justice majority characterized as interference with liberty of contract and the resulting doctrine was characterized as "substantive due process."[18] As already noted, this defeat led legal progressives like Brandeis and Kelley to shift their strategy, and focus on enacting state legislation that limited only the hours of women workers. The role of women as mothers of future citizens, and the more "delicate" physical and emotional nature of women, would provide courts with a hook. They could find that the inherent police power of the state to protect the health and safety of women workers, was constitutionally valid, even though it limited liberty of contract. The legal progressives hoped that this approach would create a doctrinal "wedge." Eventually courts might be inclined to expand their view of appropriate police power, to include the regulation of all employer-employee relationships, not just those of female workers.[19]

This strategy was successful with the court's decision in *Muller v. Oregon* in 1908.[20] Brandeis, Kelley, and other legal progressives wrote and submitted what has become known as the "Brandeis Brief"—a written argument grounded in empirical social science, an approach to legal advocacy relatively unknown in American jurisprudence until that point.[21] In *Muller*, the court upheld an Oregon statute, which regulated the working hours of women employees, as a valid use of the state's police power. The decision rested, in part, on the characterization of women as physically different from men:

> [I]n structure of body, in the functions to be performed by each, in the amount of physical strength, in the capacity for long-continued labor, particularly when done standing, the influence of vigorous health upon the future wellbeing of the race, the self-reliance which enables one to assert full rights, and in the capacity to maintain the struggle for subsistence. This difference justifies a difference in legislation, and upholds that which is designed to compensate for some of the burdens which rest upon her.[22]

The *Muller* court, in an intriguing passage, invoked the fact that Oregon was one of the western states that had denied women the vote. While insisting that fact was not dispositive, the *Muller* court seemed to hint that Oregon's failure to give women the vote bolstered the court's physical difference and "difference in functions" arguments for "protecting" women in the workplace. The *Muller* court took pains to say that they had not discussed, "the denial of the elective franchise in the State of Oregon" because, while that fact might indicate, "a lack of political equality in all things with her brother, that is not of itself decisive." The court added that its decision to uphold protective maximum-hour legislation for women, "runs deeper, and rests in the inherent difference between the two sexes, and in the different functions in life which they perform."[23]

Muller was a victory for the legal progressives and social feminists, but in its language lay the seeds for continued paternalism toward women. This approach concerned many neutrality feminists. They saw the language of physical and functional difference, in the first paragraph cited above, as a potential legal basis for withholding rights. Yet, the *Muller* court's noting that women in Oregon could not vote was significant. It arguably implied that, once women were enfranchised, such protective legislation would no longer be necessary or justified because women would be politically equal with men. They could then presumably decide, through the ballot box, whether to elect legislators partial to protective legislation or not.

After the February 1921 NWP annual convention discussed in Chapter 2, "Validity," concluded, the NWP moved ahead on a new federal amendment, the ERA. Its position was that this amendment would prevent states from abridging or denying civil, political, and legal rights, based solely on sex. And after its 1920 Victory Convention, NAWSA became the NLWV, focused on voter education and supporting the Sheppard-Towner Maternity and Infancy Protection Act of 1921, providing federal funds for maternal and child health. It also supported the new child labor amendment being spearheaded by Florence Kelley and the NCL, thus aligning itself with the social feminists. Paul and Kelley shared a preference for federal amendments as a means to legal and social reform. Both had put their full efforts into ratification of the Nineteenth Amendment as part of the NWP and they had seen success in 1920. Kelley and Paul shared an understanding that the courts had not been bastions of equality for women. The judicial trend of using the common law tradition, and precedent, to deter reform was an insight the two female lawyers understood far better than their male counterparts.[24] For example, when Kelley began advocating for the child labor amendment, which would give Congress explicit authority to regulate child labor, she got pushback from her allies on protective legislation. Felix Frankfurter and his dean at Harvard Law School, Roscoe Pound, "opposed any such amendment as too radical. Instead Frankfurter and his allies argued that the [National Consumers League] should continue to draft legislation around court decisions. When Kelley would not accept such advice, the Frankfurter contingent refused to further participate in her efforts." Some scholars have observed that this split, "may hearken back to the difference between those male legal progressives and realists who were so steeped in law that they could not abandon the common law and traditional Constitutional Arguments, and the many women legal reformers who, from their own experience, viewed courts, the common law, and even the Constitution as significant obstacles to reform."[25]

While Kelley turned toward the child labor amendment, Paul and other NWP members began to draft the ERA.[26] The initial drafts of the ERA included language that prohibited the federal and state governments from enacting or maintaining legislation, which enshrined any political, civil, or legal disabilities or inequalities "on account of sex or marriage." Paul tried to assuage concerns from legal progressives, like Frankfurter and Kelley, about the language in what she called the "Lucretia Mott Amendment," named after the fellow Quaker and woman suffrage pioneer.[27] Legal progressives and social feminists were alarmed by the possibility that the laissez-faire, pro-business US Supreme Court would use the language to strike down protective legislation as unconstitutional.

It is fairly clear that Paul personally opposed protective legislation for women. She was afraid that its rationale that women were "different" was inherently dangerous for the future of women's equality under the law.[28] That antipathy and her single-minded focus drove her decision to move forward with her "blanket amendment" in 1923.[29] The transcripts of oral interviews with Paul many years later reveal her feelings about those women she called the "special labor law ladies," like Kelley and Ethel Smith, legislative secretary for the National Women's Trade Union League.[30] Paul said that they, "objected to the Equal Rights Amendment on the ground that they'd worked very hard to get special protection for women and this would be wiped out." Paul noted that she tried to reassure Kelley that "it *wouldn't* be wiped out because equality in laws affecting industry could be made by every state to apply equally, under the Equal Rights Amendment, to men and women employees. Any benefit that occurred would be beneficial to any person—we thought."[31]

Kelley had been a member of the NWP's National Advisory Council, working for a federal suffrage amendment. But she was to become an ardent foe of Paul's after ratification. Unlike her break with Kelley, Paul did retain close ties to Maud Younger, a member of the NWP, but also an influential leader in the labor movement for protective legislation for women. Before joining Paul and the NWP, Younger herself had used the legal strategy of bringing a series of test cases to push the courts to uphold an eight-hour law for women in California. As Paul recalled Younger's history, "She did everything, I guess, that was done—succeeded in getting through an eight-hour law for women in California, which I suppose was one of the first that was ever passed in the country. It was then challenged—its validity and so on—and I suppose presumably by people who were in some way involved in restaurants or hotels that tried to have the law thrown out." Paul went on to note that the law was challenged all the way up to the US Supreme Court, and that Younger had, "carried it there herself and financed the whole campaign and paid all the expenses, largely; maybe other people helped, but she was always supposed to be the main person back of this. The eight-hour law was sustained by the Supreme Court, for women." As a consequence, Paul added that Younger was regarded by the people in, "this protective labor law group as the mother of the eight-hour law for women."[32]

Paul went on to describe how she subsequently met Younger, and invited her to come join the NWP in Washington to work for the Nineteenth Amendment, which Younger did. After ratification of the suffrage amendment, Younger was torn by her allegiance to the labor movement and the movement's position on Paul's new ERA. In the end, as Paul said, Younger chose the NWP. "[Younger] thought a long time about it and she finally decided this was the right principle, and that all the efforts she'd been making for women in industry had been right, in her opinion, and they ought to be extended for everybody, not make it for one sex."[33] Thus, the NWP was not monolithic in its views, but it clearly became associated with the neutrality view during the debates over the ERA.[34]

Paul made repeated overtures, through Maud Younger and others, to Frankfurter, Kelley, and Pound.[35] Pound was not only Frankfurter's dean at Harvard Law School, he was a close confidante of Frankfurter. Pound's prestige would lend great weight to the new amendment, if he were to support its language. Paul tried to negotiate language that would alleviate their concerns. In addition to Younger, Paul made these overtures through Elsie Hill and Albert Levitt, a Harvard Law School graduate and young law professor, who was later to become Hill's husband. Hill had taken over the role as chairman of the new NWP, after the 1921 convention. Paul had been reluctant to take the helm of the new organization, since she was trying to pay off the old NWP's debt and attend law school at the same time. In a June 9, 1921, Western Union telegram to Frankfurter, Hill wrote with regard to the ERA, "Reply received. Will you stop in Washington on return if possible or arrange conference. Have conferred repeatedly with Florence Kelley but she sailed for Europe Saturday. We are determined to avoid difficulties suggested and of course need your help."[36] The reply Hill referred to was a letter from Frankfurter dated June 7, 1921, on stationery from the Hotel Cleveland where he was staying. In the letter, Frankfurter noted that the version of the ERA that Hill had asked him to review was:

[H]ighly dangerous . . . in that it may bring into question a permissive field of legislature [sic] such as the minimum wage in favor of women which cannot be based solely "on the basis of the physical constitution of women." I quite understand that you do not intend to cut down the so-called "police power" but . . . the form in which you have attained your end begets new difficulties.[37]

Frankfurter went on to suggest that he could not give Hill any actual suggested language to fix the problems with which he was concerned. He was under too much "pressure." And the task was one that required "considerable delicacy." He could only say, "that the amendment in its present form is fraught with mischief that I know you are anxious to avoid."[38]

Similarly, in a letter from Levitt to Pound, Levitt asked, if Congress were to pass "an act forbidding the employment of women in lead factories" whether the phrase "shall not be denied or abridged on account of sex" would render such a hypothetical statute unconstitutional.[39] Levitt suggested to Pound that it would not, since one could argue that the statute was enacted to protect the national welfare, not women. In good law student fashion, Levitt tried to curry favor with his former dean (and reference for law teaching positions) when he wrote that Pound's advice was "really tremendous" and that Levitt's recent visit with Pound had been "good fun."[40]

Pound wrote back to Levitt and suggested particular language. Levitt wrote to Paul that Pound had said that Levitt could show his letter to whomever Levitt wanted but that Pound was not ready to write something for publication yet. Pound suggested that the NWP should take the public position that they wanted to, but should concede that the "the facts of nature and industry" justified differences "in the exercise of the police power." He suggested that the NWP should have their supporters in Congress reiterate this position and add a specific provision to that effect in the proposed legislation, to the effect that "This article shall not be interpreted as preventing legislation in the exercise of the police power or for the protection of women in industry." However, Pound warned that the last clause would raise "a great outcry."[41]

By some accounts, Albert Levitt drafted more than seventy-five versions of the ERA. None drew consensus and, in 1923, Alice Paul gave up and found two members of Congress who agreed to introduce her amendment.[42] The final 1923 version, introduced in December, provided that "Men and women shall have equal rights throughout the United States and every place subject to its jurisdiction."[43] Levitt felt embarrassed and betrayed, when Paul publicly asserted that Pound and Frankfurter had approved the language in the final version of the amendment submitted to Congress. Neither Pound nor Frankfurter had actually done so. Nevertheless, Levitt went on to marry Elsie Hill, and he continued to support the NWP. Hill's efforts to persuade Kelley and Frankfurter to, at the very least, not oppose the ERA came to naught. In the end, Kelley, a long-time ally of Paul in the fight for suffrage, condemned Paul as a "fiend."[44] Former NAWSA leader Carrie Chapman Catt, who had long had a similar antipathy toward Paul; and NAWSA's successor, the NLWV, sided with Kelley and vigorously opposed the ERA.

While Frankfurter and Kelley were wrangling with Paul about the ERA, they were all also deeply involved in a case moving through the courts in which an employee challenged a statute setting a minimum wage for women. *Adkins v. Children's Hospital of the District of Columbia* wound its way through the Court of Appeals for the District of Columbia in 1922, and ended up in the US Supreme Court in 1923.[45] The court's approach in the *Adkins* decision was informed by the two major factions on the court at the time, reflecting the differences in the scope of the police power laid out in *Lochner* and in *Muller*, more than a decade before. When *Adkins* came before the court in 1923, a recent shift in membership solidified the *Lochnerian* "substantive due process" wing of the court and its approach to social legislation in the realm of labor relations. "The upshot was something of a reign of terror for state and federal legislation." The replacement of Chief Justice Edward White with William Howard Taft in 1921 and three additional appointments over the next two years, including George Sutherland, Pierce Butler, and Edward Sanford to replace Justices Day, Pitney, and Clarke had consequences for protective legislation. Day and Pitney, "had frequently voted with Holmes, Brandeis, and Clarke to sustain social legislation against due process attacks." And, significantly, Alice Paul had worked with George Sutherland on the federal suffrage amendment, prior to 1920, and had sought his opinion, after 1920, about the impact of the ERA on protective legislation, before he was appointed to the Supreme Court.[46] New Justices Sutherland, Butler, and Sanford, "tended to cast their lot with Van Devanter, McReynolds, and McKenna" who supported the idea of using substantive due process to invalidate such state legislation. "[T]hus a vocal minority became a solid majority [in favor of substantive due process] within a two-year period."[47]

During the time Frankfurter was being consulted by NWP members on the ERA, he became the lawyer for the Washington, DC, Minimum Wage Board. Congress had enacted a statute authorizing the board, and giving it the authority to set a minimum wage for women employed in the District. That statute was challenged by Willie Lyons, a woman who worked as an elevator operator. Lyons asserted that she had been fired when her employer was forced to pay her twice her wage as a result of the minimum wage set by the board. They could hire a man for less. The litigation that ensued found Frankfurter arguing for the validity of the minimum wage law and Lyons's attorneys, Challen and Wade Ellis, arguing that it was unconstitutional, under the Fifth Amendment's due process clause, because it interfered with Lyons's liberty to contract for her labor. Frankfurter countered that such liberty could be constitutionally constrained by a valid exercise of the police power inherent in the state, especially when it came to regulating the wages of women.[48] It is notable that the Ellis brothers met with Paul, who shared NWP literature with them that Challen Ellis later cited in his oral argument in *Adkins*.[49]

The statute was upheld by the trial court. That decision was followed by an appeal to the Circuit Court of Appeals for the District of Columbia. After one hearing that affirmed the trial court, the statute was subsequently invalidated by the appeals court at a second hearing in *Children's Hospital v. Adkins*.[50] The statute gave the District extensive authority to intervene in the private employer-employee relationship. It authorized the District of Columbia commissioners to appoint a three-member "minimum wage board." That board was given the authority to investigate the status of women's wages in the District and to then actually set a minimum wage for women as a result of finding wages inadequate. Any employer who did not abide by that wage could be held guilty of a crime, punishable not only by a fine but by imprisonment. The significant power vested in the board allowed them, "to examine the books of every individual or corporation, employing women in the District of Columbia, to ascertain the names of women employees and the wages paid, a register of which every employer is required to keep."[51]

The language used in the appeals court's opinion, illustrated its fear about the consequences of extending the police power to authorize state intervention in private business relationships. It echoed concerns about creating a slippery slope toward socialism and anarchy that beset the nation in the 1920s:

> The tendency of the times to socialize property rights under the subterfuge of police regulation is dangerous, and if continued will prove destructive of our free institutions. It should be remembered that of the three fundamental principles which underlie government, and for which government exists, the protection of life, liberty, and property, the chief of these is property; not that any amount of property is more valuable than the life or liberty of the citizen, but the history of civilization proves that, when the

citizen is deprived of the free use and enjoyment of his property, anarchy and revolution follow, and life and liberty are without protection.[52]

In striking down the District statute and handing Frankfurter and social feminists like Kelley, a very public defeat, the court of appeals again characterized the act in question as one that gave the state the power to "socialize" property. The court warned of the slippery slope created by interpreting the police power to authorize the state to, "fix the wage which the citizen must accept, or choose idleness, or, as in the case of Willie Lyons, be deprived of the means of earning a living." The court warned that "it is but a step to a legal requirement that the industrious, frugal, economical citizen must divide his earnings with his indolent, worthless neighbor." And not only would such a constitutional interpretation lead to socialism, "[t]he modern tendency toward indiscriminate legislative and judicial jugglery with great fundamental principles of free government, whereby property rights are being curtailed and destroyed, logically will, if persisted in, end in *social disorder and revolution* [emphasis added]." The appeals court cautioned that no one should, "imagine for a moment that our civilization is such that property rights can thus be socialized without the grossest abuse of the privileges granted, or that the restraint of the abuses can be left with safety to legislative or judicial discretion."[53]

In an extensive dissent, Chief Justice Smyth countered with a defense of an expansive view of the state's police power. Smyth argued that the Fifth and Fourteenth Amendments simply protected against the state taking one's property, without the proper procedural safeguards. If the state abided by the correct process, the due process clause was not intended to limit its power to legislate for the public welfare. Citing the US Supreme Court's decision in *Barbier v. Connolly*, Smyth considered the scope of the Fourteenth Amendment.[54] It said, 'But neither the amendment—broad and comprehensive as it is—nor any other amendment, was designed to interfere with the power of the state, sometimes termed its police power, to prescribe regulations to promote the health, peace, morals, education, and good order of the people, and to legislate so as to increase the industries of the state, develop its resources, and add to its wealth and prosperity.' "[55]

The US Supreme Court eventually accepted certiorari in *Adkins v. Children's Hospital*.[56] It upheld the court of appeals's decision to invalidate the statute, despite its own decision in *Muller v. Oregon*, upholding a statute providing maximum work hours for women.[57] *Adkins* was decided on due process grounds, but it used the Nineteenth Amendment as a constitutional reference point for women's progress.[58] Justice Sutherland wrote the opinion for the court.[59] He invoked the Nineteenth Amendment, proclaiming that "[i]n view of the great—not to say revolutionary—changes which have taken place since [*Muller*], in the contractual, political, and civil status of women, culminating in the Nineteenth Amendment, it is not unreasonable to say that these differences have now come almost, if not quite, to the vanishing point."[60] Justice Sutherland reasoned that while the physical differences between men and women could be recognized in appropriate cases, women could not be subjected to restrictions on their liberty to contract which were not imposed on men.[61] To uphold this legislation, according to Justice Sutherland, "would be to ignore all the implications to be drawn from the present day trend of legislation" that "emancipates" women from special treatment.[62] One could argue that the implicit suggestion by the *Muller* court in 1908—that Oregon's denial of suffrage to women was relevant though not dispositive—gave some support to the majority's decision in *Adkins*. Fifteen years after Muller, the *Adkins* court was arguing the logical extension of that suggestion. The government's special protection of women was no longer warranted since women had become full citizens, and could now vote to protect their own interests.

Both Justice Taft and Justice Holmes dissented, questioning Justice Sutherland's invocation of the Nineteenth Amendment. Justice Taft noted, "I am not sure from a reading of the opinion whether the court thinks the authority of *Muller v. Oregon* is shaken by the adoption of the Nineteenth Amendment. The Nineteenth Amendment did not change the physical strength or limitations of women upon which the decision in *Muller v. Oregon* rests."[63] Justice Holmes further contended that *Muller* was good law, reasoning that "[i]t will need more than the Nineteenth Amendment to convince me that there are no differences between men and women, or that legislation cannot take those differences into account."[64]

Justice Brandeis recused himself. As a leading progressive lawyer, Brandeis had been the architect of the successful outcome in *Muller* in 1908, and "his daughter Elizabeth served on the District of Columbia Minimum Wage Board."[65] Ironically, Brandeis had also been the author of the majority opinion in *Leser v. Garnett*, the case that upheld the validity of the Nineteenth Amendment. The Nineteenth Amendment was the very same amendment now being invoked for the proposition that women no longer needed the protective legislation that Brandeis and his protégé, Frankfurter, had fought so hard to establish.

Joan Zimmerman has argued that the *Adkins* decision represented, "the sanction of the Supreme Court for [Alice Paul's] view of equality. In fact, Sutherland's termination of the dependent woman theory had gone almost too far. His broad claims for the Nineteenth Amendment's emancipation of women had almost undermined the need for the ERA."[66] This view is buttressed by a telegram from Felix Frankfurter, the lawyer on the losing side in *Adkins*, to Florence Kelley. Frankfurter's telegram to Kelley read, "Confidential: Most ominous part of the opinion is suggestion that *Muller* doctrine has been supplanted by nineteenth amendment . . . Upshot would be adoption Alice Paul theory of constitutional law plus invalidity of legislation affecting industrial relations of either men or women."[67]

As noted previously, the "Alice Paul theory" of constitutional law referenced by Frankfurter was one of formal equality, whereby the Constitution simply guaranteed equality of opportunity and not equality of outcomes. "Class legislation" that singled out groups for disparate treatment—even advantageous treatment—was anathema under this view of how equality should be defined under the Constitution. Alternatively, legal progressives viewed constitutional equality as a doctrine that allowed for and sometimes required, affirmative assistance to those in society—like female factory workers—who were at a disadvantage. As Florence Kelley said, "Let's not begin by meaningless words. 'Equality' where this is no equality is as terrible a thing for the defenseless workers as the cry of 'peace' where there is no peace."[68] As a social feminist, Kelley embraced a constitutional interpretation allowing for a proactive state.[69] "In contrast to the laissez-faire state, Kelley advocated an activist state, one that pursuant to the Fourteenth Amendment had affirmative duties to its citizens: "[It] was the state's obligation to foster the health and well-being of its citizens."[70] Such an interpretation validated state intervention in the workplace, to level the playing field for women disadvantaged by poverty and class. This "substantive" view of equality was seen as dangerous by middle- and upper-class women, especially those who were making some progress as professionals in law, medicine, and business. In their view, the inability to compete on the same terms as men—due to government intervention in the form of minimum-wage and maximum-hour legislation—was deeply problematic and ensured continued inequality. This was especially true, when the government's exercise of the police power to enact such legislation was justified on the basis of women's fragile physical nature. The US

Supreme Court in *Adkins* had come down squarely on the side of those, like Alice Paul, who rejected a constitutional definition of equality that allowed for differential legislative treatment based on sex.[71]

In addition to solidifying formal equality as the definition of the type of equality guaranteed by the US Constitution, Reva Siegel has argued *Adkins* signaled the Nineteenth Amendment had potentially broad implications:

> Reasoning from this standpoint, *Adkins* interpreted the Amendment as a change in the Constitution with significance for other bodies of constitutional doctrine. The *Adkins* opinion pointed to shifts, "in the contractual, political and civil status of women culminating in the Nineteenth Amendment," and treated this positive account of the ratification campaign normatively—as a reason for similarly transformative interpretation of the due process jurisprudence of the Fifth and Fourteenth Amendments. *Adkins* thus offers the first synthetic interpretation of the Nineteenth Amendment. The opinion understands the suffrage amendment as bringing about a major change in the terms of women's citizenship, a change having implications for the way the Court interprets diverse bodies of constitutional law.[72]

But this expansive view, "never gathered significant momentum."[73] The interesting question is why that "thick" conception of the Nineteenth Amendment did not gain traction. Rather, a "thin" conception emerged by the end of the 1920s. After 1931, the Nineteenth Amendment itself was rarely cited by American courts and, when it was, it was invoked as simply a rule governing voting. Several strategic choices by both the social feminists and the neutrality feminists help explain this puzzle. The social feminists, like Kelley, for obvious reasons, were afraid of the *Adkins* court's reasoning. The defeat of protective legislation, although later softened in a case shortly thereafter, remained deeply problematic for their constitutional agenda.[74] So they were not likely to support this "thicker" understanding of the Nineteenth Amendment since it was a potent weapon against their goals. And the neutrality feminists, like Paul, were already deeply invested in an equal rights amendment as the path to full civil, political, and legal equality for women. The hint that such goals may already have been achieved might have been a reason why they did not embrace *Adkins* and take it further. If the Nineteenth Amendment had already accomplished the goals of full equality, what was the argument for an equal rights amendment? As some scholars have said,

"Yet even the NWP, who hailed the decision as a victory for their principles, might have hesitated. They were, after all, just inaugurating a campaign for the elimination of legal disabilities when Sutherland announced that these very contractual, political, and civil differences had, 'now come almost, if not quite, to the vanishing point.' "[75] At the time of the *Adkins* decision in April 1923, Paul was also still negotiating with the social feminists and legal progressives around the ERA, as the *Adkins* litigation was going on, hoping to at least secure their agreement not to oppose, if not support, the proposed amendment. Zimmerman has noted that Paul wanted to keep her work with the Ellis brothers around *Adkins* secret for that reason.[76] So Paul's failure to immediately capitalize on the victory in *Adkins* for a potentially thicker conception of the Nineteenth Amendment, may be, in part, be due to these concerns.

Another way to help explain the emergence of a thin conception, after the glimpse of a thicker understanding of the constitutional meaning and scope of the Nineteenth Amendment in *Adkins,* is that *Adkins* dealt with economic rights or, as supporters of the liberty of contract theory might argue, civil rights. But in either case, it was not about political rights. And the prevailing view of the time was that those two categories of rights were distinct. So the thick conception of the *Adkins* court around economic or civil rights, was unlikely to be applied to political rights, despite Sutherland's intoning, "[i]n view of the great—not to say revolutionary—changes which have taken place since [*Muller*], in the contractual, political, and civil status of women, culminating in the Nineteenth Amendment, it is not unreasonable to say that these differences have now come almost, if not quite, to the vanishing point."[77] His statement did not comport with the facts on the ground. States were resisting the extension of political rights, other than voting, to women at the time Sutherland wrote the opinion in *Adkins*. As discussed in Chapter 5, "Voting and Jury Service" and in Chapter 6, "Voting and Holding Public Office," in 1923, there were state courts using statutory construction to hold that voting was *not* coextensive with jury service or public officeholding and, thus, those political rights were not automatically extended to women, simply by ratification of the Nineteenth Amendment.

Political rights other than voting, like jury service and holding public office, had been distinguished in the debates about the scope of the Fourteenth and the Fifteenth Amendments. It presumably took enactment of the Fifteenth Amendment, and related enforcement legislation, to provide a basis for the Supreme Court's protecting jury service for African American men, in cases like *Strauder* and *Neal.* The mere enactment of the Fourteenth Amendment was understood to be limited to civil rights rather than to encompass political rights. But without enforcement legislation under the Nineteenth Amendment, no similar cases came before federal courts. "Notably, the United States Supreme Court did not rule on the issue, perhaps in part because the jury trial requirements of the Bill of Rights were not understood at that time to apply against the states."[78] In addition, the construction cases analyzed in Chapter 5, "Voting and Jury Service," demonstrate that "[r]arely did any of these early jury cases involve federal constitutional claims, perhaps because dicta in a nineteenth-century Supreme Court case involving race discrimination appeared to foreclose them."[79] In the few that did raise potential or actual Fourteenth Amendment claims, based on women's citizenship as opposed to the defendant's right to a representative jury, those claims were not successful.

The energy spent by the social feminists and the neutrality feminists around introduction of the ERA in December 1923 helps explain, in part, the puzzle of the emergence of a thin conception. The pivot to the ERA, and the resulting stalemate, took energy and focus away from the development of the Nineteenth Amendment, as the former suffragists got tangled up in the ERA battle. In the aftermath of *Adkins*, the divide deepened, and the acrimony between neutrality feminists like Paul and social feminists like Kelley, became entrenched. That perception that enormous effort was being wasted in this battle, is illustrated in the following description of Justice Brandeis's wife asking Dean Acheson, then clerking for Brandeis, to visit Paul to try to bridge the divide.

> Dean Acheson, a Harvard graduate and young Washington lawyer, best captured the bitterness of the controversy. A mission of reconciliation left him "sat on by all sides." Mrs. Brandeis, wife of the justice, had dispatched him to talk to Paul because leading NCL members were "distressed about the waste of effort involved in a row with Alice Paul."[80]

Combined with the NWP's move away from enforcement legislation, given its perceived need for white southern votes for the proposed ERA, this "waste of energy" in the battle between the neutrality feminists and the social feminists (and other legal progressives), sheds some light on the puzzle around why the thin conception of the Nineteenth Amendment prevailed by the end of the decade.[81] Each of the former national suffrage organizations continued to work in state legislative arenas, through their state chapters, to remove political, civil, and legal discrimination and extend rights. Yet neither organization was much in the courts, in the early years after ratification, invoking a thicker conception of the Nineteenth Amendment as the basis an expansion of women's political, civil, or legal equality.[82]

8

The Nineteenth Amendment Today

The change in the legal status of women wrought by the Nineteenth
Amendment was radical, drastic, and unprecedented. While it is to
be given full effect in its field, it is not to be extended by implication.
— *Commonwealth v. Welosky* (Massachusetts Supreme Judicial
Court 1931)

By the end of the decade following ratification of the Nineteenth Amendment,
the number of state cases construing the Nineteenth had slowed, and a
thin conception of its meaning and scope had emerged. As discussed in
Chapter 5, "Voting and Jury Service," in 1931, the Massachusetts Supreme
Judicial Court (SJC) construed the Nineteenth Amendment narrowly in
Commonwealth v. Welosky, rejecting the argument that its ratification extended to jury service.[1] *Welosky* has been identified by scholars as a test case,
where, "the MA-NWP took a new approach: attempting to change the law via
a judicial route," supported by the MA-LWV in this strategy.[2] Frustrated by
the slow pace of state legislative change, the groups worked together and, in
amicus briefs, argued for the court to construe the Nineteenth Amendment
as extending to jury service. When the court failed to embrace a thicker version of the Nineteenth Amendment and find that the amendment extended
beyond voting to jury service, the national NWP became involved. They arranged for a petition for certiorari in the US Supreme Court. But when it
denied that petition in 1932, the Supreme Court effectively left the thin conception as the prevailing interpretation at the end of the decade following
ratification.[3]

There were only a handful of federal cases in later decades that construed,
or even invoked, the Nineteenth Amendment. Some of those cases embraced
the narrow construction of the Nineteenth Amendment, adopted by many
state courts in the decade after ratification. These included *Breedlove
v. Suttles* in 1937, "the only Supreme Court case to directly decide whether

Constitutional Orphan. Paula A. Monopoli, Oxford University Press (2020). © Paula A. Monopoli.
DOI: 10.1093/oso/9780190092795.001.0001

a state law violated the Nineteenth Amendment.[4] As discussed in Chapter 4, "A Self-Executing Amendment," the *Breedlove* court addressed the question of women paying a required poll tax. The court held that the tax provisions did not violate the Nineteenth Amendment.[5] While several voting rights cases decided after *Breedlove* evinced a "nascent thick understanding" of the Nineteenth, the Supreme Court focused its reasoning in subsequent sex discrimination cases on the Fourteenth Amendment, rather than on the Nineteenth.[6] For example, the Supreme Court's final decisions on women and jury service, *Taylor v. Louisiana* in 1975 and *J.E.B. v. Alabama ex rel. T.B.* in 1994, reasoned from the Fourteenth Amendment, for the proposition that state laws around jury service could not differentiate on the basis of sex, and that sex was "an unconstitutional proxy for juror competence and impartiality."[7] Thus, as the twentieth century unfolded, federal courts expanded women's political and civil rights, but they did so on the basis of the Fourteenth Amendment, rather than the Nineteenth Amendment. The Nineteenth Amendment became somewhat of a constitutional orphan in American jurisprudence, rarely interpreted or cited as foundational to the court's analysis of underlying constitutional doctrine.[8]

The story of who is vested with full citizenship, as a matter of constitutional identity, in American history is complex and contested.[9] The previous chapters have described the role of national suffrage organizations, like the NWP and NAWSA/NLWV, in that story, in terms of the part they played in the emergence of a thin conception of the Nineteenth Amendment, during the decade following its ratification. The chapters evaluate the impact of the former suffragists' strategic choices and divisions on that conception, and connect those choices up with the amendment's constitutional development.[10] And they focus on explaining *how* that thin conception of the Nineteenth Amendment emerged, taking into account the impact of race, gender, and class on questions of federalism, women's citizenship, and the constitutional meaning of equality. So what does that story of the former suffragists and the Nineteenth Amendment in the decade after its ratification tell us about how we should, as a normative matter, interpret the Constitution today? The centennial of the ratification of the Nineteenth Amendment is a useful moment to reflect on that question, and to consider the contemporary scholarship that engages it.

Democratic legitimacy is derived from the consent of the governed. The Nineteenth Amendment expanded the political community, in terms of who was eligible to give that consent, by extending that right to women by protecting their eligibility to vote.[11] And enhancing democratic legitimacy was clearly one rationale for enacting the Nineteenth Amendment. After years of resisting a federal suffrage amendment, President Woodrow Wilson was forced to acknowledge that it was hollow to deploy the idea of protecting democracy abroad, as a rallying cry to justify US intervention in World War I, when half of American adults at home did not have the vote. His speech to the Senate in 1918 was a significant step in the effort to eventually enact the Nineteenth Amendment, in June 1919.[12] Neil Siegel highlights the role that enhancing democratic legitimacy played in Wilson's support of suffrage, and he argues that the Nineteenth Amendment should be construed in that light. In the context of the suffrage movement, and given the political conditions on the ground in 1920, Siegel reviews a number of important questions about women's rights today, concluding:

> The Nineteenth Amendment, whether read purposively, structurally, and aspirationally in light of its history or synthetically with the Equal Protection Clause, does not determine a uniquely correct answer to all of the above questions, whether that answer is found in constitutional politics or in constitutional law. But the Nineteenth Amendment, including its history, bears on the proper resolution of those questions. That is because the Amendment—if only it would be noticed—calls upon Americans to ask themselves what it means to take women seriously as the equals of men, in both family life and public life.[13]

In 2020, enhancing democratic legitimacy is one of the dominant issues in public political discourse. And recent scholarship, around revisiting the Nineteenth Amendment as a tool for shoring up that principle in our republic, demonstrates the link between 1920 and 2020. One might bring a feminist lens to this exercise in constitutional interpretation, "giving preference to interpretive choices that are less inclined to disproportionately disadvantage women."[14] Such an approach might begin with a direct extension of the Nineteenth Amendment to current voting rights practices. In that context, Rick Hasen and Leah Litman offer an argument for a thicker conception of the Nineteenth itself, and a thick conception of the congressional power to enforce the amendment.[15] "A 'thin' conception of the Nineteenth Amendment maintains that the amendment merely prohibits states from enacting laws that abridge a woman's ability to vote, once the state decides to hold an election. And a 'thin' conception of Congress's power to enforce the

Nineteenth Amendment maintains that Congress may only supply remedies for official acts that violate the Amendment's substantive guarantees."[16] Embracing a synthetic interpretive approach, Hasen and Litman argue that the Nineteenth Amendment "does more."[17] They argue that a thicker understanding is consistent with the text, the history, and a synthetic reading of the Constitution's history of expanding voting rights over time.[18] Hasen and Litman outline how this thicker conception would, "allow voting rights plaintiffs to attack restrictive voting laws burdening women, especially when those laws burden young women of color" and "redeem the Amendment from some of its racist origins . . ." This, in turn, "reinforces the democratic legitimacy of the Constitution."[19] Section two's enforcement clause provides the authority for Congress to protect such voters and ensure their political equality.[20] Building on recent scholarship by Steve Kolbert, which details the history of the enforcement clause debates,[21] Hasen and Litman map, "a litigation strategy premised on a revived Nineteenth Amendment within the scope of a cluster of new voting rights claims."[22] In addition, they argue that both the text and the history of the Nineteenth Amendment lend support to the proposition that "the national government [should have] a key role in ensuring equal voting rights regardless of gender. The amendment mandated gender equality in voting on a national scale, with federal protection and congressional enforcement power to be wielded against resisting states."[23]

This new scholarship builds on the foundational work of Reva Siegel's "She the People: The Nineteenth Amendment, Sex Equality, Federalism, and the Family." In that article, Siegel built the case for a synthetic reading of the Fourteenth Amendment together with the Nineteenth Amendment.[24] "Today, women's struggle for enfranchisement plays no role in the ways we understand or interpret the Constitution. Even though the quest for the vote spanned generations and provoked the most sustained dialogue about women's position in the constitutional community that the nation has ever conducted, the Nineteenth Amendment has been utterly excluded from the constitutional canon."[25] Siegel argued that the "Nineteenth Amendment was the product of a wide-ranging, multigenerational debate over the terms of women's citizenship in a democratic constitutional order."[26] Thus, "debates over 'the woman question' are part of the ratification history of the Nineteenth Amendment; at the same time, they are part of the post-ratification history of the Fourteenth Amendment, akin to the civil rights movement of the Second Reconstruction."[27] In her article, Siegel applied a synthetic reading to the Supreme Court's decision in *United States v. Morrison*, to demonstrate how a thicker interpretation of the Nineteenth, one that understands the Nineteenth as having an impact on other constitutional doctrines, could change both constitutional reasoning and outcomes.[28]

In her most recent scholarship, "The Nineteenth Amendment and the Democratization of the Family," Siegel extends that sociohistoric argument, focusing on the institutional history of the Nineteenth.[29] She suggests that history was deeply rooted in inequalities in the family itself. And it can be read to support a constitutional approach, which acknowledges that the Nineteenth Amendment is a basis for equal citizenship among family members, and is an "intersectional claim on equal protection." She envisions an approach that "look[s] beyond the Court's traditional case law enforcing Section One of the Fourteenth Amendment." Siegel notes that Justice Ginsburg, writing for the court in 1996 in *United States v. Virginia*, signaled that kind of shift when she, "turned to the story of suffrage struggle to explain the intermediate scrutiny-sex discrimination framework," connecting the history of woman suffrage to the history of laws that discriminated against women. The majority in *United States v. Virginia*, "ruled that the Equal Protection Clause forbids state action that perpetuates subordination of this kind: 'Sex classifications . . . may not be used, as they once were . . . to create or perpetuate the legal, social, and economic inferiority of women.'" Arguing that the court should apply a thicker conception of the Nineteenth to its reasoning under the Fourteenth, Siegel suggests ways in which, "we can begin to read the Nineteenth Amendment together with the Reconstruction Amendments, informed by the voices and concerns of the disenfranchised as well as the enfranchised, as we enforce the Constitution in a wide variety of contexts."[30] Those contexts include rights beyond political rights and include voting, the regulation of pregnancy and contraception, and protecting women from gender-motivated violence. Acknowledging that the current Supreme Court is unlikely to revisit cases like *United States v. Morrison*, Siegel concludes instead with a call for Congress to hold hearings to consider the scope of its powers to legislate women's equal citizenship pursuant to, "the Commerce Clause, Fourteenth Amendment, and the Nineteenth Amendment." She concludes that such authority supports enactment of legislation, like the "Pregnant Workers Fairness Act" providing for reasonable accommodations for pregnant women workers, law that is built on the assumption that women will continue employment in the marketplace, rather

than on gender schemas about their retreating to the private sphere after becoming mothers.[31]

Steven Calabresi and Julia Rickert have suggested an original public
meaning approach to interpreting the Nineteenth Amendment.[32] They,
too, endorse a synthetic reading of the Nineteenth with the Fourteenth
Amendment. The result is a capacious view of the Fourteenth that concludes
that women had full political rights upon ratification of the Nineteenth
Amendment.[33] Since voting was viewed as the apex of political rights, rights
like jury service and holding public office were subsumed within voting.
Thus, as a matter of constitutional interpretation, Calabresi and Rickert
reason that women had the right to sit on juries and hold public office immediately after ratification in 1920, despite the fact that some state courts did
not recognize this in the decade after ratification, nor did federal courts until
well into the 1970s. They conclude that an original public meaning approach
to this synthetic reading of the Nineteenth Amendment, together with the
Fourteenth, expands the anti-caste norm that underlies the Fourteenth, to
prohibit laws that abridge civil, as well as political rights, on the basis of sex.[34]

Finally, Tracy Thomas and Elizabeth Katz have given recent accounts of
how the debates, catalyzed by the nineteenth-century women's rights movement, around civil rights like property ownership in the context of marriage,
and political rights like officeholding, shaped law.[35] Such accounts help sit-
uate the Nineteenth Amendment in historical context and teach us how racial, gender, and class concerns informed its narrow construction by state
courts, before and after ratification. For attitudinal and institutional reasons,
or for reasons of state sovereignty, many of those courts cabined the impact
of the Nineteenth, and sanctioned only a thin conception of the Nineteenth,
devoid of much, if any, intersection with the Fourteenth Amendment. But a
deeper understanding of those state cases, and the social conditions around
race, gender, and class in the era in which they were decided, is helpful in
explaining how that thin conception emerged, and why modern courts
should apply a thicker conception of the Nineteenth Amendment.

The scholarship described in this chapter offers new ways in which the
Nineteenth Amendment can be understood to extend women's constitutional rights beyond voting. And in persuading contemporary courts to
reason around a thicker conception, it might be useful to suggest that previous courts gave too much weight to one factor over another, when faced
with interpreting the Nineteenth Amendment. Rather than focusing primarily on the implications of the Nineteenth for federalism, courts should seek

to divine what Congress intended in enacting the Nineteenth Amendment, in terms of the scope of women's citizenship and gender equality. There were extensive debates around woman suffrage, both in Congress and in public discourse, for more than seventy years preceding its ratification. Thus, one might plausibly suggest to today's courts that Congress meant the Nineteenth Amendment to be more than simply a check on state or federal power to deprive women of the mechanism for selecting representatives. This is especially true in light of the fact that fifteen states had already extended full suffrage to women prior to ratification of the federal amendment. In other words, the Nineteenth was not a "negative" amendment in the sense of simply preventing state action. Rather, Congress meant the amendment to operate in a positive manner, redefining who was part of the governing group—the People—in a broad sense, with all of the implications that such a positive reading might entail.

We still face the issue of how much Congress and the courts should embrace neutrality as the goal, or how much they should accommodate either physical difference or different social conditions around being female. For example, interpretation of federal legislation like Title VII of the Civil Rights Act of 1964, as applied to pregnancy, remains a matter of litigation and legislation.[36] As the scholars noted in this chapter have argued, reasoning from an understanding of the Nineteenth Amendment as an extension of full citizenship, and as a democratic reconstruction of the family, might help resolve that debate. Congressional authority to legislate, in traditionally state spheres like domestic violence and criminal law, may look different in light of an understanding of the Nineteenth Amendment as an expression of Congress's authority to protect women as citizens. Courts might also reason differently about the disparate impact of facially neutral state, local, and private employer veterans' preferences in employment on women, in an era of endless war, if they focused on the questions of women's citizenship and gender equality rather than federalism. Finally, state and federal restrictions on women's reproductive rights look very different when the lens is changed, from federalism, to the question of women as full citizens, entitled to equality of outcomes in their economic and intimate lives.

* * *

The Nineteenth Amendment enfranchised 26,500,000 women.[37] Some have called it, "the single biggest democratizing event in American history."[38] With 31,500,000 men eligible to vote prior to the amendment, the near-doubling of potential voters changed the size and composition of the American electorate in profound ways.[39] So, at one level, the Nineteenth Amendment was a significant success in terms of constitutional reform. Yet, on another level, the promise of that foundational change in American democracy was not fully realized.

Gretchen Ritter suggests that "*Why* suffrage failed to transform women's citizenship remains a puzzle."[40] One piece of that puzzle may be found in an account of the decade after ratification, one which concludes that it was a thin conception of the federal suffrage amendment that emerged at the end of that decade. The previous chapters describe *how* that amendment came to be understood in its most narrow sense, as a matter of constitutional interpretation. The chapters offer an account of the strategic choices made by the NWP and NAWSA/NLWV. These include their quick pivot away from the Nineteenth Amendment, and the NWP's perceived need for white southern political support for a new federal amendment and state reform legislation. This account is a means to understand, in part, why the thin conception of the Nineteenth Amendment prevailed in the decade after its ratification. One is left to imagine how, if the former suffragists had moved more slowly, and had worked together for a longer period post-ratification to put meat on the bones of the spare amendment, what might have been accomplished. Seasoned lawyers like Florence Kelley, working together with talented organizers like Alice Paul; and African American suffragists like Mary Church Terrell and Ida B. Wells-Barnett, on enforcement legislation and test cases around female voter suppression in the South, could have been a powerful alliance in terms of trying to persuade courts to embrace a thicker conception of the Nineteenth Amendment.[41] Given the political, social, and economic bent of the courts in the 1920s and their role as institutional actors preserving a constitutional regime still grounded in patriarchy, those courts might well have resisted such a thick conception. But the opportunity to do so was limited because such an alliance did not happen, no federal forum for litigation was created by congressional enforcement legislation, and state courts were left without specific federal direction as to whether the amendment was meant to protect political rights beyond voting, like jury service and public office holding. Thus, the thinner interpretation of the Nineteenth Amendment was left to prevail by the end of the decade:

> The citizenship established for women under the Nineteenth Amendment . . . was a citizenship of limited rights, limited expectations,

and broad space for state regulation of its specifics . . . The alternative (and never realized) vision articulated by rights advocates was of a citizenship grounded in political rights, like voting and jury service. Instead they got a citizenship in which, at the barest level, women were men's equals and could not be excluded from voting, or eventually, from serving on juries. But the failure to exclude did not constitute an argument for inclusion.[42]

As noted in the Introduction, the lack of unified feminist pressure and divisions within the women's movement are significant in understanding how law fails to develop, or develops in counterproductive ways.[43] The lack of unified pressure by the suffragists post-ratification, and their deep division over a new amendment, help explain the puzzle of why a thin conception of the Nineteenth Amendment emerged at the end of the decade following rat-ification. "[T]he rights advocates of the 1920s quickly recognized the inade-quacies of what they had won, and were drawn into other campaigns . . . Once women had the vote; they were supposed to be full citizens. Yet this did not occur."[44] The "other campaigns" included the push for the ERA. Had neu-trality feminists and social feminists worked together in the period immedi-ately after ratification to more securely ground the Nineteenth Amendment in the federal and state legal fabric, later efforts to build a constitutional ju-risprudence of gender equality and to ratify the ERA might have come more quickly, and might have been more successful.[45] Although it was finally passed by Congress in 1972, the ERA failed to be ratified in 1982.[46] There is a theory that it could be ratified, if three more states ratified, even though its deadline has passed. And three more states have now done so.[47] If courts reject these additional three state ratifications as coming too late, we should consider whether a thicker conception of the Nineteenth Amendment might serve as an effective substitute.

As an empirical matter, the Nineteenth Amendment and its tremendous expansion of the electorate did not have a significant impact on the outcome of presidential elections for many years after its ratification.[48] However, in 1980 the so-called gender gap in voting began to emerge.[49] Women as a bloc began to swing presidential elections.[50] Since 1980, women have consistently voted more Democratic than have men. And, since 1992, they have con-sistently voted majority-Democratic. It is clear from the data that African American women voters, as a bloc, were responsible for President Obama winning the female vote in 2008 and 2012.[51] They turned out in fewer num-bers in 2016.[52] So while women overall voted for the first female major party candidate in 2016, and 94% of African American women voted for her, the majority of white women did not, with 53% of them voting for Donald Trump."[53] In that divided voting pattern, there is the echo of white suffragists turning their backs on African American suffragists, in the immediate aftermath of ratification of the Nineteenth Amendment.[54]

As Reva Siegel concludes in her argument for a resurrection of the Nineteenth Amendment as a constitutional tool:

> What difference does it make to criticize a Supreme Court decision by the lights of a constitutional amendment so rarely cited that reference to it prompts many, if not most, constitutional law scholars to ask: "Which one is that?" In the short run, quite plainly, it makes no practical difference at all. But the exercise may prompt us to wonder about the conventions of reasoning that regulate the Constitution's meaning, both as a narrative and as a constellation of decision-rules that guide our social practice.[55]

In engaging in such an exercise, one could focus on the role of Congress in the story of how a thin conception of the Nineteenth Amendment emerged by the end of the decade following its ratification, in its failure to enact enforcement legislation. Or one could highlight the role of the state actors, state court judges who cabined the scope of the Nineteenth by strict construction of the amendment. This book illuminates the role of two former national suffrage organizations, as significant institutional actors in civil society, in that story. It suggests their strategic choices in moving quickly away from the Nineteenth, and toward a new amendment and state legislative reform as tools to effectuate women's equality, played a role in solidifying the thin conception of the Nineteenth Amendment. In all of these accounts, there was arguably a "missed constitutional opportunity" that could be recaptured by the adoption of a thicker, more robust reading of the Nineteenth Amendment today, either alone or in conjunction with the Fourteenth Amendment.[56] Such a reading has the potential to make substantive gender equality a constitutional reality for American women, more fully reflecting the description of the ratification of the Nineteenth Amendment in 1920 as, "a long-resisted, fully deliberated, collective commitment to include women as equal members of the constitutional community."[57]

Notes

Introduction

1. *See* National American Woman Suffrage Association, *Victory: How Women Won It, A Centennial Symposium, 1840–1940* (New York: H.W. Wilson Co., 1940), 153. The Tennessee ratification documents had been quietly sent over to Colby's residence to avoid attention. On August 25, 1920, NWP Headquarters Secretary Emma Wold wrote to Harriet Stanton Blatch, "We are now awaiting the arrival of certification papers from Tennessee, and we hope that Secretary Colby will stay in retirement until he can sign the proclamation so that he may avoid being served with injunction papers." Emma Wold to Harriet Stanton Blatch, 25 August 1920, box II: 6, National Woman's Party Records, Manuscript Division, Library of Congress. The concern was about legal action by groups opposed to ratification of the amendment. *See* Maud Wood Park, *Front Door Lobby*, edited by Edna Lamprey Stantial (Boston: Beacon Press, 1960), 276.
2. As used in this book, NWP refers both to the original party formed by Alice Paul and Lucy Burns in 1916 and the "new" National Woman's Party, formed in February 1921. While the new chair was Elsie Hill, it is clear from the record that Alice Paul was still the guiding force behind decisions about strategy in the new party. Note that several sections from this Introduction also appear in Paula A. Monopoli, "The Constitutional Development of the Nineteenth Amendment in the Decade Following Ratification," *ConLawNOW 11* (2020): 61–73.
3. "At four o'clock on the morning of August twenty-sixth, the certificate from Tennessee reached Washington, when where [*sic*] the Solicitor-General, who sat up all night waiting for it, made the examination needed before the signature of the Secretary of State could be affixed. Shortly after eight, that same morning, Mrs. Catt, on her way back from Tennessee, arrived [*sic*] in Washington, and the first thing she did was to telephone to the office of the Secretary of State. Mrs. Harriet Taylor Upton and I were in the room with her and heard her ask him whether the Tennessee certificate had been received. In a moment she put down the telephone, turned to us, and said, 'The Secretary has signed the Amendment and he wants us to go over to his office and see the Proclamation before he sends it out.'" Park, *Front Door Lobby*, 276.
4. Under the US Constitution, states are granted the power to define who is eligible to vote in federal or state elections, other than criteria included in the "voting amendments." U.S. Const. amend. XIV, § 2; U.S. Const. amend. XV (race); U.S. Const. amend. XIX (sex); U.S. Const. amend. XXVI (age).
5. Native Americans, who were not already eligible to become citizens through other means like marrying white men, did not become citizens until 1924 when President Calvin Coolidge signed the Indian Citizenship Act of 1924. Pub L. No. 68-175, 43

Stat. 253 (1924). Some Asian immigrants became eligible for naturalization under the Magnuson Act of 1943 (also known as the Chinese Exclusion Repeal Act of 1943.) But many others were not eligible for naturalization until the Immigration and Naturalization Act of 1952. Pub. L. No. 82-414, 66 Stat. 163.

6. *See generally* Chapter 3, "Enforcement Legislation." Note that like African American women, Latinas and other women of color in various parts of the country were often prevented from voting by devices like literacy tests and poll taxes.

7. There were also a number of white women who were not able to vote in that first post-ratification presidential election. *See* J. Kevin Corder and Christina Wolbrecht, *Counting Women's Ballots: Female Voters from Suffrage through the New Deal* (New York: Cambridge University Press, 2016), noting that "restrictive interpretations of registration rules (ratification had occurred after registration deadlines in a number of states) denied women access to the ballot in Arkansas, Georgia, Mississippi, and South Carolina in 1920, delaying women's participation in presidential elections in those states until 1924," *citing* Harold F. Gosnell, *Why Europe Votes* (Chicago: University of Chicago Press, 1930).

8. It should be noted that state and local chapters of both the National Woman's Party and the National American Woman Suffrage Association and its successor, the National League of Women Voters, were engaged in advocacy that was often distinct from the national leadership's efforts. So when describing "suffragists" or "suffrage organizations," I am referring to the national organizations and their leadership. The laudable efforts of the hundreds of state and local chapters are beyond the scope of this book.

9. Elsie M. Hill to Helen Peters, 25 May 1921, box II: 12, National Woman's Party Records, Manuscript Division, Library of Congress.

10. *See* NAWSA, *Victory*, 153.

11. A Lexis-Nexis search (January 1, 2020) indicated that there are 622 judicial opinions that cite the Nineteenth Amendment, with 291of those in state courts and 331 in federal courts. The number of US Supreme Court opinions that cite the Nineteenth Amendment is 39. It is interesting to compare that with the same search for the Fifteenth Amendment, which has virtually the same text as the Nineteenth. That search turns up 2,845 total citations, with 2,734 of those coming after 1920. The split between federal and state courts is more skewed, with 439 state courts and 2,406 federal courts citing the Fifteenth Amendment. Finally, there are 194 citations to the Fifteenth Amendment in US Supreme Court decisions.

12. *See* Reva B. Siegel, "She the People: The Nineteenth Amendment, Sex Equality, Federalism, and the Family," *Harvard Law Review* 115 (2002): 945–1046, wherein Siegel argues for a more synthetic interpretation of the Nineteenth and Fourteenth Amendments based on a sociohistoric reading of the suffrage amendment in American constitutional history. Siegel notes the more robust conception of the Nineteenth Amendment embraced in some federal cases like Adkins v. Children's Hospital but observes that view faded quickly and the amendment became simply a "nondiscrimination rule governing voting." Ibid., 953. This book adds to that insight by offering an account of how that thick conception faded so quickly. It examines the role of the major suffrage organizations in that account. It suggests that their strategic

choices to shift immediately to other goals, and withdraw from active support of pending enforcement legislation, played a role in the amendment's limited constitutional development in the decade after ratification.

13. Strauder v. West Virginia, 100 U.S. 303 (1880), in which the court reversed the decision of the West Virginia Supreme Court, holding that a state statute that only allowed white male persons to serve as jurors was unconstitutional under the Fourteenth Amendment's equal protection clause and affirming the power of Congress to enact enforcement legislation pursuant to the fifth clause of the Fourteenth. The court unfortunately stated that states could still exclude jurors based solely on sex. Neal v. State of Delaware, 103 U.S. 370, 404–405 (1881), in which the court affirmed Strauder and invoked the Fifteenth Amendment as well as the Fourteenth. In his dissent, Justice Field argued that the fifth clause of the Fourteenth Amendment did not give Congress the authority to enact "the fourth section of the act of March 1, 1875, c. 114," providing that no citizen should be denied the right to serve on a jury due to race, color, and previous condition of servitude. There was no similar federal enforcement legislation pursuant to the section two of the Nineteenth Amendment that could have ensured a uniform conclusion by all state courts who considered the question of whether voting was coextensive with jury service.

14. *See* Steven G. Calebresi and Julia T. Rickert, "Originalism and Sex Discrimination," *Texas Law Review* 90 (2011): 1, 89–90, noting southern politicians' belief that "[t]he Nineteenth Amendment would precipitate a 'second reconstruction' in the South," and their "fear of a second reconstruction inspired by Bolshevists, female voters and African-Americans ..."

15. Adkins v. Children's Hospital, 261 U.S. 525 (1923), *overruled in part by* West Coast Hotel Co. v. Parrish, 300 U.S. 379 (1937). These cases involved challenges to protective legislation that required employers to abide by maximum hour and minimum wage legislation. The US Supreme Court upheld a maximum hour law in Muller v. Oregon, 208 U.S. 412 (1908). However, in 1923 the court distinguished a minimum wage law as unrelated to the physical differences between men and women that justified its decision in *Muller*. And it found such a minimum wage law unconstitutional. *See Adkins*, 261 U.S. 525.

16. I am using the term "neutrality feminist" to describe suffragists, like Alice Paul, who embraced the view that the Constitution should be interpreted to simply invalidate any "class legislation" that treated men and women differently, in order to render equality. I use the term "social feminist" to describe feminists, like Florence Kelley, who believed that the police power inherent in the Constitution, to provide for the general health and welfare of the populace, justified legislation that recognized the asymmetry of power based on both sex and class. These feminists held the view that such legislation rendered equality of outcomes, a more substantive definition of constitutional equality.

17. *See, e.g., Adkins*, 261 U.S. 525, in which Justice Sutherland, a laissez-faire adherent who had advised Alice Paul on drafting the Equal Rights Amendment when he was a senator, wrote the majority opinion striking down the District of Columbia's minimum wage law. *See* Siegel, "She the People," 1014.

18. One way we might characterize the protective labor legislation cases, is as a debate about whether our Constitution merely guarantees a neutral or "formal" approach to equality, that is, ensuring that women simply have the same opportunities as men. Or, whether our Constitution should be interpreted to ensure "substantive" equality, that is, similar outcomes that take into account differences between men and women.

19. *See, e.g.,* Young v. United Parcel Service, Inc., 575 U.S. 206 (2015), interpreting the Pregnancy Discrimination Act amendments to Title VII of the Civil Rights Act of 1964.

20. Siegel, "She the People," 1022.

21. Ibid.

22. Jeannette Rankin (R-Montana) was the first woman elected to Congress, and the only one to vote in 1918 on the text of the bill that later became the Nineteenth Amendment. *See* James J. Lopach and Jean A. Luckowski, *Jeannette Rankin: A Political Woman* (Boulder: University Press of Colorado, 2005), 146.

23. For example, President Wilson, after initially being opposed to a federal suffrage amendment, arguably changed his position only when it became essential to his war effort to do so. *See* Neil S. Siegel, "Why the Nineteenth Amendment Matters Today: A Guide for the Centennial," *Duke Journal of Gender, Law and Policy* 27 (2020): 235, 243–244, describing Wilson's shift from opponent to supporter of the federal suffrage amendment and suggesting reasons why he might have changed his position.

24. Vicki Schultz, "Taking Sex Discrimination Seriously," *Denver University Law Review* 91 (2015): 995, 1003.

25. Ibid. Some scholars have argued that a similar lack of support from women's rights organizations for the private right of action under the Violence Against Women Act (VAWA) was, in part, to blame for its eventual demise at the hands of the US Supreme Court. *See* Caroline S. Schmidt, "What Killed the Violence Against Women Act's Civil Rights Remedy before the Supreme Court Did?," *Virginia Law Review* 101 (2015): 501, 530–533.

26. One potential direct application is to state laws that require the payment of fees and fines by those convicted of felonies, prior to reinstatement of voting rights. These laws are preconditions on voting that arguably have a disparate impact on women, given the gender pay gap. For synthetic applications, *see* Reva B. Siegel, "The Nineteenth Amendment and the Democratization of the Family," *Yale Law Journal Forum* 129 (2020): 450, 482–489, for several "ways in which an institutional understanding of the Nineteenth Amendment can guide the Court's interpretation of the Equal Protection Clause." Siegel cites Justice Ginsburg's majority opinion in United States v. Virginia, 518 U.S. 515 (1996), as one that "invite[s] synthetic interpretation." Ibid., 484.

27. Leser v. Garnett, 114 A. 840 (Md. 1921), *affirmed*, 258 U.S. 130 (1922). Fairchild v. Hughes, 258 U.S. 126 (1922).

28. *See* Commonwealth v. Welosky, 177 N.E. 656 (Mass. 1931), in which amicus briefs were filed.

29. *Adkins* was later overturned by West Coast Hotel Co. v. Parrish, 300 U.S. 379 (1937).

Chapter 1

1. Louise R. McKay to Alice Paul, 22 August 1920, box II: 6, National Woman's Party Records, Manuscript Division, Library of Congress.

2. J. E. Milholland to Alice Paul, 20 August 1920, box II: 6, National Woman's Party Records, Manuscript Division, Library of Congress. Note that the battle for suffrage was not over for Native American women who did not become eligible for citizenship until 1924 and for many Asian immigrant women who did not become eligible for naturalization until the 1940s and 1950s. And, as described in later chapters, African American women and Latinas, who were citizens, continued to face de facto barriers to voting, like poll taxes and literacy tests, well into the 1960s.

3. Milholland's daughter, Inez, was a suffragist who marched alongside Alice Paul in 1913. Inez fell ill while on a suffrage speaking tour and died in 1916, before ratification had been achieved. Thus, Milholland concluded his congratulatory letter to Paul with the sentence, "So I am speaking for the whole Milholland Family, the Living and the Dead." Ibid.

4. *See also* Reva B. Siegel, "The Nineteenth Amendment and the Democratization of the Family," *Yale Law Journal Forum* 129 (2020): 450–495. Siegel argues that "The debate about women voting in the decades after the founding centrally concerned the family. A male head of household was enfranchised to represent his wife, children, and other members of the household. A woman's claim to vote was a challenge to this system of 'virtual representation,' and for this very reason, a claim for democratic reconstruction of the family." Ibid., 452.

5. Sam Roberts, "The Roles of Men and New York State in Women's Suffrage," *New York Times*, 1 November 2017. Despite their virulent anti-suffrage stance, "even the antisuffragist *New York Times* chronicled [the NWP members'] jail experiences daily and admitted that Alice Paul's willingness to die in jail had changed the nation's opinion of suffrage and suffragists." Katherine H. Adams and Michael L. Keene, *Alice Paul and the American Suffrage Campaign* (Urbana and Chicago: University of Illinois Press, 2008), xv. "The Camden Courier said of these women: '. . . [The National Woman's Party] certainly put it over for it was they who helped put through the House of Representatives the resolution calling for a suffrage amendment to the Constitution . . .'" Ibid.

6. Suffrage is generally defined as the right to vote in an election. *Merriam Webster's Collegiate Dictionary*, 11th ed., s.v. "suffrage." It has various etymologies: "late 14c., 'intercessory prayers or pleas on behalf of another,' from Old French *sofrage* 'plea, intercession' (13c.) and directly from Medieval Latin *suffragium*, from Latin *suffragium* 'support, ballot, vote; right of voting; a voting tablet,' from *suffragari* 'lend support, vote for someone,' . . . The meaning 'political right to vote' in English is first found in the U.S. Constitution, 1787." *Online Etymology Dictionary*, s.v. "suffrage," https://www.etymonline.com/word/suffrage.

7. Many suffragists spoke in terms of the ratification of the Nineteenth Amendment as securing their "political" freedom as opposed to full social, economic, and legal equality. In a telegram from one supporter to Alice Paul, the sender noted, "the long

struggle of American women for political freedom is at and [*sic*] end." Telegram from Bertha W. Fowler to Alice Paul, 27 August 1920, box II: 6, National Woman's Party Records, Manuscript Division, Library of Congress. And Alice Paul herself wrote, "The women who have been working for the enfranchisement of all women through the passage of the National Suffrage Amendment express to you their deep appreciation of the splendid aid which California women voters have given in the campaign for the political freedom of women." Telegram from Alice Paul to Mrs. John R. Haynes, acting chairman, California League of Women Voters, 28 August 1920, box II: 6, National Woman's Party Records, Manuscript Division, Library of Congress.

8. *See* Tracy A. Thomas, "More Than the Vote: The Nineteenth Amendment as Proxy for Gender Equality," *Stanford Journal of Civil Rights and Civil Liberties* 15 (forthcoming 2020) (draft at 1–2, https://papers.ssrn.com/sol3/papers.cfm?abstract_id=3364546).

9. *See* Aileen S. Kraditor, *The Ideas of the Woman Suffrage Movement, 1890–1920* (New York: Columbia University Press, 1965), 2. Some argue that it dates back further to 1837. *See* Barbara F. Berenson, *Massachusetts in the Woman Suffrage Movement* (Charleston, SC: The History Press, 2018), 11–12.

10. *See* Thomas, "More Than the Vote" (draft at 1).

11. *See generally* Berenson, *Massachusetts in the Woman Suffrage Movement.*

12. *See* Thomas, "More Than the Vote (draft at 2).

13. Prior to the Nineteenth Amendment, fifteen states had given women full voting rights in both federal and state elections. Another twelve allowed women to vote for presidential electors, but did not extend full suffrage. And yet other states had given women other sorts of partialized voting, for example, school or tax and bond suffrage. *See* "Centuries of Citizenship: A Constitutional Timeline," National Constitution Center, https://constitutioncenter.org/timeline/html/cw08_12159.html. So even before the Nineteenth Amendment was ratified, women could vote for 339 of 531 presidential electors. *See* National American Woman Suffrage Association, *Victory: How Women Won It, A Centennial Symposium, 1840–1940* (New York: H. W. Wilson, 1940), 164.

14. A new suffrage wave began in 1910 and extended over the next eight years to Washington (1910), California (1911), Arizona (1912), Kansas (1912), Oregon (1912), Montana (1914), Nevada (1914), New York (1917), Michigan (1918), Oklahoma (1918), and South Dakota (1918). *See* "Centuries of Citizenship."

15. *See* Rosalyn Terborg-Penn, *African-American Women in the Struggle for the Vote, 1850–1920* (Bloomington: Indiana University Press, 1998), 88–89; *see also* Paula Giddings, *When and Where I Enter: The Impact of Black Women on Race and Sex in America* (New York: Amistad, 1984), 93–94.

16. Terborg-Penn, *African-American Women in the Struggle for the Vote*, 128–135.

17. J.D. Zahniser and Amelia R. Fry, *Alice Paul: Claiming Power* (New York: Oxford University Press, 2014), 108–109.

18. Mary Walton, *A Woman's Crusade: Alice Paul and the Battle for the Ballot* (New York: Palgrave Macmillan, 2010), 10.

19. While in this country "suffragettes" would have been deemed pejorative as the diminutive form of "suffragist," in Britain the term was used to distinguish the militant

Pankhurst branch from the less militant branch of the suffrage movement headed by Millicent Fawcett and others. The term was actually embraced by the militant British suffragists and used by them to describe themselves. *See* Katy Steinmetz, "Everything You Need to Know about the Word 'Suffragette,'" *Time Magazine*, 22 October 2015, https://time.com/4079176/suffragette-word-history-film/.

20. Adams and Keene, *Alice Paul and the American Suffrage Campaign*, 4.

21. Mickle Paul to Tacie Paul, 14 December 1909. Alice Paul Papers, 1785–1985; MC 399 box 14, folder 210, Schlesinger Library, Radcliffe Institute, Harvard University.

22. Tacie Paul to Christabel Pankhurst, 2 December 1909. Alice Paul Papers, 1785–1985; MC 399 box 14, folder 210, Schlesinger Library, Radcliffe Institute, Harvard University.

23. Zahniser and Fry, *Alice Paul*, 125.

24. *See* Lynda G. Dodd, "Parades, Pickets, and Prison: Alice Paul and the Virtues of Unruly Constitutional Citizenship," *Journal of Law and Politics* 24 (2008): 339, 377–379, describing Paul's break with NAWSA and concluding that "Despite Paul's efforts to remedy the situation, NAWSA began issuing demands that led Paul and Burns to conclude that they could no longer pursue their federal amendment campaign under its auspices." Ibid., 379.

25. Zahniser and Fry, *Alice Paul*, 188.

26. Walton, *A Woman's Crusade*, 133.

27. Akhil Amar has described this moment as, "the single biggest democratizing event in American history . . . Even the most extraordinary feats of the Founding and Reconstruction eras had involved the electoral empowerment and/or enfranchisement of hundreds of thousands, not millions." Akhil Reed Amar, *America's Constitution: A Biography* (New York: Random House, 2005), 419, *cited in* Neil S. Siegel, "Why the Nineteenth Amendment Matters Today: A Guide for the Centennial," *Duke Journal of Gender Law and Policy* 27 (2020): 235, 235 n. 3.

28. *See* National American Woman Suffrage Association, *Victory*, 146.

29. *See* ibid.

30. Kraditor, *Ideas*, 9.

31. Leser v. Garnett, 258 U.S. 130 (1922), affirming 114 A. 840 (Md. 1921).

Chapter 2

1. The lawsuit that was the primary test case for validity was filed in the Maryland Court of Common Pleas, and that decision was appealed to the highest court in Maryland, the Court of Appeals, which affirmed the lower court. Leser v. Garnett, 114 A. 840, 844 (Md. 1921).

2. "The Woman's Party was disbanded as a suffrage organization, having accomplished its work, at our national convention in February. It immediately reorganized under the same name to work for the welfare of women in other ways. The new organization . . . is taking as its first work, the removal of all the legal disabilities of women." Alice Paul to Miss S. Ada Flatman, 26 May 1921, box II: 12, National Woman's Party Records, Manuscript Division, Library of Congress.

3. "The National American Woman Suffrage Association is no longer functioning as an organization. Its work is done and its officers and headquarters are merely engaged in closing its business. We have, however, a successor, which is our own organization under another Board, and that is the League of Women Voters." Carrie Chapman Catt to Samuel Gompers, 20 September 1921, ProQuest History Vault. Women's Studies. Struggle for Women's Rights, Organizational Records, 1880–1990 (hereinafter ProQuest Struggle for Women's Rights) Papers of the League of Women Voters, folder 002637-003-0454. Yet, the original organization continued to have a legal existence. In a 1940 publication celebrating one hundred years of the woman suffrage movement, it is noted that "The National American Woman Suffrage Association is an incorporated body and remains intact . . . The Board of Officers in July 1940 are: Carrie Chapman Catt, President, . . . The Board of Directors: Mrs. J.C. Cantrill Kentucky . . . The National Headquarters, 1624 Grand Central Terminal Building, 70 East 45th Street, New York City." *See* National American Woman Suffrage Association, *Victory: How Women Won It, A Centennial Symposium, 1840–1940* (New York: H. W. Wilson Co., 1940), 158.

4. This litigation upholding the validity of the ratification of the Nineteenth Amendment also included Hawke v. Smith, 253 U.S. 221 (1920), which reversed a decision by the Supreme Court of Ohio that the constitution of the State required submission of the issue of ratification of the Nineteenth Amendment to a referendum by the people, because such a referendum was inconsistent with the process set out in Article V of the US Constitution.

5. *See, e.g.*, B.V. Hubbard, *Socialism, Feminism, and Suffragism, the Terrible Triplets, Connected by the Same Umbilical Cord, and Fed from the Same Nursing Bottle* (Chicago: American Publishing Co., 1915), http://www.loc.gov/resource/rbnawsa. n6027 (dedicated "to the innumerable multitude of motherly women, who love and faithfully serve their fellow men with a high regard for duty, a veneration for God, respect for authority, and love for husband home and heaven . . ."). The author argues that feminism is a "twin sister of Socialism" and that "Socialists and Feminists are universally and without exception suffragettes." And he adds that "Socialism, aided by Feminism and Suffragism, aims to overthrow the philosophy of the ages, and destroy our theory of family and school governments, and our system of public justice, and substitute in their places atheistic anarchy." Ibid.

6. Helen Kendrick Johnson, *Woman and the Republic: A Survey of the Woman-Suffrage Movement in the United States and a Discussion of the Claims and Arguments of its Foremost Advocates* (New York: The Guidon Club, 1913). In this anti-suffrage book (owned by Carrie Chapman Catt and donated with her papers to the Library of Congress), the author argues that women like Anne Hutchinson, Elizabeth Cady Stanton, Susan B. Anthony, and others were "reenacting the Temptress and the Fall." Ibid., 266–267.

7. "Because Catt expected that NAWSA's work to secure the suffrage would soon be finished, she used the Jubilee Convention of 1919 to organize NAWSA's successor, the National League of Women Voters. NAWSA estimated its membership above two million." Jacqueline Van Voris, *Carrie Chapman Catt: A Public Life* (New York: The Feminist Press, 1987), 153.

8. Ibid., 157.

9. Convention Minutes, p. 3. Victory Convention of the National American Woman Suffrage Association and the First National Congress of the League of Women Voters, Chicago, 12–18 February 1920. Papers of the League of Women Voters, 1918–1974, Part II, Series A: Transcripts and Records of National Conventions, 1919–1944, and of General Councils, 1927–1943 ProQuest Struggle for Women's Rights, folder: 002634-001-0079.

10. Ibid., pp. 5 and 9.

11. Ibid., 5. "That the Board of Officers so constituted shall have full charge of the remainder of the ratification campaign, all necessary legal proceedings and shall dispose of files, hooks, data, property and funds (if any remain) of the Association subject to the further instruction of this convention. The Executive Council shall be subject to call by the Board of Officers if necessary; . . . Whereas, The question of the legality of referendum by petition or Federal Amendments is pending in the Federal Supreme Court and will not be heard before March 1, therefore be it resolved, That if the Court holds such referenda to be legal and referenda campaigns are in consequence instituted (a) each of the 48 states be urged to pledge itself to furnish a competent experienced man or woman campaigner and defray all expenses of their representatives; (h) that each state be assessed for its due proportion of the necessary campaign fund; (c) that the Board of Directors be authorized to appoint a national campaign committee, if one be found necessary." Ibid. Convention Minutes, p. 5, 12–18 February 1920.

12. Ibid., 14–16.

13. "[Catt's] goal was worldwide amity to exclude war forever through an international nexus of viable democratic institutions." Jacqueline Van Voris, *Carrie Chapman Catt: A Public Life* (New York: The Feminist Press 1987), 171.

14. J.D. Zahniser and Amelia R. Fry, *Alice Paul: Claiming Power* (New York: Oxford University Press, 2014), 320.

15. Alice Paul to Miss Mary Burnham, 28 August 1920, box II: 6, National Woman's Party Records, Manuscript Division, Library of Congress.

16. "From September 1920 through February 1921, the party's inner circle, the National Executive Committee, met monthly to hash out resolutions to present at the grand convention in February, where the future form and goals (if any) of the party were ostensibly to be decided by the delegates present. While Paul gave many of her followers the impression that she was too exhausted to go on leading them, her predilections guided preparations." Nancy F. Cott, "Feminist Politics in the 1920s: The National Woman's Party," *Journal of American History* 71 (1984): 43–68, 47, and n. 9, *citing* National Executive Committee, National Woman's Party minutes, 10 September, 8 October, 16 November, 10 December, 1920, 22 January, 24 February 1921; reel 114, part A, series 2, National Woman's Party Papers, 1913–1974.

17. Minutes of 10 September 1920, Meeting of National Executive Committee pp. 1–2, National Woman's Party Papers, Part I: 1913–1974, Series 2: Minutes, Legal Papers, and Financial Records, 1912–1972, series: Minutes, 1917–1972, folder: National Executive Committee Minutes, February 1917–August 1921, ProQuest Struggle for

Women's Rights, folder: 002614-114-0757. The five lawsuits included what the party members called, "the Ohio Referendum Case, the Injunction Suit, the Tennessee Case, and the Maryland case." *See* Proceedings of the February 1921 National Woman's Party Convention Transcript, Alice Paul Papers, 1785–1985; MC 399 box 2, folder 318 at 26, Schlesinger Library, Radcliffe Institute, Harvard University.

18. Mary Walton, *A Woman's Crusade: Alice Paul and the Battle for the Ballot* (New York: Palgrave Macmillan, 2010), 246.

19. Ibid.

20. Amy E. Butler, *Two Paths to Equality: Alice Paul and Ethel Smith in the ERA Debate, 1921–1929* (Albany: State University of New York Press, 2002), 56, noting also that "The stage was set for conflict, however, because behind the scenes Paul and her supporters had already established the agenda that they would pursue for the remainder of the 1920s. While event participants assumed that their views would influence future directions of the party, Paul ultimately rejected all proposals for cooperation and publicly announced that her organization would pursue state equal rights bills as well as a federal equal rights amendment." Ibid., 56–57.

21. Ibid., 6, *citing* Kathryn Kish Sklar's biography of Florence Kelley, noting Sklar "portrays Kelley as a woman who . . . sought remedial legislation as an alternative to the late-nineteenth-century conservative judicial doctrine that 'refused to recognize class as a valid basis for public policies.' That strategy used sex-specific laws for the class-specific purposes of changing the jurisprudence of laissez-faire and its attendant protection of freedom of contract. By challenging legal conservatism, according to Sklar, Kelley worked to enhance women's economic status in the labor force and to restructure the relationship between the state, employers and employees." Ibid., 6 n. 15, *citing* Kathryn Kish Sklar, *Florence Kelley and the Nation's Work: The Rise of Women's Political Culture, 1830–1900* (New Haven, CT: Yale University Press, 1995), 256–258.

22. Muller v. Oregon, 208 U.S. 412 (1908).

23. Christine Lunardini, *From Equal Suffrage to Equal Rights: Alice Paul and the National Woman's Party, 1920–1928* (Lincoln, NE: ToExcel Press, 1986, 2000), 52.

24. Ibid., 153.

25. Butler, *Two Paths to Equality*, 58, *citing* the minority report submitted by Murray, "requesting that convention proceedings include recognition of the remaining political inequalities that affect African-American women, especially in the South."

26. Cott, "Feminist Politics in the 1920s," 53.

27. Butler, *Two Paths to Equality*, 56. *See also* Cott, "Feminist Politics in the 1920s," 47. "In December [1920 Paul] told the National Executive Committee that Sue Shelton White (a lawyer and vigorous party worker since 1917), who had been surveying sex discriminations in state legal codes, had drawn up a 'blanket bill' that 'could be introduced in Congress and each legislature to sweep away these discriminations' and 'could be offered at the final convention as a possible piece of work for the future.' Despite the contrary efforts of a few who wished for a broader-ranging program . . . the leadership moved undeviatingly toward the majority resolution offered at the convention: that the party disband but immediately regroup under the same

name, with its 'immediate work' being 'the removal of the legal disabilities of women.'" And "Paul had been experimenting with forms of a constitutional amendment to end sex discrimination in law even before the convention gave its mandate." Cott, "Feminist Politics in the 1920s," 56.

28. *See* Reva B. Siegel, "She the People: The Nineteenth Amendment, Sex Equality, Federalism, and the Family," *Harvard Law Review* 115 (2002): 947–1046.

29. Lunardini, *From Equal Suffrage to Equal Rights*, 157, noting the absence of the National American Woman Suffrage Association (NAWSA), the NWP's chief organizational rival. Ibid., 158.

30. Proceedings of the February 1921 National Woman's Party Convention Transcript. Alice Paul Papers, 1785–1985; MC 399 box 2, folder 318 at 1, Schlesinger Library, Radcliffe Institute, Harvard University.

31. Jennifer K. Brown, "The Nineteenth Amendment and Women's Equality," *Yale Law Journal* 102 (1993): 2175–2204.

32. Proceedings of the February 1921 National Woman's Party Convention Transcript, Alice Paul Papers, 1785–1985; MC 399 box 2, folder 318 at 3, Schlesinger Library, Radcliffe Institute, Harvard University.

33. Ibid., 4.

34. Lunardini, *From Equal Suffrage to Equal Rights*, 159.

35. Proceedings of the February 1921 National Woman's Party Convention Transcript, Alice Paul Papers, 1785–1985; MC 399 box 2, folder 318 at 58, Schlesinger Library, Radcliffe Institute, Harvard University.

36. Ibid., 61.

37. *See* Gretchen Ritter, "Jury Service and Women's Citizenship before and after the Nineteenth Amendment," *Law and History Review* 20 (2002): 479–515 at 481, *citing* Reva B. Siegel, "Collective Memory and the Nineteenth Amendment: Reasoning about the 'Woman Question' in the Discourse of Sex Discrimination," in *History, Memory, and the Law*, edited by Austin Sarat and Thomas R. Kearns (Ann Arbor: University of Michigan Press, 1999).

38. *See* Cott, "Feminist Politics in the 1920s," 51, describing Emma Wold's response to Mary White Ovington, couched in terms of "feminist" versus "racial" issues as appropriate for debate at the convention.

39. Proceedings of the February 1921 National Woman's Party Convention Transcript, Alice Paul Papers, 1785–1985; MC 399 box 2, folder 318 at 106–108, Schlesinger Library, Radcliffe Institute, Harvard University.

40. Ibid.

41. Ibid.

42. Ibid.

43. Ibid., 111–112. After the convention, "Murray declined to serve on the party's new National Advisory Council, 'in view of certain phases of the recent convention,' and ended her subscription to the party newspaper." *See* Cott, "Feminist Politics in the 1920s," 54.

44. Butler, *Two Paths to Equality*, 58 nn. 8 and 9. Florence Kelley was a member of the National Association for the Advancement of Colored People (NAACP).

45. Note that Ethel Smith of the National Women's Trade Union League also spoke of the plight of twelve million wage-earning women in the United States. Smith stated that she was also a member of the Minimum Wage Board of the District of Columbia and in that capacity warned women that if they split on the question of protective legislation for women workers, they were "playing into the hands of the employers." She noted that the employers had threatened to take away contributions to the party if the convention adopted a platform that supported protective legislation and were trying to split the women's movement into "two camps." Smith made clear that her organization supported such legislation in both Congress and the states. Proceedings of the February 1921 National Woman's party Convention Transcript, Alice Paul Papers, 1785–1985; MC 399 box 2, folder 318 at p. 85, Schlesinger Library, Radcliffe Institute, Harvard University.

46. Lunardini, *From Equal Suffrage to Equal Rights*, 160 nn. 36 and 37, citing National Woman's Party convention transcript, pp. 15–18. Unfortunately, Kelley "came to perceive her one-time ally Alice Paul as a "fiend" whose only purpose was to hinder the women's movement and undo twenty years of labor legislation." Ibid., 162.

47. Proceedings of the February 1921 National Woman's Party Convention Transcript, Alice Paul Papers, 1785–1985; MC 399 box 2, folder 318 at pp. 78–79, Schlesinger Library, Radcliffe Institute, Harvard University.

48. Ibid., 79.

49. Ibid., 67.

50. Ibid.

51. Ibid., 30.

52. Proceedings of the February 1921 National Woman's Party Convention Transcript, Alice Paul Papers, 1785–1985; MC 399 box 2, folder 318 at p. 67, Schlesinger Library, Radcliffe Institute, Harvard University.

53. Lunardini, *From Equal Suffrage to Equal Rights*, 160 nn. 36–37, citing party convention pp. 15–18 and *New York Times*, 18 February 1921. While the split over protective legislation seems clear at the convention, some scholars like Lunardini have argued that the scope of the impact of this emerging division was not identified at the convention. Ibid., 160.

54. Anita L. Pollitzer to Mrs. Frank H. Bachman, 21 May 1921, box II: 12, National Woman's Party Records, Manuscript Division, Library of Congress.

55. Alice Paul to Miss S. Ada Flatman, 26 May 1921, box II: 12, National Woman's Party Records, Manuscript Division, Library of Congress.

56. Elsie M. Hill to Mrs. J. Lincoln Dearing, 22 May 1921, box II: 12, National Woman's Party Records, Manuscript Division, Library of Congress, quoting Albert Levitt, then a young law professor at the University of North Dakota's law school.

57. Elise M. Hill to Miss Mary B. Nelson, 26 May 1921, box II: 12, National Woman's Party Records, Manuscript Division, Library of Congress, noting that "the program adopted at the convention was for the removal of the legal disabilities of women as the first step in the removal of all the remaining forms of subjection. 'All forms of subjection' will make the new campaign very much broader, although more difficult than the campaign for suffrage." So NWP leaders did understand they were taking on a tougher fight.

58. Initial drafts of the equal rights amendment included language that forbid discrimination based both on sex and on marital status. The final version, introduced in 1923 after two years of negotiation between the neutrality feminists like Paul and the social feminists, like Florence Kelley, described in Chapter 7, "Defining Equality," did not include any reference to marriage.

59. Anita L. Pollitzer to Mrs. James Ginns, 28 May 1921, box II: 12, National Woman's Party Records, Manuscript Division, Library of Congress.

60. *See* NWP to Mrs. B.T. Martin, 21 August 1920, noting that the old NWP had fifty thousand members. *But see* Anita L. Pollitzer to Mrs. John Rogers, 24 May 1921, box II: 12, National Woman's Party Records, Manuscript Division, Library of Congress noting that as of 24 May 1921, the new NWP had only 281 members. *See also* Lunardini, *From Equal Suffrage to Equal Rights*, 202 n. 8. "At a congressional hearing in 1925, Mabel Vernon testified that the number of party members at that time hovered around 20,000. If that figure is correct, and even that may be somewhat generous, fully two-thirds of the members resigned from the organization after 1920 or never joined the new organization." Ibid., *citing* Hearings of the House Committee on the Judiciary on the Equal Rights Amendment, 68th Congress, 2nd Sess. (1925).

61. Anita L. Pollitzer to Mrs. Frank H. Bachman, 21 May 1921, box II: 12, National Woman's Party Records, Manuscript Division, Library of Congress.

62. Felix Frankfurter to Elsie M. Hill, 7 June 1921, box II: 12, National Woman's Party Records, Manuscript Division, Library of Congress.

63. Elsie M. Hill to Miss Alice Hunt, 4 June 1921, box II: 12, National Woman's Party Records, Manuscript Division, Library of Congress.

64. *See generally* Butler, *Two Paths to Equality*, chap. 5.

65. Proceedings of the February 1921 National Woman's Party Convention Transcript, Alice Paul Papers, 1785–1985; MC 399 box 2, folder 318 at 59, Schlesinger Library, Radcliffe Institute, Harvard University. Mrs. Donald R. Hooker of Maryland, presenting the majority report of the Executive Committee said, "You will say, many of you, how can we go on? Alice Paul will not go on as our leader, how can we proceed with no one to lead us to the light?" Ibid.

66. *See also* Cott, "Feminist Politics in the 1920s," 62. "When the Supreme Court in 1923 used reasoning consonant with the party's to invalidate the minimum-wage law covering women in the District of Columbia, the party's new newspaper, *Equal Rights*, applauded but deferred: 'It is not within the province of the Woman's Party, as a purely feminist organization, to discuss the constitutional question involved or to discuss the merits of minimum wage legislation as a method of bettering labor conditions. On these points we express no opinion.' Just as black voting rights had been judged outside the 'purely feminist'; so was the betterment of labor conditions. That single-mindedness made the party virtually anathema to labor and the Left. In the 1920s context of Republican domination, with business in the saddle and with labor interests losing out in both trade union organization and state protection, to express no policy but equal rights for women was to affirm the status quo in every other respect. Although party members did not hold consistently laissez-faire views, the single-mindedness of their espousal of equal rights made them appear to. While the

party was able to hold on through the 1920s to a few of its longtime members who had vital interests in changing conditions for the working masses, it could not recruit new ones with its insistence on 'purely feminist' claims." Ibid.

67. *See* Siegel, "She the People," proposing a synthetic reading of the Nineteenth and the Fourteenth Amendments.

68. Lunardini, *From Equal Suffrage to Equal Rights*, 165.

69. In her article supporting protective legislation, Mary Anderson called women like Paul "theoretical feminists" to distinguish them from social feminists who supported protective legislation. See *Good Housekeeping*, September 1925, 52–53, *cited in* Richard Chused and Wendy Williams, *Gendered Law in American History* (Durham, NC: Carolina Academic Press, 2016), 918.

70. "I cannot go to Squirrel Inn as I am studying law and cannot get away. I am taking double work by going to both George Washington University law school and Washington College of Law. One place has classes in the evening and one has classes in the day. By doing this I can graduate next summer I think. This is what I am trying to do." Alice Paul to Tacie Paul, 5 July 1921, Alice Paul Papers, 1785–1985; MC 399 box 2, folder 30, Schlesinger Library, Radcliffe Institute, Harvard University. She describes the new headquarters on First Street that the NWP has acquired and notes that she is living at the headquarters. *See also* Christine Lunardini, *Alice Paul: Equality for Women* (Boulder, CO: Westview Press 2013), 152. Paul "earn[ed] her LLB from the Washington College of Law in 1922. She went on the earn a master's of law from American University in 1927 and a doctorate in civil law also from American University, in 1928."

71. Butler, *Two Paths to Equality*, 135, n. 38, noting that Paul's PhD dissertation at the University of Pennsylvania in 1912, "The Legal Position of Women in Pennsylvania," was sold by the party to educate the public about the need for equal rights legislation. And Paul's dissertation at American University was titled, "Towards Equality: A Study of the Legal Position of Women in the United States."

72. Muller v. Oregon, 208 U.S. 412 (1908).

73. Jacqueline Van Voris, *Carrie Chapman Catt: A Public Life* (New York: The Feminist Press, 1987), 143–144.

74. Anita Pollitzer to Mrs. Rebecca Lee, 7 June 1921, box II: 12, National Woman's Party Records, Manuscript Division, Library of Congress, describing the effort to collect sufficient funds to secure funds to take full possession of "this beautiful strategic location."

75. The original state-by-state approach of the National American Woman Suffrage Association (NAWSA) was anathema to Alice Paul who broke with NAWSA to push for a federal amendment. This issue was the impetus for Paul's strategic split with NAWSA in 1914 and it is difficult to overestimate its significance to Paul and her legacy as a suffrage leader.

76. The resolution passed at the convention contemplated that the NAWSA board would wind down the affairs of the organization, but not until final ratification and lawsuits challenging such ratification were finally settled. "[T]he Board of Officers shall render a quarterly account of the procedure, and an annual report of all funds in its possession

duly audited by certified accountant, to the women who in February 1920, compose its Executive Council. When its work is completed and its final report has been accepted by these presidents, it may by formal resolution dissolve." Convention Minutes, p. 5, Victory Convention of the National American Woman Suffrage Association and the First National Congress of the League of Women Voters, Chicago. 12–18 February 1920. ProQuest Struggle for Women's Rights, folder: 002634-001-0079.

77. U.S. Const. art. V.

78. Proceedings of the February 1921 National Woman's Party Convention Transcript, Alice Paul Papers, 1785–1985; MC 399 box 2, folder 318 at 26, Schlesinger Library, Radcliffe Institute, Harvard University. *See also* Clement E. Vose, *Constitutional Change: Amendment Politics and Supreme Court Litigation Since 1900* (Lexington, MA: Lexington Books, 1972), 53–63.

79. Leser v. Garnett, 258 U.S. 130 (1922).

80. Leser v. Garnett, 114 A. 840, 845 (Md. 1921), quoting Neal v. Delaware, 103 U.S. 370, 389–390 (1881).

81. Leser v. Garnett, 258 U.S. 130, 136–137. In Fairchild v. Hughes, 258 U.S. 126 (1922), a companion case of Leser v. Garnett decided the same day and discussed in Chapter 3, "Enforcement Legislation," the court addressed the question of a plaintiff's standing to challenge the ratification of the Nineteenth Amendment. The plaintiff was a member of the American Constitutional League, a group advocating for the states' right to determine elective franchise. The plaintiff alleged that the Nineteenth Amendment could not be validated by ratification of thirty-six state legislatures, and challenged the Secretary of State's forthcoming proclamation of ratification. While the plaintiff argued that this proclamation would not be conclusive of the amendment's validity, it would "lead election officers to permit women to vote in states whose Constitutions limit suffrage to men." He further challenged the "force bill" introduced in the Senate, which imposed fines and imprisonment on any person who refused to allow women to vote, to be enforced by the Attorney General. If the amendment were validated, the plaintiff warned, "[f]ree citizens would be deprived of their right to have such elections duly held, the effectiveness of their votes would be diminished, and election expenses would be nearly doubled. Thus irremediable mischief would result." The trial court dismissed the case, and while the appeal was pending, the thirty-sixth state legislature ratified the amendment and the Secretary of State proclaimed the amendment's ratification. The DC Court of Appeals also dismissed the case, reasoning that the amendment's validity rested on the ratification of the states, not the Secretary of State's proclamation. The Supreme Court, in Justice Brandeis's unanimous opinion, decided the case on the issue of standing, reasoning that the plaintiff had no interest on which to ground standing, and finding the case was "frankly a proceeding to have the Nineteenth Amendment declared void. In form it is a bill in equity; but it is not a case" within the Article III requirement of "case or controversy." The plaintiff alleged that the proclamation that would "mislead" election officers into allowing women to vote, but the court pointed out that the plaintiff, "is not an election officer; and the state of New York, of which he is a citizen, had previously amended its own Constitution so as to grant the suffrage to women, and had ratified this

amendment." The plaintiff thus lacked standing, because the general right he and all citizens have to require that government be administered legally and efficiently "does not entitle a private citizen to institute in the federal courts a suit to secure by indirection a determination whether a statute, if passed, or a constitutional amendment, about to be adopted, will be valid." *Fairchild* is often cited in later cases addressing standing. Ibid.

82. Marbury v. Madison, 5 U.S. (1 Cranch) 137 (1803).

83. Marbury met regularly with a group of prominent Baltimoreans that included Woodrow Wilson when Wilson lived in Baltimore as a PhD candidate at Johns Hopkins. Garrett Power, "Eugenics, Jim Crow and Baltimore's Best," *Maryland Bar Journal*, December 2016, 4. Note that many legal progressives, including social feminists like Florence Kelley, did not share Marbury's Darwinian views.

84. Power, "Eugenics," 4.

85. Myers v. Anderson, 238 U.S. 368 (1915).

86. William L. Marbury, "The Limitations upon the Amending Power," *Harvard Law Review* 33 (1919): 223, 230–233.

87. Ibid., 223–224.

88. William L. Frierson, "Amending the Constitution of the United States," *Harvard Law Review* 33 (1920): 659, 661–662.

89. This argument has been the subject of an ongoing scholarly debate that continues to the present day. *See generally* Richard Albert, Constitutional Amendments: Making, Breaking, and Changing Constitutions (New York: Oxford University Press 2019), chap. II "The Boundaries of Constitutional Amendment."

90. Frierson, "Amending the Constitution of the United States," 666.

91. William L. Marbury, "The Nineteenth Amendment and After," *Virginia Law Review* 7 (1920): 1, 3. *See also* Siegel, "She the People," 1004–1006, for discussion of Marbury's theory and his role in Leser v. Garnett.

Chapter 3

1. The so-called Force Acts were a "series of four acts passed by Republican Reconstruction supporters in the Congress between 31 May 1870, and 1 March 1875, to protect the constitutional rights guaranteed to blacks by the Fourteenth and Fifteenth Amendments. The major provisions of the acts authorized federal authorities to enforce penalties upon anyone interfering with the registration, voting, officeholding, or jury service of blacks; provided for federal election supervisors; and empowered the president to use military forces to make summary arrests. [The] act[s] resulted in more than 5,000 indictments and 1,250 convictions throughout the South. In subsequent Supreme Court decisions, various sections of the acts were declared unconstitutional." *See* "Force Acts: United States [1870–1875]," *Encyclopaedia Britannica*, https://www.britannica.com/topic/Force-Acts.

2. *See* Neal v. Delaware, 103 U.S. 370 (1881) *citing* Virginia v. Rives, 100 U.S. 313 (1880), and Ex parte Virginia, 100 U.S. 339 (1880), and *affirming* Strauder v. West

Virginia, 100 U.S. 303 (1880), in which the court reversed the decision of the West Virginia Supreme Court and held that a state statute that only allowed white male persons to serve as jurors was unconstitutional under the Fourteenth Amendment's equal protection clause and affirming the power of Congress to enact enforcement legislation pursuant to the fifth clause of the Fourteenth. In dicta, the court unfortunately stated that states could continue to exclude jurors based solely on sex. In Neal v. Delaware, 103 U.S. 370 (1881), the court invoked the Fifteenth Amendment as well as the Fourteenth. In his dissent, Justice Field argues that the fifth clause of the Fourteenth did not give Congress the authority to enact, "the fourth section of the act of 1 March 1875, c. 114" providing that no citizen should be denied the right to serve on a jury due to race, color and previous condition of servitude. Neal, 404–405.

3. Prior to the Nineteenth Amendment, fifteen states had given women full voting rights in both federal and state elections. Another twelve allowed women to vote for presidential electors, but did not extend full suffrage. And yet other states had given women other sorts of partialized voting, for example, school or tax and bond suffrage. *See* "Centuries of Citizenship: A Constitutional Timeline," *National Constitution Center*, https://constitutioncenter.org/timeline/html/cw08_12159.html. So even before the Nineteenth Amendment was ratified, women could vote for 339 of 531 presidential electors. *See* National American Woman Suffrage Association, *Victory: How Women Won It, A Centennial Symposium, 1840–1940* (New York: H. W. Wilson, 1940), 164.

4. Ibid., 153.

5. Note that poor white women also faced obstacles to voting, like the poll tax. And all women in Georgia could not vote in 1920 because, "In Georgia, where the state laws require that prospective voters register six months before the election, the women [did] not take part in the November election. The Attorney General held that women could register at a later date and vote, but he [was] overruled." J.E. C. Bryant, "Southern Women Vote," *The Suffragist: Official Organ of the National Woman's Party*, Vol. III, No. 11 (November 1920), 286. *See also* J. Kevin Corder and Christina Wolbrecht, *Counting Women's Ballots: Female Voters from Suffrage through the New Deal* (New York: Cambridge University Press, 2016): 3, n. 1, noting that "restrictive interpretations of registration rules (ratification had occurred after registration deadlines in a number of states) denied women access to the ballot in Arkansas, Georgia, Mississippi, and South Carolina in 1920, delaying women's participation in presidential elections in those states until 1921," and *citing* Harold F. Gosnell, *Why Europe Votes* (Chicago: University of Chicago Press, 1930).

6. Rosalyn Terborg-Penn, *African American Women in the Struggle for the Vote, 1850–1920* (Bloomington: Indiana University Press, 1998), 146.

7. The Nineteenth Amendment shared the same text as the Fifteenth, with the exception of the word "sex":

> The right of citizens of the United States to vote shall not be denied or abridged by the United States or by any state on account of sex. Congress shall have power to enforce this article by appropriate legislation. U.S. Const. amend. XIX.

The right of citizens of the United States to vote shall not be denied or abridged by the United States or by any State on account of race, color, or previous condition of servitude. The Congress shall have power to enforce this article by appropriate legislation. U.S. Const. amend. XV.

8. Everette Swinney, "Enforcing the Fifteenth Amendment, 1870–1877," *The Journal of Southern History* 28 (1962): 202, 204–205.

9. Swinney, "Enforcing the Fifteenth Amendment," 207–209, *citing* United States v. Cruikshank, 25 Fed. Cas. 707, 710 (D. La. 1874) (No. 14,897).

10. United States v. Cruikshank, 92 U.S. 542, 543 (1875). The indictments were a response to the Colfax massacre in which over one hundred black men were killed.

11. Swinney, "Enforcing the Fifteenth Amendment," 207–209. *See also* James Gray Pope, "Snubbed Landmark: Why United States v. Cruikshank (1870) Belongs at the Heart of the American Constitutional Canon," *Harvard Civil Rights-Civil Liberties Law Review* 49 (2014): 385–447 (describing the significance of *Cruikshank* and its causal connection to "national civil rights enforcement authority"). Ibid., 413, n. 176.

12. Garth Pauley, *LBJ's American Promise: The 1965 Voting Rights Address* (College Station: Texas A&M University Press, 2007), 32, *cited in* Vanessa A. Holloway, *In Search of Federal Enforcement: The Moral Authority of the Fifteenth Amendment and the Integrity of the Black Ballot, 1870-1965* (Lanham, MD: University Press of America, 2015), 2.

13. Rosalyn Terborg-Penn, *African American Women in the Struggle for the Vote, 1850–1920* (Bloomington: Indiana University Press, 1998), 151.

14. Paula Giddings, *When and Where I Enter: The Impact of Black Women on Race and Sex in America* (New York: Amistad Press, 1984), 123.

15. Terborg-Penn, *African American Women in the Struggle for the Vote*, 152.

16. Ibid., 153.

17. Ibid.

18. Ibid.

19. Ibid.

20. Ibid., 146–147.

21. *See* Steven G. Calabresi and Julia T. Rickert, "Originalism and Sex Discrimination," *Texas Law Review* 90 (2011): 1, 90–92, noting southern politicians' belief that "[t]he Nineteenth Amendment would precipitate a 'second reconstruction' in the South . . ." and "fear of a second reconstruction inspired by Bolshevists, female voters and African-Americans . . ."

22. Anne Firor Scott has noted the post-ratification efforts of some southern suffragists to reform the poll tax and even raise money to help women voters pay it. "The poll tax was the subject of dual concern. Women's groups opposed the tax, but in the meantime they set out to collect money for the payment of poll taxes in order to increase the number of qualified voters." Anne Firor Scott, "After Suffrage: Southern Women in the Twenties," *The Journal of Southern History* 30, No. 3 (1964): 298, 311–312.

23. Library of Congress, "NAACP Victory in Guinn v. United States," *NAACP: A Century in the Fight for Freedom*, http://www.loc.gov/exhibits/naacp/founding-and-early-years.html#obj23.

24. The Congressional Record indicates that an enforcement bill was submitted as early as 4 May 1920 (before ratification) by Sen. James Watson (R-IN). S. 4323 was referred to the Senate Committee on the Judiciary, 59 Cong. Rec. 6494 (4 May 1920), and no further action was taken on the bill.

25. *The Suffragist: Official Organ of the National Woman's Party* 3, No. 11 (December 1920), 301.

26. Ibid.

27. *See* Scott, "After Suffrage."

28. *The Suffragist: Official Organ of the National Woman's Party*, 301, describing the issues around registration deadlines in other states as well.

29. In the November 1920 issue of *The Suffragist*, Mary White Ovington pleaded for subscribers (presumably members of the NWP) to join her in her cause: "We must not rest until we have freed black as well as white of our sex. Will not those who wish to see this come to pass write me to that effect? There are only a few of us in this Negro cause and we need the knowledge that you have gained in your long campaigns." *The Suffragist: Official Organ of the National Woman's Party* 3, No. 10 (November 1920): 279–280.

30. The author of an undated letter to the editor of *The State*, in Columbia, South Carolina, identified himself as "An Alabamian [who] appeals to the assembly of South Carolina, and all the other Southern states." The tenor of his letter is that they had a solemn duty, under the oath they swore to uphold the state constitution, to resist ratification of the Nineteenth Amendment because it included an enforcement clause akin to that under the Fourteenth and Fifteenth. The author wrote, "Think, men, of South Carolina, think of your 'simple great ones gone forever and ever by!' Would they have tolerated for one moment even the proposal of this curse, to revive the 14th and 15th amendments, adding a third, and worst of all, with the pitiable excuse of 'political expediency' to further our humiliation . . . You have had a white man's government, best for both races." ProQuest History Vault. Civil Rights and the Black Freedom Struggle (hereinafter ProQuest Civil Rights). NAACP Papers, Women's suffrage, folder 001517-002-0678.

31. "An Editorial," *The Suffragist: Official Organ of the National Woman's Party* 3, No. 11 (December 1920): 301.

32. Steve Kolbert, "The Nineteenth Amendment Enforcement Power (But First, Which One Is the Nineteenth Amendment, Again?)," *Florida State University Law Review* 43 (2016): 507, 544–546.

33. Ibid., 545.

34. Ibid., 544–546.

35. Bernadette Cahill, *Alice Paul, the National Woman's Party and the Vote* (Jefferson, NC: McFarland & Company, 2015), 96 n. 8, *citing* "Wants New Suffrage Act: Woman's Party Will Urge the Passage of an Enforcement Measure," *New York Times*, 6 November 1920.

36. "Proceedings of Congress and Committees in Brief," *Washington Post*, 31 December 1920, p. 6.

37. Fairchild v. Hughes, 258 U.S. 126 (1922).

38. Leser v. Garnett, 258 U.S. 130 (1922).
39. *Fairchild*, 258 U.S. 126, 128.
40. *See* Laura Free, *Suffrage Reconstructed: Gender, Race and Voting Rights in the Civil War Era* (Ithaca, NY: Cornell University Press, 2015), 130–134. *See also* Calabresi and Rickert, "Originalism and Sex Discrimination," 66–70. "In Section Two, the Reconstruction Framers inserted the word *male* into the Constitution for the first time, explicitly privileging males over females with respect to voting rights." Calabresi and Rickert take the position that "[t]he Nineteenth Amendment changed all this, however, when it reinstated the Constitution's sexual neutrality by nullifying the use of the word *male* in Section Two." Ibid., 66.
41. Free, *Suffrage Reconstructed*, 131.
42. Free, *Suffrage Reconstructed*, 130–134.
43. There was also a failed effort to include women in the Fifteenth Amendment. *See* Free, *Suffrage Reconstructed*, 162–165.
44. Minor v. Happersett, 88 U.S. 162 (1875).
45. Giddings, *When and Where I Enter*, 123–124.
46. Ibid., 125.
47. Ibid., 127. Although it should be noted that white southern suffragists were not monolithic in this regard. Some later supported repeal of barriers to African American women voting, like poll taxes, in the wake of ratification of the Nineteenth. *See* Scott, *After Suffrage*.
48. Giddings, *When and Where I Enter*, 127.
49. Geoffrey C. Ward and Ken Burns, *Not for Ourselves Alone: The Story of Elizabeth Cady Stanton and Susan B. Anthony* (New York: Alfred A. Knopf, 1999), 215.
50. Clay and Gordon went on to play a significant role in leading the opposition to the Tennessee legislature's vote, making it the thirty-sixth state to ratify the Nineteenth Amendment. *See* Elaine Weiss, *The Woman's Hour: The Great Fight to Win the Vote* (New York: Viking/Penguin, 2018), 208–209.
51. Terborg-Penn, *African American Women in the Struggle for the Vote*, 130–131.
52. Giddings, *When and Where I Enter*, 120, 127–128.
53. Ibid., 129.
54. As early as November 1920, Mary White Ovington was quoted in the NWP newspaper, *The Suffragist*: "During the many years that the women of the United States have struggled for the ballot, I have often appealed to suffrage workers and their leaders for help in battling against the disfranchisement [*sic*] of the negro. The answer I have received has been invariably the same, 'We must have a single issue: we cannot intrude the negro questions until the battle is over. When the fight is won, then will be the time to ask us to take up the cause of the negro women.' Well, the battle is over. The women of the country have received the vote." Crystal Eastman, "What Next," *The Suffragist: Official Organ of the National Woman's Party* 3, No. 10 (November 1920): 278–286, 279.
55. Nancy F. Cott, "Feminist Politics in the 1920s: The National Woman's Party," *Journal of American History* 71 (1984): 43–68, 51. Cott goes on to suggest that Paul did try to include African American women in a limited way, "Wold emphasized that it was the definition of the convention program rather than lack of concern about blacks that

caused this refusal. She encouraged the appointment of black women as delegates who could speak from the floor. Headquarters did make efforts to facilitate the inclusion of blacks in state delegations, and when a black woman from Virginia, probably fearing segregation, inquired, "how will the arrangements be for the colored delegates in this convention," Wold replied for Paul that black delegates would have exactly the same arrangements as white delegates and would be seated with their state delegations. Paul also conferred with Hallie Brown, Terrell, and other black women leaders about representation of the National Association of Colored Women's Clubs at the ceremony unveiling the sculptures and reached agreement on a "representation of their race" satisfactory to the black women, according to Paul." Ibid.

56. The NWP Executive Committee Minutes of 14 May 1920, note the moment when the NWP officially approved a motion to endorse the introduction of an enforcement bill. While the record is only partially readable due to serious deterioration, marked by [] below, the words that are left indicate that attorney Shippen Lewis shared it with the Solicitor General. Alexander King was the Solicitor General until May 1920, he was succeeded by George Sutherland, senator from Utah and subsequently an associate justice of the United States Supreme Court. Sutherland had worked with Alice Paul on both the suffrage amendment and the equal rights amendment. Lewis, son of prominent NWP member Dora Lewis (see below) worked with the NWP to draft the enforcement legislation:

> [] to enforce the provisions of the suffrage [] read by Mrs. Lewis. Mrs. Wainwright made a [] Mrs. Gardner seconded, that this Act which has [] Shippen Lewis and submitted to Solicitor General [] Sutherland: former President of the American Bar [] pushed through Congress. Motion was carried. A Copy of Enforcement Act is appended.

> Minutes of 14 May 1920, Meeting of National Executive Committee p. 2, National Woman's Party Papers, Part I: 1913–1974, Series 2: Minutes, Legal Papers, and Financial Records, 1912–1972; series: Minutes, 1917–1972; folder: National Executive Committee Minutes, February 1917–August 1921, ProQuest Struggle for Women's Rights, folder: 002614–114-0757. Dora Lewis was a prominent member of the NWP, holding a number of leadership positions. She was one of the NWP members jailed for suffrage. In a letter to her son, dated 26 May 1920, Dora Lewis, who was then national ratification chairman of the NWP, wrote that "Mrs. Catt has engaged Mr. Charles E. Hughes to look after the interests of the Suffragists." (From 1910 to 1916, Hughes had served as an associate justice of the US Supreme Court and he served again as chief justice from 1930 to 1941.) Dora Lewis asked Shippen Lewis to meet with Hughes to work together to protect the ratification and prevent referenda. Dora Lewis to Shippen Lewis, 26 May 1920, Ibid., National Woman's Party suffrage correspondence, folder: 002620–079-0223.

57. Amy E. Butler, *Two Paths to Equality: Alice Paul and Ethel Smith in the ERA Debate, 1921–1929* (Albany: State University of New York Press, 2002), 58, citing the minority report submitted by Murray "requesting that convention proceedings include recognition of the remaining political inequalities that affect African-American women, especially in the South."

58. Cott, "Feminist Politics in the 1920s," 53.
59. Terborg-Penn, *African American Women in the Struggle for the Vote*, 156.
60. Ibid.
61. Ibid., 169.
62. ProQuest Civil Rights. NAACP Papers, Women's Suffrage folder 8 February 1921–3 April 1921, folder: 001517-002-0850.
63. Giddings, *Where and When I Enter*, 169, n.34, *citing* Resolutions re: National Woman's Party, 15–18 February 1921, NAACP files, Suffrage, Library of Congress.
64. *See* Amelia Fry, "Conversations with Alice Paul: Woman Suffrage and the Equal Rights Amendment," Oral History Project, The Bancroft Library, University of California Berkeley, 1976, http://content.cdlib.org/view?docId=kt6f59n89c&doc.view=entire_text, 134–135.
65. Mary White Ovington to Alice Paul, 4 January 1921, ProQuest History Vault. NAACP Papers. National Woman's Party and voting rights, folder 001517-002-0484.
66. Florence Kelley to Mary White Ovington, 22 December 1920, Ibid.
67. Mary Winsor to Mary White Ovington, 31 December 1920, Ibid.
68. Emma Wold to Harriet Stanton Blatch, 29 December 1920, Ibid.
69. Harriet Stanton Blatch to Mary White Ovington re: Emma Wold, 29 December 1920, Ibid.
70. Proceedings of the February 1921 National Woman's Party Convention Transcript, Alice Paul Papers, 1785–1985; MC 399 box 2, folder 318 at 15, Schlesinger Library, Radcliffe Institute, Harvard University.
71. *See* Fry, "Conversations with Alice Paul," pp. xiv–xv. "Her ability to set strategy rapidly and unerringly is one of the most astounding things about her. About two years before the interview Alice had asked me to come to Washington to do a week of lobbying for the Equal Rights Amendment in Congress. I happily agreed. First of all, I believed in the cause. I also wanted to see what it was like to work under Alice Paul. Alice, then age eighty-five, had a running record in her head of every congressman. She knew almost anything that she needed to know about his past actions on the ERA and his operations with other congressmen. She usually knew the attitudes of wives, secretaries, and administrative assistants. She knew that Mrs. Alan Cranston had her hair coiffed in a particular place where Alice sometimes went. (Belmont House was across the parking lot from the Senate Office Building.) Thus had she become acquainted with Mrs. Cranston, and it was through Mrs. Cranston that she had been working to get Senator Cranston's approval of the Equal Rights Amendment."
72. Proceedings of the February 1921 National Woman's Party Convention Transcript, Alice Paul Papers, 1785–1985; MC 399 box 2, folder 318 at 36, Schlesinger Library, Radcliffe Institute, Harvard University.
73. Adams and Keene, *Alice Paul and the American Suffrage Campaign*, xviii. *See also* Bernadette Cahill, *Alice Paul, the National Woman's Party and the Vote: The First Civil Rights Struggle of the 20th Century* (Jefferson, NC: McFarland & Company, 2015), 148–152.
74. Adams and Keene, *Alice Paul and the American Suffrage Campaign*, 118.

75. Ibid.

76. Ibid., 118, 123.

77. Mary Walton, *A Woman's Crusade: Alice Paul and the Battle for the Ballot* (New York: Palgrave Macmillan, 2010), 247. *See also* Reva B. Siegel, "She the People: The Nineteenth Amendment, Sex Equality, Federalism and the Family," *Harvard Law Review* 115 (2002): 947, 1008, n. 190, "[F]or an account of the National Woman's Party's legislative aims, see Nat'l Woman's Party, Declaration of Principles, Equal Rights, Feb. 17, 1923, at 5. For an assessment of the movement's legislative accomplishments at the decade's end, see Report of Legislative Work from 1921 to 1929, Equal Rights, Jan. 4, 1930, at 379. As of 1924, the League of Women Voters reported that its state affiliates had secured enactment of eighty-six bills that would work to remove 'legal discriminations against women.' Nat'l League of Women Voters, A Record of Four Years in the National League of Women Voters 1920-1924, at 23 (1924)."

78. *See* NWP to Mrs. B.T. Martin, 21 August 1920, noting that the old NWP had fifty thousand members. *But see* Anita L. Pollitzer to Mrs. John Rogers, 24 May 1921, noting that, as of 24 May 1921, the new NWP had only 281 members. Box II: 12, National Woman's Party Records, Manuscript Division, Library of Congress. *See also* Christine Lunardini, *From Equal Suffrage to Equal Rights: Alice Paul and the National Woman's Party, 1920–1928* (Lincoln, NE: toExcel Press, 1986, 2000), 153, n. 8 at 202. "At a congressional hearing in 1925, Mabel Vernon testified that the number of NWP members at that time hovered around 20,000. If that figure is correct, and even that may be somewhat generous, fully two-thirds of the members resigned from the organization after 1920 or never joined the new organization." *citing* Hearings of the House Committee on the Judiciary on the Equal Rights Amendment, 68th Congress, 2nd Sess. (1925). Ibid.

79. Adams and Keene, *Alice Paul and the American Suffrage Campaign*, 141–142.

80. *See* Cott, "Feminist Politics in the 1920s," 51, *citing* National Executive Committee, National Woman's Party, minutes, 16 May 1921, reel 114, part A, series 2. Ibid., n. 23.

81. National Executive Committee, National Woman's Party, minutes, 16 May 1921, box II: 197, National Woman's Party Records, Manuscript Division, Library of Congress.

82. Extending the Right of Suffrage to Women, Hearings Before the Committee on Woman Suffrage, House of Representatives, 65th Congress, 2d Session, on H. J. Res 200. 3, 4, 5, and 7 January 1918 (Washington, DC: Government Printing Office 1918), 143–148.

83. Neither of the House or Senate bills introduced in the 66th Congress were reported out of committee. There was a House bill introduced in the 67th Congress, H.R. 24 (Bill to enforce provisions of the 19th Amendment with respect to the elective franchise). Introduced again by Rep. Fess (R-OH) and referred to H.R. Comm. On Woman Suffrage, 61 Cong. Rec. 87 (11 April 1921). But there was no companion Senate bill filed and the bill went no further.

84. Note that congressional intent in enacting the Reconstruction Amendments was often fleshed out in cases like United States v. Cruikshank, 92 U.S. 542 (1875), Strauder v. West Virginia, 100 U.S. 303 (1880), and Neal v. Delaware, 103 U.S. 370

(1881), due, in part, to the need to parse the meaning of the enforcement legislation enacted pursuant to those amendments.

85. *See generally* Kolbert, "The Nineteenth Amendment Enforcement Power"; Richard L. Hasen and Leah M. Litman, "Thin and Thick Conceptions of the Nineteenth Amendment Right to Vote and Congress's Power to Enforce It," *Georgetown Law Journal* 19th Amendment Special Edition (forthcoming 2020), draft available at https://papers.ssrn.com/sol3/papers.cfm?abstract_id=3501114.

86. Terborg-Penn, *African American Women in the Struggle for the Vote*, 155.

87. Anne Firor Scott, "Epilogue," in *Votes for Women: The Struggle for Suffrage Revisited*, edited by Jean H. Baker (New York: Oxford University Press, 2002), 192.

88. Ibid., 193.

Chapter 4

1. *See, e.g.*, Hawthorne v. Turkey Creek School District, 134 S.E. 103 (Ga. 1926).

2. U.S. Const., Article I, Section 2.

3. Roger C. Hartley, *How Failed Attempts to Amend the Constitution Mobilize Political Change* (Nashville, TN: Vanderbilt University Press, 2017), 78.

4. Minor v. Happersett, 88 U.S. 162 (1875).

5. Several other cases in immediate aftermath of ratification mentioned the Nineteenth Amendment in more tangential ways. *See, e.g.*, Rice v. Board of Aldermen of City of Woonsocket, 112 A. 175 (R.I. 1920), wherein the Supreme Court of Rhode Island considered a petition for writ of certiorari regarding the legality of an election that took place less than three months after the Nineteenth Amendment was ratified. Aline Belanger, a married woman, owned in fee simple a property in her own name, with her husband only a tenant by curtesy. Her husband, Anthony Belanger, was elected to the office of alderman in that election. The Rhode Island Constitution conferred the right to vote on male citizens twenty-one years and older who owned (or rented) property worth at least $134, a provision the Nineteenth Amendment modified to include both men and women. The court, in its statutory construction, held that while Anthony Belanger's "estate" could not qualify any other person to vote, the term "estate" included his curtesy interest, and thus the statute did not deprive him of the right to vote, since no one shared this curtesy interest. *See also* McComb v. Robelen, 116 A. 745 (Del. Ch. 1922), wherein the Delaware Chancery Court referred to the Nineteenth Amendment, but did not directly interpret it. The case involved an election dispute, in which seventy-eight votes were alleged to be submitted by voters that were not "qualified" as provided by the statute. The question was whether there was a difference between "qualified" and "registered" voters. The court used the Nineteenth Amendment to illustrate the difference, noting that prior to the passage of the Nineteenth Amendment, women who paid school taxes were permitted to vote, although they were not permitted to register to vote.

6. Brown v. City of Atlanta, 109 S.E. 666 (Ga. 1921).

7. Ibid., 666–667.

8. Ibid., 671.

9. Ibid., 672.

10. Ibid., 672–673.

11. Ibid.

12. Stephens v. Ball Ground School District, 113 S.E. 85 (Ga. 1922).

13. Ibid., 85.

14. Ibid.

15. Ibid., 85–86.

16. Ibid.

17. Stewart v. Cartwright, 118 S.E. 859 (Ga. 1923).

18. Ibid., 861.

19. In re Graves, 30 S.W.2d 149 (Mo. 1930).

20. Ibid., 150.

21. Ibid.

22. Ibid.

23. Ibid.

24. Ibid., 151.

25. Ibid.

26. Ibid., 153.

27. Ibid.

28. Ibid., 152.

29. Ibid.

30. Ibid., 154.

31. Hartley, *How Failed Attempts to Amend the Constitution Mobilize Political Change*, 78–79.

32. Ibid., 79.

33. Ibid.

34. In assessing whether a constitutional amendment (either federal or state) is self-executing, courts ask "whether a constitutional provision is so complete that there is no need (and hence no authority) for legislative action on that subject." Second, does a person have a "direct right of action under the constitution to remedy a violation of constitutional rights because there is no other adequate remedy available under state law." Frayda Bluestein, "Self-Executing Constitutional Provisions," *Coates' Canons: NC Local Government Law*, 23 March 2011, https://canons.sog.unc.edu/self-executing-constitutional - provisions.

35. Graves v. Eubank, 87 So. 587 (Ala. 1921). This case is referred to as *Eubank* to distinguish it from the prior decision discussed in this chapter, *In re* Graves, 30 S.W.2d 149, 150 (Mo. 1930).

36. Ibid., 587.

37. Ibid.

38. Ibid.

39. For courts to determine that a constitutional provision is self-executing, the court:

> must articulate or supply a rule that is sufficient to give effect to the underlying rights and duties intended by the framers. A constitutional provision must be regarded as self-executing if the nature and extent of the right conferred and the liability imposed are fixed by the constitution itself so that they can be determined by an examination and construction of its terms, and there is no language indicating that the subject is referred to the legislature for action. In another test to determine whether a constitutional provision is self-executing, a court asks whether the constitution addresses the language to the courts or to the legislature; if addressed to the courts, it is self-executing.

"Constitutional Law," *Corpus Juris Secundum*, Sections 128–130.

40. *Eubank*, 87 So. 587, 588.

41. Similar issues continue to arise in the context of federalism. When the Supreme Court recently held that states could not deny marriage to same-sex couples, it did not spell out how that new constitutional norm affected state statutes that raised corollary issues like parentage. State courts were forced to grapple with the impact of that federal constitutional decision on long-standing state common law or statutory law regarding presumptions about the husband of a wife being deemed the legal father of a child born during a marriage. Should the word "husband" be read to include a female spouse in a same-sex marriage? These kinds of statutory interpretation issues implicate the nature of constitutional actions by the federal government, and the scope of the impact of such actions on both federal and state constitutional law. They also implicate "rules of construction" under state law that may cabin when courts are allowed to ignore terms like "male" in a particular statute. *See* Paula A. Monopoli, "Inheritance Law and the Marital Presumption after *Obergefell*," *Estate Planning & Community Property Law Journal* 8 (2016): 437.

42. *Eubank*, 87 So. 587, 588.

43. Guinn v. United States, 238 U.S. 362 (1915).

44. *Eubank*, 87 So. 587, 588 (*citing* Guinn v. United States, 238 U.S. 362 (1915)).

45. *Eubank*, 87 So. 587, 588–589.

46. Ibid., 590 (McClellan, J., dissenting).

47. Stuard v. Thompson, 251 S.W. 277 (Tex. Civ. App. 1923).

48. Ibid., 279.

49. Ibid.

50. Ibid.

51. Ibid.

52. Ibid.

53. Ibid., 281 (*citing* Solon v. State, 114 S.W. 349 (Tex. Crim. App. 1908)).

54. *Stuard*, 251 S.W. 277, 281.

55. The *Stuard* court also opened the door to a discussion of the constitutionality of requiring poll taxes as a precondition to voting. The court notes that poll or capitation taxes had been a revenue-generating tool for state governments since before the Revolution and had not been held to, "conflict with the constitutional provisions requiring uniform and equal taxation, though in particular instances they may be

invalid or lacking in uniformity." However, "[s]ome of the states have made the payment of poll taxes condition precedent of the right to exercise the elective franchise. Statutes imposing this limitation have been held to be constitutional, but, being in derogation of common right, have usually been strictly construed." Ibid. This raises the issue discussed in the previous chapter, as to whether the NWP or NAWSA/NLWV could have joined forces with the NAACP and the NACW to challenge poll taxes, as a device to block African American women from exercising their newly won franchise under the Nineteenth Amendment.

56. *Stuard*, 282.
57. Ibid.
58. Davis v. Warde, 118 S.E. 378 (Ga. 1923).
59. Ibid., 390.
60. Ibid., 395.
61. Ibid., 394.
62. Ibid.
63. Brown v. Atlanta, 109 S.E. 666 (Ga. 1921).
64. *Davis*, 118 S.E. 378, 394 (*citing* Brown v. Atlanta).
65. Ibid.
66. *Hawthorne*, 134 S.E., 103.
67. Ibid., 105.
68. Ibid.
69. Ibid., 106.
70. Ibid.
71. Ibid.(*citing* Brown v. Atlanta, 109 S.E. 666 (Ga. 1921)).
72. *Hawthorne*, 134 S.E., 106.
73. Ibid.
74. Ibid.
75. Ibid.
76. Ibid.
77. Taaffe v. Sanderson, 294 S.W. 74 (Ark. 1927).
78. Ibid., 75.
79. Ibid.
80. Ibid., 77.
81. Ibid.
82. Ibid.
83. Ibid.
84. Ibid., 78.
85. Ibid.
86. Ibid., 79.
87. People *ex rel.* Murray v. Holmes, 173 N.E. 145 (Ill. 1930).
88. Ibid., 146.
89. Ibid.
90. Ibid.
91. Ibid.

92. Ibid., 147.
93. Ibid.
94. People ex. rel. Fyfe v. Barnett, 150 N.E. 290 (Ill. 1925).
95. *Murray*, 173 N.E. 145, 148.
96. Ibid.
97. Ibid.
98. Ibid., 147–148.
99. Ibid.
100. Breedlove v. Suttles, 302 U.S. 277 (1937).
101. Richard L. Hasen and Leah M. Litman, "Thin and Thick Conceptions of the Nineteenth Amendment Right to Vote and Congress's Power to Enforce It," *Georgetown Law Journal* 19th Amendment Special Edition (forthcoming 2020), draft available at https://papers.ssrn.com/sol3/papers.cfm?abstract_id=3501114, draft at 6. In Harper v. State Board of Elections, 383 U.S. 663 (1966), "the *Harper* majority did not overrule the part of *Breedlove* that approved gender discrimination in the application of the poll tax. The court has never returned to the issues, leaving *Breedlove* to be at least nominally good law on the meaning of the Nineteenth Amendment right to vote." Ibid.
102. Breedlove v. Suttles, 302 U.S. 277 (1937), *overruled by* Harper v. Virginia State Board of Elections, 383 U.S. 663 (1966).
103. Ibid., 280.
104. Ibid.
105. Ibid., 282.
106. Ibid., 283.
107. Ibid., 284.
108. Reva B. Siegel, "The Nineteenth Amendment and the Democratization of the Family," *Yale Law Journal Forum* 129 (2020): 450, arguing that "the Nineteenth Amendment transformed We the People—not simply by adding voters, but by democratizing the family so that women could represent themselves in the state." Ibid., 451.
109. Proceedings of the February 1921 National Woman's Party Convention Transcript, Alice Paul Papers, 1785–1985; MC 399 box 2, folder 318 at 106, Schlesinger Library, Radcliffe Institute, Harvard University. The majority report of the NWP February 1921 convention stated, "Owing to the fact that women have not yet won full civil and economic freedom and equality we recommend; That the National Woman's Party, having accomplished the object for which it was created, now disband; that a new organization be created; that the immediate work of the new organization be the removal of the legal disabilities of women. That the political freedom of women having been won in the United States, the women here assembled now consecrate themselves to seeing that this freedom be not lost in any association of nations that may be established, and to work for the absolute equality of men and women." The new NWP Constitution set out the goal of the new organization, "The enfranchisement of women having been won in the United States, the object of this association

shall be to secure equality of women with men in the United States and in any international government that may be established." Ibid., 137. *See also* Convention Minutes, pp. 18–23, Victory Convention of 1920, and the First National Congress of the League of Women Voters, Chicago, Feb 12, 1920–Feb 18, 1920. Papers of the League of Women Voters, 1918–1974, Part II, Series A: Transcripts and Records of National Conventions, 1919–1944, and of General Councils, 1927–1943, ProQuest Struggle for Women's Rights, folder: 002634-001-0079.

110. *See, e.g.,* Telegram from Elizabeth G. Kalb to State Attorney General of Virginia, 25 August 1920, box I: 6, National Woman's Party Records, Manuscript Division, Library of Congress. "Please wire collect ruling whether Virginia ennabling[*sic*] not passed by legislature at special session for Virginia women enfranchised by constitutional amendment is valid at this time also what will be poll tax provisions for women voters this fall." Ibid. Similar letters and telegrams referencing the poll tax were sent to other southern state attorneys general like North Carolina. Telegram from Elizabeth Kalb to Attorney General of North Carolina, 30 August 1920, box I: 6, National Woman's Party Records, Manuscript Division, Library of Congress.

111. *See* Frederic D. Ogden, *The Poll Tax in the South* (Tuscaloosa: University of Alabama Press, 1958), 177. "Examination of the form of the tax indicated that the tax tends to bear more harshly on women than men and analysis . . . disclosed that more white women had been prevented from voting by the tax than either white men or Negroes." Ibid.

112. Note that African American suffrage organizations like the NACW did in fact work with organizations like the NAACP to combat voter suppression devices like poll taxes. "Black women fought the efforts to render their vote meaningless not only at the polls but though the Suffrage Department of the NAAACP and the NACW." Paula Giddings, *When and Where I Enter, The Impact of Black Women on Race and Sex in America* (New York: Amistad, 1984), 168. And local and state chapters of the NLWV were very involved in later decades in poll tax repeal efforts across the south. *See* Ogden, *The Poll Tax in the South*, 233 (Noting that much of the reform effort around poll taxes was done by women's groups, including the state League of Women Voters in Alabama in 1953. "Because of the veteran exemption, they concluded that the tax requirement fell most heavily upon [women]. With something of the vigor and sense or righteousness of suffragettes, they organized to repeal the poll tax.").

113. At their pivotal conventions, both the NWP and the NLWV stated that their future mission should include enacting state legislation to make it clear that women could serve on juries or hold public office. So they were committed to reform through legislation but did not discuss litigating the scope of the Nineteenth Amendment vis-à-vis these political rights. *See, e.g.,* NAWSA Victory Convention Minutes, p. 3, folder: 002634-001-0079, National American Woman Suffrage Association Victory Convention of 1920, and the First National Congress of the League of Women Voters, 12–18 February 1920 ("Laws should provide that women be subject to jury service . . .").

Chapter 5

1. In Graves v. Eubank, the government argued that the federal suffrage amendment could not serve to levy a state tax. But the Alabama Supreme Court held that the Nineteenth Amendment put women on an equal footing, and altered state laws not only directly about voting but about any preconditions to voting like payment of the poll tax. *See* Graves v. Eubank, 87 So. 587, 588 (Ala. 1921). In essence, this case can be read to apply the Nineteenth Amendment to other state constitutional doctrine, like the general taxing power. But note that in Breedlove v. Suttles, 302 U.S. 277 (1937), *overruled by* Harper v. Virginia State Board of Elections, 383 U.S. 663 (1966), the Supreme Court reasoned that the Nineteenth Amendment did not serve to regulate taxes, and to interpret it as the plaintiff suggested "would make the amendment a limitation upon the power to tax." Ibid., 283. Thus, some of the early state cases following ratification can be read, like *Adkins v. Children's Hospital*, discussed in Chapter 7 "Defining Equality," to suggest a more expansive reading of the Nineteenth Amendment on constitutional doctrine other than voting.

2. In her article "'A Woman Stumps Her State': Nellie G. Robinson and Women's Right to Hold Public Office in Ohio," *Akron Law Review* 53 (2019): 313, 320, n. 37. Elizabeth Katz contrasts the deep scholarship around jury service and its "contested connection to suffrage" with the paucity of scholarship around public officeholding. As examples of the most significant jury service scholarship, Katz cites:

   > Linda Kerber, *No Constitutional Right to Be Ladies: Women and the Obligations of Citizenship* (New York: Hill and Wang, 1998), 124–220; Joanna L. Grossman, "Women's Jury Service: Right of Citizenship or Privilege of Difference?," *Stanford Law Review* 46 (1994): 1115; Gretchen Ritter, "Jury Service and Women's Citizenship before and after the Nineteenth Amendment," *Law and History Review* 20 (2002): 479; Jennifer K. Brown, "The Nineteenth Amendment and Women's Equality," *Yale Law Journal* 102 (1993): 2175; Holly J. McCammon, *The U.S. Women's Jury Movements and Strategic Adaptation: A More Just Verdict* (New York: Cambridge University Press, 2014); Cristina Rodriguez, "Clearing the Smoke-Filled Room: Women Jurors and the Disruption of an Old-Boys' Network in Nineteenth-Century America," *Yale Law Journal* 108 (1999): 1805; Vikram David Amar, "Jury Service as Political Participation Akin to Voting," *Cornell Law Review* 80 (1995): 203, 241–242.

3. Ritter, "Jury Service and Women's Citizenship," 480–481. *See also* Andrew Guthrie Ferguson, "The Jury as Constitutional Identity," *UC Davis Law Review* 47 (2014): 1105, 1127, citing Vikram Amar and Barbara Babcock for the idea that the suffragists struggle had always been about both the vote and jury service. Babcock said they were the "twin indicia of full citizenship" and Ferguson concludes that "those interested in redefining constitutional identity used jury service as a symbol of constitutional equality." Ibid., 1127–128, *citing* Barbara Allen Babcock, "A Place in the Palladium: Women's Rights and Jury Service," *University of Cincinnati Law Review* 61 (1993): 1139, 1164. *See also* Tracy A. Thomas, "More than the Vote: The Nineteenth Amendment as Proxy for Gender Equality," *Stanford Journal of Civil*

Rights and Civil Liberties 15 (forthcoming 2020) draft at https://papers.ssrn.com/sol3/papers.cfm?abstract_id=3364546.

4. Katz observes that "some treatments assume or claim that the Amendment clearly encompassed or inevitably built toward other political rights," Katz, "A Woman Stumps Her State," 319, citing as an example Akhil Reed Amar, "The Bill of Rights as a Constitution," *Yale Law Journal* 100 (1991): 1131 in which Amar reasons that "Once suffrage rights are extended, corresponding and coextensive changes must occur in juries and militias." Ibid., 1202.

5. Proceedings of the February 1921 National Woman's Party Convention Transcript, Alice Paul Papers, 1785–1985; MC 399 box 2, folder 318 at 27, Schlesinger Library, Radcliffe Institute, Harvard University. Note that while the NWP may have tracked state cases, it did not become directly involved in many of them until the end of the decade in *Commonwealth v. Welosky*.

6. Ibid., 28.

7. Gretchen Ritter, *The Constitution as Social Design: Gender and Civic Membership in the American Constitutional Order* (Stanford, CA: Stanford University Press, 2006), 102–103.

8. Ibid.

9. Strauder v. West Virginia, 100 U.S. 303 (1880). *See also* Ritter, *The Constitution as Social Design*, 105. Ritter argues that in *Strauder*, "[j]ury service was treated as a civil right. The Court states that the purpose of the Fourteenth Amendment was to grant the freedmen 'all the civil rights that the superior race enjoy.'"

10. Ibid., 307. *See* Jennifer Brown, "It might appear that the principle of equality and fairness that animated the holding in *Strauder* would guarantee women's equal participation on juries based on the Fourteenth Amendment alone, without any consideration of suffrage, at least in cases involving female defendants. Yet *Strauder* did not provide women any such guarantee; rather, the Court stated in dicta that a state "may confine the selection [of jurors] to males," and repeated the contention, made in its earlier Fourteenth Amendment jurisprudence, that the amendment was addressed solely to race discrimination. Brown, "The Nineteenth Amendment and Women's Equality," 2188–2189.

11. Neal v. Delaware, 103 U.S. 370, 389 (1881).

12. Ibid., 408 (Field, J., dissenting).

13. Ibid., 407–408.

14. The Force Bills are discussed generally in Chapter 3, "Enforcement Legislation." More specifically, "[S]ection 1 of the Civil Rights Act of 1870 . . . prohibits racially discriminatory voter qualifications: '[A]ll citizens of the United States who are or shall be otherwise qualified by law to vote at any election by the people in any State, Territory, district, county, city, parish, township, school district, municipality, or other territorial subdivision, shall be entitled and allowed to vote at all such elections, without distinction of race, color, or previous condition of servitude; any constitution, law, custom, usage, or regulation of any State or Territory, or by or under its authority, to the contrary notwithstanding.'" Jonathan Mitchell, "Textualism and the Fourteenth

Amendment," *Stanford Law Review* 69 (2017):1237, 1266–1267, *citing* Civil Rights Act of 1870, ch. 114, § 1, 16 Stat. 140, 140.

15. Mitchell, "Textualism," 1270–1271, citing Civil Rights Act of 1875, §4, and noting, "The text of this statutory prohibition extends to every grand and petit jury, in every civil and criminal case in state or federal court. And it governs *every* "person" charged with "any duty" in the selection or summoning of jurors. That includes not only prosecutors and judges but also private attorneys who wield peremptory strikes to exclude jurors on account of their race. Of course, the Citizenship Clause did not establish this right to jury service as a self-executing matter. It has long been understood that only a subset of the citizenry is eligible for jury service; children and convicted felons are excluded, and women were excluded when the Fourteenth Amendment was ratified. A constitutional guarantee of citizenship does not by itself guarantee one's status as a juror. But the enforcement power and the Necessary and Proper Clause allow Congress to legislate against juror exclusions if Congress concludes that those discriminatory measures undermine one's status as a full and equal citizen." Ibid.

16. Ibid.

17. Ibid.

18. McCammon, *The U.S Women's Jury Movements*, 42–43. "In fact, the investigation of the jury movements pursued here reveals that activists considered state legislatures to be the crucial decision-making body on the issues, although in a few instances proponents pursued test cases in the state courts. Rarely, though, was litigation successful." Ibid., 43.

19. Ibid., 43. In her work, McCammon focuses on the strategic choices by former suffrage movement actors and other women's organizations and the link between those choices and their ability to achieve their stated goal of enacting state statutes granting women the equal right to sit on juries. She notes various "judicial studies" on state and federal cases in the area of jury service, including Grossman, Ritter, and Brown, but adds to those by analyzing the "women's activism surrounding jury reform" and "developments in statutory law, the latter of which, as will be seen, activists deemed critical to gaining women's inclusion on juries." Ibid., 34. McCammon argues that "while many have suggested that women's political activism evaporated or declined significantly after the enactment of suffrage, the state level jury movements show that advocacy to broaden women's legal rights continued well after 1920, and into the 1950s and 1960s, right up until women's efforts to pass an Equal Rights Amendment began to intensify." Ibid., 35.

20. Ibid., 44.

21. Ibid., 45. This is notable because African American women would have been within the ambit of both the Nineteenth and the Fifteenth Amendments, raising the possibility of using the Civil Rights Act of 1875's specific mandate about protecting jury service. And there were cases like State v. Bray, 95 So. 417 (La. 1923) that involved an African American female defendant. This "double coverage" might have made for a stronger test case, using African American women as a "wedge" much like women were used as a class in test cases around protective legislation. But it is understandable that the energy of former African American suffragists was focused on more

fundamental issues like disenfranchisement and lynching. McCammon adds that some of the resistance to extending jury service "was fear on the part of some county [League] members that white and colored women would be forced to serve on the same jury," citing a Maryland League's Legislative Committee report as to one reason the bill in that state had failed. McCammon, *The U.S Women's Jury Movements*, 45–46.

22. Note that there were cases that came up in states that enacted suffrage laws before the Nineteenth Amendment as well. These earlier cases are gathered in Gretchen Ritter and Jennifer Brown's work and set the stage for the debate in the states over the impact of the Nineteenth Amendment on the corollary right to serve on juries.

23. *See* Joanna Grossman, "Women's Jury Service: Right of Citizenship or Privilege of Difference?," *Stanford Law Review* 46 (1994): 1115, 1160, arguing that most of the jury service cases from ratification of the Nineteenth Amendment to the present day have focused on the defendant and the "representativeness" of the jury rather than on the excluded juror and her citizenship rights.

24. People v. Barltz, 180 N.W. 423 (Mich. 1920).

25. Ibid., 424.

26. Ibid.

27. Ibid.

28. Ibid., 425.

29. Ibid., (citing Rosencrantz v. Territory, 5 P. 305 (Wash. Terr. 1884)).

30. *Barltz*, 180 N.W. 423, 426.

31. Ibid.

32. Ibid., 426–427.

33. Ibid.

34. Commonwealth v. Maxwell, 114 A. 825 (Pa. 1921).

35. Ibid., 825.

36. Ibid.

37. Ibid.

38. Ibid., 826.

39. Ibid., 826–827.

40. Ibid., 829.

41. Ibid.

42. Ibid., 827.

43. Ibid., 827–828, (*citing* People v. Barltz, 180 N.W. 423 (Mich. 1920)).

44. Ibid., 828.

45. In a fascinating passage, the *Maxwell* court felt the need to justify its conclusion, which was the polar opposite of that of its colleagues on the Massachusetts Supreme Judicial Court in In re Opinion of the Justices, 130 N.E. 685 (Mass. 1921). This nod may simply have been a collegial way to avoid criticizing the SJC's analysis that the common law trial by jury contemplated men and thus the Nineteenth Amendment had no automatic impact on the Massachusetts jury statute, without further legislative action:

> While it is true the Supreme Court of Massachusetts, in giving an advisory opinion to the Legislature of that state recently determined that, under its

Constitution and existing statutes, women are not liable to jury duty, yet the opinion in question holds, as we do, that the qualification of jurors is a matter not constitutionally fixed, but within the control of the Legislature, and that the General Assembly of that state is authorized to make a change in the statutory law upon the subject, so as to render women liable to jury duty. The only difference between their conclusion and the one reached by us is that we hold our existing legislation sufficient in itself to meet the situation while they think a further statute is required. Had the Massachusetts legislation been similar to that in Pennsylvania, which is not the case, their conclusion might possibly have accorded with ours; but, however, that may be, the decision under discussion is in no sense binding upon us, notwithstanding the high respect in which we hold the tribunal which rendered it.

Ibid., 829.
46. Ibid.
47. Palmer v. State, 150 N.E. 917 (Ind. 1926).
48. Ibid., 917.
49. Ibid.
50. Ibid.
51. Ibid., 917–918.
52. Ibid., 918.
53. Ibid.
54. Ibid., (*citing* Neal v. Delaware, 103 U.S. 370 (1881)).
55. *Palmer*, 919.
56. Ibid.
57. Ibid.
58. Wilkinson v. State, 151 N.E. 690 (Ind. 1926).
59. Ibid., 690.
60. Ibid.
61. *Palmer*, 917.
62. *Wilkinson*, 151 N.E. 690, 691.
63. Ibid.
64. Cleveland, C., C. & St. L. Ry. Co. v. Wehmeier, 170 N.E. 27 (Ohio. Ct. App. 1929).
65. Ibid., 28.
66. Ibid.
67. Ibid.
68. Ibid.
69. Ibid., 28–29.
70. Ibid.
71. Ibid.
72. Ibid.
73. In re Opinion of the Justices, 130 N.E. 685 (Mass. 1921).
74. Ibid., 685–686.
75. Ibid., 686.
76. Ibid., 686–687.
77. Ibid., 687.

78. Ibid.
79. Ibid., 687–688.
80. Ibid., 688.
81. Ibid., 685.
82. Ibid., 687.
83. Ibid., 688.
84. State v. James, 114 A. 553 (N.J. Err. & App. 1921).
85. Ibid., 554–555.
86. Ibid., 555.
87. Ibid.
88. Ibid.
89. Ibid., 556.
90. Ibid.
91. Ibid.
92. Ibid., 555.
93. Ibid., 556 (*citing* In re Opinion of the Justices, 130 N.E. 685 (Mass. 1921)).
94. *James*, 556.
95. State v. Mittle, 113 S.E. 335 (S.C. 1922).
96. Ibid., 336–337.
97. Ibid.
98. Ibid., 337–338.
99. Ibid., 337.
100. Ibid.
101. Ibid.
102. Ibid.
103. Ibid.
104. Ibid.
105. Ibid., 338.
106. State v. Bray, 95 So. 417 (La. 1923).
107. Ibid.
108. Ibid.
109. Ibid., 417–418.
110. Ibid., 418.
111. Ibid.
112. Ibid., 418–419.
113. Ibid., 417.
114. Ibid., 418.
115. Ibid. Note that the Equal Protection Clause of the Fourteenth Amendment would not be extended by the US Supreme Court to laws that discriminated based on sex until 1971, in Reed v. Reed, 404 U.S. 71 (1971).
116. Ibid., 419.
117. Ibid, 417.
118. State v. Dreher, 118 So. 85 (La. 1928).
119. Ibid., 92.

120. Ibid.
121. Ibid., 93.
122. Ibid.
123. Ibid.
124. Ibid.
125. Ibid.
126. Ibid., 115 (O'Niell, C.J., dissenting).
127. People *ex rel.* Fyfe v. Barnett, 150 N.E. 290 (Ill. 1925). Fyfe is noted as a test case in McCammon, *The U.S Women's Jury Movements*, 43. Notably, Fyfe was the vice president of the state chapter of the League of Women Voters and presumably selected a female lawyer, Elizabeth Perry, since this was a test case. *See* John A. Lupton, "Illinois Supreme Court History: Women and Juries," *Illinois Courts Connect*, 26 March 2019, https://courts.illinois.gov/Media/eNews/2019/032619_SCHistory.asp.
128. *Fyfe*, 150 N.E. 290.
129. Ibid.
130. Ibid., 292.
131. Ibid.
132. Ibid.
133. Ibid.
134. Ibid., 290–291.
135. Ibid., 291–292.
136. Ibid., 292 (*quoting* Uphoff v. Industrial Board of Illinois, 111 N.E. 128 (Ill. 1915)).
137. *Fyfe*, 292.
138. Ibid.
139. Ibid., 291.
140. The NLWV pamphlet "Survey of the Legal and Political Status of Women" (circa 1922) instructed state chapters in their legislative campaigns to be wary of "blanket" legislation and pin down legislators on its effects. The pamphlet instructed members to ask legislators to state their positions on whether "If there should be an amendment to the United States or to your State constitution declaring 'No political, civil or legal disability or inequality on account of sex or marriage shall exist,' would this not repeal your minimum wage law or women's eight hour law and law for the sanitary regulation of factories employing women and even take the legal chair from under the tired woman clerk?" League of Women Voters Papers, ProQuest Struggle for Women's Rights, folder: 002637-004-0083.
141. Ritter, "Jury Service and Women's Citizenship," 503, *citing* Louise M. Young, *In the Public Interest: The League of Women Voters, 1920–1970* (Westport, CT: Greenwood Press, 1989), 56. "By the middle of the 1920s it was increasingly evident that the courts and legislatures were resistant to further extensions of women's rights in this area."
142. Commonwealth v. Welosky, 177 N.E. 656 (Mass. 1931). McCammon traces the Massachusetts League of Women Voters efforts, but notes that "[f]or much of the 1920s, the Massachusetts branch of the National Woman's Party was merely an observer and not a participant in the state's jury movement, working instead on an

equal rights bill. In 1930, however, the MA-NWP decided after growing frustration with the legislative response to the MA-LWV's efforts that it would try its hand at winning a place on juries for Massachusetts women. Although the MA-NWP supported the League in its efforts to win a jury law via legislative channels, MA-NWP leaders also took a new approach: attempting to change the law via a judicial route. The MA-NWP worked with Boston attorney George E. Roewer to select a 'test case' to take before the Massachusetts Supreme Judicial Court to determine whether this alternative avenue of action could bring the matter to fruition." McCammon, *The U.S Women's Jury Movements*, 111. McCammon notes that the MA-LWV "supported the MA-NWP in the case by filing a test brief." Ibid. McCammon cites a January 17, 1930 letter from Bernita Shelton Matthews of the National Woman's Party to Alma Lutz of the state branch opining that such a test case might bring attention to the issue, but doubting whether it would achieve more than that. Matthews noted "that she had reviewed a handful of other such cases around the nation and found that the judiciary channel had thus far not borne fruit in the overall effort to change jury statues." McCammon, *The U.S Women's Jury Movements*, 111–113. After losing the case at the Supreme Judicial Court and having certiorari denied by the United States Supreme Court, "the MA-NWP did not participate further in the Massachusetts jury campaign and instead returned to its work on an equal rights bill." McCammon, *The U.S Women's Jury Movements*, 112.

143. Only a few cases even mentioned the Fourteenth Amendment or enforcement legislation. While *Mittle* implied that some defendants might have a Fourteenth Amendment claim, the male defendant in that case was not a member of the excluded class. State v. Mittle, 113 S.E. 335, 338 (S.C. 1922). *Bray* noted explicitly that in the absence of enforcement legislation similar to that enacted under the Fourteenth Amendment, it certainly could not find women entitled to sit on juries. State v. Bray, 95 So. 417, 418 (La. 1923). And in *Dreher*, the dissenting chief justice suggested that Congress might not even have the power to enact legislation extending the right for women to serve on juries. State v. Dreher, 118 So. 85, 115 (La. 1928) (O'Niell, C.J., dissenting).

144. *See* letter from George E. Roewer, Rower & Bearak (attorney representing Mrs. Welosky in Commonwealth v. Welosky) to Burnita Shelton Matthews, 16 October 1931, National Woman's Party Papers, ProQuest Struggle for Women's Rights, folder: 002613-047-0097. Matthews was a Washington, DC, lawyer and the chair of the National Woman's Party Lawyers Council. The letter is responding to Matthews's prior letters inquiring about the cost of having Roewer's firm pursue the petition for certiorari. He notes the fee for the petition stage and suggests that she might consider having someone involved in the NWP write the brief instead. The Massachusetts state branch of the NWP had chosen to take the case to the state SJC, despite the national NWP's view that not much more than publicity would be gained by taking the test case there. But after they lost, Matthews's letter to Roewer suggests that the national NWP got more involved, at least to the extent of arranging and financing the petition for certiorari and filing a petition to file an amicus brief (as did the National Association of Women Lawyers). The petition for certiorari was

filed by Joseph Bearak, George Roewer's law partner, so it appears Matthews chose to use Roewer & Bearak for that purpose. The US Supreme Court eventually denied certiorari, refusing to review the Massachusetts SJC opinion that did not extend jury service to women, thus leaving the decision to stand.

145. Commonwealth v. Welosky, 177 N.E. 656 (Mass. 1931), *cert. denied*, 284 U.S. 684 (1932).

146. *Welosky*, 664.

147. *Bray*, 95 So. 417, 418.

148. *Dreher*, 118 So. 85, 115 (O'Niell, C.J., dissenting).

149. McCammon, *The U.S Women's Jury Movements*, 43–44 ("A number of years later Dorothy Kenyon and Pauli Murray wrote a lengthy proposal for the American Civil Liberties Association for remedial federal legislation to place women, both white and black, as well as black men on state juries (*citing* Dorothy Kenyon and Pauli Murray, The Case for Equality in State Jury Service: Memorandum in Support of ACLU Proposal to Amend S. 2923 (Civil Rights Protection Act of 1966)—to Deal with Exclusion of Women from Service on State Juries. Unpublished manuscript, American Civil Liberties Union). Yet most of women's pressure on authorities to change jury law took place at the state level.").

150. Ferguson, "The Jury as Constitutional Identity," 1131, *citing* Taylor v. Louisiana, 419 U.S. 522 (1975); and J.E.B. v. Alabama, 511 U.S. 127, 140 (1994).

151. Ritter, "Jury Service and Women's Citizenship," 480–481.

Chapter 6

1. Elizabeth D. Katz, "'A Woman Stumps Her State': Nellie G. Robinson and Women's Right to Hold Public Office in Ohio," *Akron Law Review* (2019): 313, *citing* Reva B. Siegel, "She the People: The Nineteenth Amendment, Sex Equality, Federalism, and the Family," *Harvard Law Review* 115 (2002): 945–1046. "[A] crucial component of the debate over women's voting rights was to challenge traditional conceptions of family life . . ." In ratifying the Nineteenth Amendment, Siegel argues that Americans "were breaking with understandings of the family that had organized public and private law and defined the position of the sexes since the founding of the republic." Siegel, "She the People," 951. Katz also cites Tracy A. Thomas, "More than the Vote: The Nineteenth Amendment as Proxy for Gender Equality," *Stanford Journal of Civil Rights and Civil Liberties* 15 (forthcoming 2020), draft at https://papers.ssrn.com/sol3/papers.cfm?abstract_id=3364546, 1–2. "Thomas explores how participants in the early women's rights movement were motivated by economic concerns and sought changes to laws and social norms regulating marriage, property and labor. The vote was the 'enforcement mechanism and the entry point for women's rights,' she argues, not the sole or even primary goal." Katz, "A Woman Stumps Her State," 318.

2. Holly J. McCammon, *The U.S Women's Jury Movements and Strategic Adaptation: A More Just Verdict* (Cambridge: Cambridge University Press, 2012), 57–58. McCammon notes that some women who supported jury service reform were wary of asking for the

right to hold public office. "For some, office holding would take women too far into the public sphere, with negative results. Some CA-FWC members believed that women running for and holding elective 'would taint women's moral image,' undermining the ideal of women as altruistic caretakers of broader society, an image that had served women well as they sought and won progressive-era reforms." Ibid., 58.

3. *See generally* ibid.; and *see* Katz, "A Woman Stumps Her State," 356–357 n. 297, listing newspaper accounts of state-focused legislative and state constitutional reform efforts. "Women to Fight Hard for Rights to Office: League Names Committee to Study Ruling Denying Voters' Eligibility," *Baltimore Sun*, 20 February 1921, 10; "Missouri Election Is Spirited Event: Vote on Amendment Allowing Women to Hold State Office May Carry," *Pantagraph* (Bloomington, Ill.), 4 August 1921.

4. Katz notes that, unlike the jury service cases, little scholarship around holding public office has been done. She recovers that history prior to ratification and suggests paths to surface post-ratification history as well. Katz, "A Woman Stumps Her State," "In the illuminating body of scholarship framing and interpreting the Nineteenth Amendment's legacy, women's right to hold public office has been a surprisingly minor component." Ibid., 318–319.

5. *In re* Opinion of the Justices, 62 Me. 596 (1873).

6. Ibid., 597–598.

7. Ibid., 601 (Dickerson, J., dissenting).

8. Ibid., 602.

9. *See* Strauder v. West Virginia, 100 U.S. 303, 307 (1880), *citing* The Slaughter-House Cases, 83 U.S. 36, 81 (1873): "The existence of laws in the States where the newly emancipated negroes resided, which discriminated with gross injustice and hardship against them as a class, was the evil to be remedied, and by it [the Fourteenth Amendment] such laws were forbidden. If, however, the States did not conform their laws to its requirements, then, by the fifth section of the article of amendment, 'Congress was authorized to enforce it by suitable legislation.' And it was added, 'We doubt very much whether any action of a State, not directed by way of discrimination against the negroes, as a class, will ever be held to come within the purview of this provision.'" And *see* Vikram Amar, "Jury Service as Political Participation Akin to Voting," *Cornell Law Review* 80 (1995): 203. "As I argue below, jury service, like voting and office holding, was conceived of as a political right, as distinguished from a civil right, and political rights were excluded from the coverage of the Fourteenth Amendment." Ibid., 204.

10. *In re* Opinion of the Justices, 62 Me. 596, 603 (1873) (Dickerson, J., dissenting). Significantly, Justice Dickerson's dissent was written in 1873, which was during the period known as the "New Departure" for American suffragists. "[A]fter ratification of the Fourteenth Amendment in 1868, [Stanton and her supporters] argued that women had the right to vote under its provision granting all citizens "privileges and immunities under the law." Thomas, "More than the Vote," 3. However, "[t]he New Departure strategy was soon halted by the U.S. Supreme Court's decision in Minor v. Happersett." Ibid. Happersett was decided in 1874. Justice Dickerson wrote his

dissent in 1873. So it may be that Dickerson explicitly invoked the Fourteenth in support of the suffragists' New Departure strategy, as he wrote his dissent in 1873.

11. *In re* Opinion of the Justices, 604.

12. U.S. Const. amend. XV. "The right of citizens of the United States to vote shall not be denied or abridged by the United States or by any State on account of race, color, or previous condition of servitude. The Congress shall have power to enforce this article by appropriate legislation."

13. Amar, "Jury Service as Political Participation," 234, quoting John M. Mathews, *Legislative and Judicial History of the Fifteenth Amendment* (Baltimore: Johns Hopkins Press, 1909), 12.

14. Preston v. Roberts, 110 S.E. 586 (N.C. 1922).

15. Ibid., 586.

16. *In re* Opinion of the Justices, 135 N.E. 173 (Mass. 1922).

17. Ibid., 174.

18. Ibid.

19. Ibid., 174–175.

20. Ibid., 175.

21. Ibid.

22. Ibid., 175–176.

23. Ibid., 176. Interestingly, the SJC refused to embrace a principle that all federal amendments would have the same sweeping, self-executing effect on the state constitution, "This principle may not be universally applicable to Amendments of the federal Constitution in their effect upon the Constitution of Massachusetts. We go no further than the case in hand and the words of our Constitution here in issue." Ibid.

24. Ibid., 175–176.

25. *In re* Opinion of the Justices, 139 A. 180 (N.H. 1927), *overruled as recognized by* Akins v. Secretary of State, 904 A.2d 702 (N.H. 2006).

26. Ibid., 181(*citing* In re Opinion of the Justices, 135 N.E. 173 (Mass. 1922)).

27. Ibid., 181–182.

28. Ibid., 182.

29. Ibid.

30. Ibid.

31. Ibid.

32. Ibid., 183.

33. Ibid.

34. Ibid. (emphasis added).

35. Ibid.

36. Ibid., 184.

37. Like jury service, state chapters of the former national suffrage organizations were on the forefront of legislative efforts to secure the right to hold public office, in the decade after ratification of the Nineteenth. And those efforts were focused predominantly in the state legislatures. *See* Katz, "A Woman Stumps Her State," 356–357 n. 297.

38. Katz, "A Woman Stumps Her State," 356, notes that "It took the Nineteenth Amendment to finally push many states to open even the most mundane official posts

to women, and many jurisdictions still resisted or remained uncertain about women's eligibility in the following years."

Chapter 7

1. Tracy A. Thomas, "More than the Vote: The Nineteenth Amendment as Proxy for Gender Equality," *Stanford Journal of Civil Rights and Civil Liberties* 15 (forthcoming 2020), draft available at https://papers.ssrn.com/sol3/papers.cfm?abstract_id=3364546, draft at 9, quoting Elizabeth Cady Stanton; *see generally* Tracy A. Thomas, *Elizabeth Cady Stanton and the Feminist Foundations of Family Law* (New York: New York University Press, 2016).
2. Thomas, "More Than the Vote," 16.
3. Vicki Schultz, "Taking Sex Discrimination Seriously," *Denver University Law Review* 91 (2015): 995, 1003.
4. As used herein, "neutrality feminists" denotes those former suffragists who adhered to legal formalism and an anti-classification approach to equality—laws should treat men and women the same—no more, no less. Courts should essentially hold state legislation to a neutrality standard in assessing whether the state was achieving equality. "Social feminists" eschewed legal formalism in favor of what was called sociological jurisprudence or legal realism, with a focus on equality of outcomes (reflecting an anti-subordination norm.) Thus, laws that treated women differently might in fact achieve equality if they leveled the playing field and were compensatory in terms of women's asymmetry of power.
5. Vivien Hart, *Bound by Our Constitution: Women Workers and the Minimum Wage* (Princeton, NJ: Princeton University Press, 1994), 111. "Legal [neutrality] feminists defined equality as identity with men in the eyes of the law, and supported the ERA. Social feminists defined equality as a social as well as a legal status, defending the unequal rights of protective legislation like the minimum wage as necessary until social equality became a reality." Ibid.
6. Hart, *Bound by Our Constitution*, 120. "The range of possibilities they [the lawyers] saw was limited by their reliance on precedent. On the other hand, they must be speculative and political about how the courts might read the same precedents in future cases. As Frankfurter reminded: 'It is not how a proposed amendment should be interpreted or would be interpreted by liberal minded judges, but how an amendment might be interpreted by an illiberal court that matters.'" Ibid.
7. Joan Zimmerman, "The Jurisprudence of Equality: The Women's Minimum Wage, the First Equal Rights Amendment, and Adkins v. Children's Hospital, 1905–1923," *Journal of American History* 78 (1991): 188–225. Thomas, "More Than the Vote," 19 n. 18; *see also* Hart, *Bound by Our Constitution*, 124 ("Animosity over the ERA in any case carried over, since counsel in the Adkins case were the very same lawyers who advised on the ERA. While Frankfurter advised the District Minimum Wage Board and the NCL prepared his brief, Children's Hospital counsel ex-governor Joseph W. Folk of Missouri briefed Alice Paul. Paul privately advised both Folk and district

lawyers Challen and Wade Ellis, who used their personal connections with the district judiciary and may have been pursuing a personal vendetta against Frankfurter."); Nancy Woloch, *A Class by Herself: Protective Laws for Women Workers, 1880s–1960s* (Princeton, NJ: Princeton University Press, 2015), 114–115 ("Representing Children's Hospital and Willie Lyons were the lawyer-brothers Wade H. Ellis and Challen Ellis . . . The Ellis brothers acquired an expert advisor from the women's movement: Alice Paul, who had met with Challen Ellis in the early 1920s to discuss the wording of an Equal Rights Amendment. Now she supplied him with National Woman's Party literature about the danger protective laws posed to women's rights; his brother cited this material in oral argument.").

8. Some have suggested that the NWP was unlikely to embrace the reasoning in *Adkins* because it almost made the ERA unnecessary. *See* Zimmerman, "The Jurisprudence of Equality," 222 ("In fact, Sutherland's termination of the dependent woman theory had gone almost too far. His broad claims for the Nineteenth Amendment's emancipation of women had almost undermined the need for the ERA.").

9. While she initially stepped away from a leadership role in the new NWP after the February 1921 convention, by October 1921 Paul had succumbed to pressure from Alva Belmont, the NWP's major financial supporter, to stay in a leadership position. *See* Alice Paul to Agnes Morey, 7 October 1921, National Woman's Party Papers, ProQuest, Struggle for Women's Rights, folder: 002613-010-0601 ("[I] am writing to say that Miss Hill is still National Chairman of the Executive Committee . . . I took the Vice Presidency at this meeting of the Council, since Mrs. Belmont seemed to insist upon this as a condition with regard to what she would do. I am still going ahead with my law work and cannot give more than a third of my time to the Woman's Party work, but in view of Mrs. Belmont's position there seemed to be nothing to do but take this office, even thought [*sic*] I cannot give much time to it.").

10. Hart, *Bound by Our Constitution*, 116. The landscape, of course, was more complex than the binary "neutrality feminist/social feminist" divide. "Women in the 1920s had different visions of feminism. By the end of the decade, the feminist label belonged to the NWP and had been ostentatiously dropped by social feminists. One view of this contested label was that feminist politics comprised women fighting for changes specifically in the condition of women. Another was that it comprised liberated women making their distinctive contribution for humanity. The first encompassed the official NWP line that a feminist organization was one working to "secure absolute equality of men and women under the law and in the administration of government." It also embraced a radical critic like Crystal Eastman who found the legalistic vision of equality inadequate. 'What,' she asked, 'do we mean by a feminist organization? It does not mean mere women juries, congressmen, etc., but it means to raise the status of women, making them self-respecting persons.'" Ibid., 116. Hart goes on to contrast the first view with that of the social feminists. "The second view of feminist politics made women agents of broad social change, by virtue of distinctive feminine qualities. Its most passionate adherents believed that world peace was the essential feminist issue. Peace feminists came closest to defining women by their biology, as people who 'gave life—not took it.' The social feminists were succinctly represented

by Mrs. Gill, of Illinois: 'By "feminism" we mean full social and economic freedom for women.'" Ibid.

11. *See, e.g.*, the anti-suffrage book by B.V Hubbard, *Socialism, Feminism, and Suffragism, the Terrible Triplets, Connected by the Same Umbilical Cord, and Fed from the Same Nursing Bottle* (Chicago: American Publishing Company, 1915). (Library of Congress Rare Book Collection, https://www.loc.gov/item/15016027/.)

12. Felix Frankfurter, "The Case of Sacco and Vanzetti," *Atlantic Monthly* 139 (March 1927): 409–432. Frankfurter went on to write a book on the case entitled *The Case of Sacco and Vanzetti: A Critical Analysis for Lawyers and Laymen* (Boston: Little, Brown and Co., 1927). Bruce Allen Murphy, *The Brandeis/Frankfurter Connection: The Secret Political Activities of Two Supreme Court Justices* (New York: Oxford University Press, 1982), 78, 383 n. 12.

13. Murphy, *The Brandeis/Frankfurter Connection*, 78–81.

14. Ibid., 39.

15. *See generally* ibid.

16. "[T]he emphasis on market liberty, the belief that market liberty could be interfered with if legislation promoted a valid public purpose, and the suggestion that valid public-purpose legislation was distinct from laws that merely promoted the interests of some classes at the expense of others—were long-standing features of nineteenth-century police powers jurisprudence." Michael Schearer, "No Ma'm: Progressive Reform as an Obstacle to Gender Equality," SSRN (April 2014), 15, https://papers.ssrn.com/sol3/papers.cfm?abstract_id=2573791, quoting Howard Gillman, *The Constitution Besieged: The Rise and Demise of Lochner Era Police Powers Jurisprudence* (Durham, NC: Duke University Press, 1993), 20. *See also* David E. Bernstein, "Class Legislation, Fundamental Rights, and the Origins of Lochner and Liberty of Contract, *George Mason Law Review* 26 (2019): 1023–1047.

17. Lochner v. New York, 198 U.S. 45 (1905).

18. Woloch, *A Class by Herself*, 36; "Formerly a 'procedural' safeguard that encompassed a citizen's right to obtain a lawyer or to call witnesses, the due process clause of the late nineteenth century became 'substantive,' a guarantee of rights against legislative intrusion . . . [This approach] offered an advantage for business." Ibid.; Hart, *Bound by Our Constitution*, 136. "Due process had at one time been taken by the court only to set standards for the means by which laws were passed and implemented— procedural due process. When the court adopted substantive due process in reviewing economic and labor legislation it assumed the right to review the purpose of legislation." Ibid.

19. This hope had some empirical basis. "One study of state and federal decisions involving protective labor legislation between 1873 (*Bradwell v. Illinois*) and 1937 (*West Coast Hotel Co. v. Parrish*) by Professor Julie Novkov found that courts struck down general, gender-neutral labor legislation nearly 50% of the time. On the other hand, the same courts struck down women's labor legislation only 21% of the time . . . themselves, the numbers suggest that courts were considerably more deferential to protective labor legislation when it focused at women." Schearer, "Progressive Reform as an Obstacle," 14, *citing* Julie Novkov, *Constituting Workers, Protecting Women: Gender, Law, and*

Labor in the Progressive Era and New Deal Years (Ann Arbor: University of Michigan Press, 2001), 29–31.

20. Muller v. Oregon, 208 U.S. 412 (1908).

21. Josephine Goldmark worked with Florence Kelley at the National Consumers League and was the sister-in-law of Louis Brandeis. She asked Brandeis to represent the State of Oregon in the *Muller* case before the US Supreme Court. For a comprehensive look at protective legislation for women and the relationships between Goldmark, Kelley, Brandeis, and Felix Frankfurter, *see generally* Woloch, *A Class by Herself.*

22. *Muller*, 208 U.S. 412, 422–423.

23. Ibid.

24. Felice Batlan, "Notes from the Margins: Florence Kelley and the Making of Sociological Jurisprudence," in *Transformations in American Legal History: Law, Ideology, and Methods*, edited by Daniel W. Hamilton and Alfred L. Brophy, vol. 2 (Cambridge, MA: Harvard University Press, 2010), 239–253, 250.

25. Ibid.

26. Others identified as co-authors of the ERA include NWP National Advisory Council member, lawyer, and social feminist Crystal Eastman. "As one of the four authors of the Equal Rights Amendment, she was also one of the few socialists to endorse it when it was introduced in 1923." American Civil Liberties Union, "Crystal Eastman," https://www.aclu.org/other/crystal-eastman. Joan Zimmerman has suggested that that lawyer Albert Levitt was the first to suggest an amendment to Paul. "On a Sunday afternoon in mid-May 1921, as Paul, Hill, and Levitt were discussing the district bill, Levitt proposed a constitutional amendment. Although Paul has been regarded as the author of the ERA, it its clear that Levitt suggested an amendment, and he wrote the first lengthy, crude version of it." Zimmerman, "The Jurisprudence of Equality," 206.

27. Hart, *Bound by Our Constitution*, 117. "Kelley and Paul discussed the ERA at a rare face-to-face meeting in December 1921, during which each woman repeatedly trumped the other's legal authorities. Paul cited her own 'high legal authorities,' and Kelley countered with 'Mr. Frankfurter and Dean Pound.' Paul read a letter from Pound 'of a later date than the one they had,' in which he had suggested 'a construing clause which he thought would protect the welfare legislation.' 'Their sole authority for opposing the amendment at all seemed to come down to Mr. Frankfurter,' Paul accused the NCL, proceeding to imply Frankfurter's utter inadequacy on grounds of partiality and arrogance. Finally, Maud Younger, NWP legislative chairman, 'turned to them and said—'Is there anyone but Mr. Frankfurter upon whom you are basing your objections?'"

28. Nancy F. Cott, "Feminist Politics in the 1920s: The National Woman's Party," *Journal of American History* 71 (1984): 43, 57, quoting Paul, "'Personally, I do not believe in special protective labor legislation for women. It seems to me that protective labor legislation should be enacted for women and men alike in a trade or in a geographic district and not along sex lines. I think enacting labor laws along sex lines is erecting another handicap for women in the economic struggle,' Alice Paul to Jane Norman Smith, November 29, 1921." Ibid. *See* ibid., generally for one of the most comprehensive

historical accounts of the negotiations among Paul, Kelley, Frankfurter, and Pound around the first ERA, in the period between 1920 and 1923.

29. The term "blanket amendment" or "blanket legislation" describes the fact the ERA did not target specific laws that discriminated against women for reform. Rather it spoke in general terms, stating that men and women shall have equal rights. This suggested to many that it would invalidate, as a constitutional matter, any law that treated men and women differently.

30. For an extensive treatment of Paul's relationship with Ethel Smith, legislative secretary of the National Women's Trade Union League, *see* Amy E. Butler, *Two Paths to Equality: Alice Paul and Ethel M. Smith in the ERA Debate, 1921–1929* (Albany: State University of New York Press, 2002).

31. *See* Amelia Fry, "Conversations with Alice Paul: Woman Suffrage and the Equal Rights Amendment," Oral History Project, The Bancroft Library, University of California Berkeley, 1976, http://content.cdlib.org/view?docId=kt6f59n89c&doc. view=entire_text, 411–412.

32. Ibid.

33. Ibid., 431–32.

34. Cott, "Feminist Politics in the 1920s," 62. "Although NWP members did not hold consistently laissez-faire views, the single-mindedness of their espousal of equal rights made them appear to." Ibid.

35. It is hard to overstate the influence of Frankfurter and Pound. Frankfurter effectively chose two Supreme Court clerks per year by recommending them to Justices Holmes and Brandeis. Frankfurter, who argued *Adkins*, and Pound, whose scholarship was cited by the dissent in the appeals court decision, ranked high among the nation's legal elite. Kelley, Frankfurter, and Pound had decades of legal experience, and Paul was just a newly minted lawyer in 1923. "Florence Kelley posited her own weighty credentials in law against the lesser professional record of Alice Paul. 'I was admitted to the Bar of Illinois and have been continuously active in the field of litigation ever since,' Kelley told the editor of the Woman's Home Companion in an indignant letter of 1922. Alice Paul, in contrast, Kelley charged, was just an upstart. 'Miss Paul . . . carries great weight with the uninitiated,' Kelley continued. 'In fact, however, as to the effects of statutes and judicial decisions, she is a newcomer fresh from the law school.'" Woloch, *A Class by Herself*, 132.

36. Telegram from Elsie Hill to Felix Frankfurter, 9 June 1921, box II: 12, National Woman's Party Records, Manuscript Division, Library of Congress.

37. Felix Frankfurter to Elsie Hill, 7 June 1921, box II: 12, National Woman's Party Records, Manuscript Division, Library of Congress.

38. Ibid.

39. Albert Levitt to Roscoe Pound, 25 May 1921, box II: 12, National Woman's Party Records, Manuscript Division, Library of Congress.

40. Ibid.

41. Albert Levitt to Alice Paul, circa 1921, box II: 12, National Woman's Party Records, Manuscript Division, Library of Congress, quoting Pound.

42. Zimmerman, "The Jurisprudence of Equality," 223. "By early November, the party had lined up two legislators willing to introduce the Equal Rights Amendment when Congress convened in early December. They were Senator Curtis, who would be Herbert Hoover's running mate in 1928, and Rep. Daniel Anthony, Susan B. Anthony's nephew. The long, confusing period of drafting the first ERA had finally ended, and the struggle over passage through Congress had begun." Ibid.

43. The 1923 version was never enacted and a new formulation was sponsored in 1943, which provided that "Equality of rights under the law shall not be denied or abridged by the United States or by any state on account of sex." It was a version of that language that was finally passed by Congress in 1972 but failed to be ratified by a sufficient number of states by the 1982 deadline.

44. Christine Lunardini, *From Equal Suffrage to Equal Rights: Alice Paul and the National Woman's Party, 1920–1928* (Lincoln, NE: toExcel Press, 1986, 2000), 162. Unfortunately, Kelley "came to perceive her one-time ally Alice Paul as a 'fiend' whose only purpose was to hinder the women's movement and undo twenty years of labor legislation." Ibid.

45. Adkins v. Children's Hospital, 261 U.S. 525, 553 (1923), *overruled in part by* West Coast Hotel Co. v. Parrish, 300 U.S. 379 (1937).

46. Zimmerman, "The Jurisprudence of Equality," 216, noting that the NWP showed drafts of the equal rights amendment to Sutherland when he was the senator from Utah. "Hill quickly confided to several supporters that she was showing the amendment to prominent lawyers, including the former Utah senator George Sutherland." Ibid., 206; *see also* ibid., 212; "Most important, Paul relied on statements from Walsh and Sutherland, both of whom insisted that the amendment would not interfere with protective legislation based on the police power. Sutherland had pointed out that if the Supreme Court wished to strike down special legislation for women, it already had the power to do so under the Fourteenth Amendment." Ibid., 216. Note that Zimmerman argues that Paul knew about the *Adkins* case from its inception in the DC superior court and the NWP had requested the briefs. *See* ibid., 211. Zimmerman also speculated "that George Sutherland knew the details of the *Adkins* case at the same time advising Paul on the ERA. It is also my speculation that Sutherland was acquainted with the Ellis brothers, Challen and Wade, Joseph Folk, Frank Walsh, and Justice Robb." Ibid., 213–214 n. 41. In fact, Zimmerman notes, "When Ethel Smith solicited Sutherland's view of the proposed ERA, Sutherland responded that he had misgivings about a blanket amendment that could create confusion in the laws regulating marriage. Sutherland thought a state-by-state elimination of specific evils would be more useful. With regard to industrial legislation for women, Sutherland responded that 'the Supreme Court might take the view that the amendment meant precisely what it said, and that a law which gave unequal advantage to women was as obnoxious to the amendment as one which was unequally to their disadvantage.' Sutherland may not have endorsed all of Paul's intentions in the ERA, but he was willing to manipulate the debate over equality for women to reinforce policies consistent with his own conservative economic and legal views." Ibid., 220.

47. David P. Currie, "The Constitution in the Supreme Court: 1921–1930," *Duke Law Journal* (1986): 65–144. "When maximum hour legislation for factory workers was approved in 1917 without so much as a citation to *Lochner v. New York*, the earlier decision seemed thoroughly discredited. When a minimum wage law for District of Columbia women succumbed to a due process assault in *Adkins v. Children's Hospital* in 1923, however, *Lochner* formed the cornerstone of Justice Sutherland's opinion. Maximum hour legislation, the Court said, had been upheld only when necessary to preserve health . . . A law forbidding nighttime employment of women in restaurants passed muster the following Term as a health measure. In its next breath, however, with only Brandeis and Holmes dissenting, the Court extinguished a law regulating the size of bread loaves in order to combat consumer fraud. A year later, six Justices joined in nullifying a law forbidding the use of shoddy in quilt manufacturing . . . Substantive due process had grown teeth such as it had never exhibited before." Ibid., 76–79.

48. Schearer, "Progressive Reform as an Obstacle," 18–19, characterizing liberty of contract as less an economic theory than "a means by which judges could draw meaningful distinctions between the legitimate police powers of the state and individual freedoms protected by the Constitution."

49. Zimmerman, "The Jurisprudence of Equality," 220. "Paul accepted an invitation to help Challen and Wade Ellis prepare their case for the Supreme Court . . . Paul apparently wanted to keep the relationship a secret; she did not openly acknowledge her involvement with Ellis until 1935. When George Gordon Battle, Alva Belmont's attorney, offered to submit a brief in the Adkins case on behalf of the National Woman's Party, Paul asked him not to intervene. Instead, she supplied materials to the Ellis brothers." Ibid.

50. Dan Ernst, "Frankfurter and DC Minimum Wage Case: The View from the Adkins Papers," *Legal History Blog*, 28 June 2012, http://legalhistoryblog.blogspot.com/2012/06/frankfurter-and-dc-minimum-wage-case.html. Note that Frankfurter lobbied Jesse Adkins to oppose Paul's ERA. "The Harvard law professor felt close enough to the Washington lawyer to urge him to 'publicly come out against the Women's Party Amendment.' (Frankfurter called this early version of the Equal Rights Amendment 'a dangerously 'liberal' proposal' that would 'romantically and blithely' sweep away the power to enact 'legislation protective of women who need it.')" Ibid.

51. Children's Hospital of District of Columbia v. Adkins, 284 F. 613, 614–615 (D.C. Cir. 1922).

52. Ibid., 622.

53. Ibid., 623.

54. Barbier v. Connolly, 113 U.S. 27 (1885).

55. *Children's Hospital v. Adkins*, 284 F. 613, 633–634 (Smyth, J., dissenting).

56. Adkins v. Children's Hosp. of the District of Columbia, 261 U.S. 525, 553 (1923), *overruled in part by* West Coast Hotel Co. v. Parrish, 300 U.S. 379 (1937).

57. Muller v. Oregon, 208 U.S. 412 (1908).

58. Hart, *Bound by Our Constitution*, 127. "The Adkins case involved the one jurisdiction, the District of Columbia, in which the Nineteenth Amendment had no effect

at all. District residents were excluded from presidential elections, unrepresented in Congress, and governed locally by an appointed board of commissioners. Men and women in the district remained equally disenfranchised until the passage of the Twenty-Third Amendment in 1961."

59. In 1916, as a senator from Utah, Sutherland had "urg[ed] the Senate to adopt a woman suffrage amendment. Division 'by the line of sex,' he told his fellow senators, was 'purely artificial' and 'certain to disappear, just as the other superstitions which in the past have denied women equal opportunities for . . . equality of legal status—and all the other unjust and intolerant denials of equality have disappeared, or are disappearing from our law and customs.' Before his own appointment to the Supreme Court, he had, like Challen Ellis, advised Alice Paul on the drafting of an ERA." Woloch, *A Class by Herself*, 116.

60. Adkins v. Children's Hosp. of the District of Columbia, 261 U.S. 525, 553 (1923), *overruled in part by* West Coast Hotel Co. v. Parrish, 300 U.S. 379 (1937).

61. Ibid.

62. Ibid.

63. Ibid., 567 (Taft, C.J., dissenting).

64. Ibid., 569–70 (Holmes, J., dissenting).

65. Schearer, "Progressive Reform as an Obstacle," 34–35.

66. Zimmerman, "The Jurisprudence of Equality," 218.

67. Telegram from Frankfurter to Kelley, 10 April 1923, NCL Correspondence 1923 folder, box 157 Frankfurter Papers, *cited in* Zimmerman, "The Jurisprudence of Equality," 222 n. 61.

68. Proceedings of the February 1921 National Woman's Party Convention Transcript, Alice Paul Papers, 1785–1985; MC 399 box 2, folder 318 at 79, Schlesinger Library, Radcliffe Institute, Harvard University.

69. Batlan, "Florence Kelley," 246. "Kelley advocated an activist state that would have affirmative duties to its citizens."

70. Ibid.

71. Note that several years later, Sutherland retreated some from his apparently absolutist position in *Adkins* when, "in Radice v. New York (1924), the Supreme Court approved a New York law that barred women's work after 10:00 p.m. in restaurants in large cities . . . Citing Muller, Justice Sutherland affirmed that the law fostered women's health and welfare." Woloch, *A Class by Herself*, 118.

72. Reva B. Siegel, "She the People: The Nineteenth Amendment, Sex Equality, Federalism, and the Family," *Harvard Law Review* 115 (2002): 947, 1016.

73. Ibid., 1118–1119. Note that Siegel also observed that several lower courts adopted a similarly expansive view of the Nineteenth Amendment: "The Supreme Court was not the only court to read the Nineteenth Amendment as embodying a sex equality norm that had implications for practices other than voting, or to suggest that the Amendment's ratification marked a break with the common law's marital status norms. For example, two years after the *Adkins* decision, a federal district court interpreted the suffrage amendment as abrogating coverture principles in federal law. Asked to apply the common law doctrine relieving a wife of liability for criminal

conduct undertaken with her husband, the judge refused, observing that 'since the adoption of the Nineteenth Amendment to the Constitution, it seems to me that the rule of common law has no application to crimes committed against the United States.' This same understanding of the Nineteenth Amendment moved a judge concurring in a federal tax case to reject the government's claim that, by marriage, a wife's tax domicile was her husband's. Citing *Adkins* for the proposition that 'woman is accorded emancipation from the old doctrine that she must be given special protection or be subjected to special restraint in her contractual and civil relationships,' the judge asserted that the Nineteenth Amendment 'covers the right of woman to select and establish a residence wherever she chooses to vote.' Other courts deciding questions concerning coverture law invoked the suffrage amendment to authorize liberalizing interpretations of the common law. In these cases, courts invoked the Nineteenth Amendment as a reason for exercising their discretion in interpreting the common law so as to restrict the authority of traditional coverture concepts." Ibid., 1116–117.

74. Woloch, *A Class by Herself,* 118, *citing* Radice v. New York, 264 U.S. 292 (1924).

75. Hart, *Bound by Our Constitution,* 129.

76. *See* Zimmerman, "The Jurisprudence of Equality," 220. Characterizing her involvement in the *Adkins* case as a "surreptitious attack," Zimmerman states that "Although the NWP papers contain many letters from lawyers, they include no correspondence between Alice Paul and Challen Ellis." Ibid. *See also* note 49.

77. Adkins v. Children's Hosp. of the District of Columbia, 261 U.S. 525, 553 (1923), *overruled in part by* West Coast Hotel Co. v. Parrish, 300 U.S. 379 (1937).

78. Vikram David Amar, "The 100-Year Anniversary of the First State Ratification of the Nineteenth Amendment: Reflections on the Breadth of Freedom from Discrimination in the 'Right to Vote,'" *Verdict Justia,* 27 June 2019, https://verdict.justia.com/2019/06/27/the-100-year-anniversary-of-the-first-state-ratification-of-the-nineteenth-amendment.

79. Deborah L. Rhode, *Justice and Gender: Sex Discrimination and the Law* (Cambridge, MA: Harvard University Press, 1989), 49.

80. Hart, *Bound by Our Constitution,* 112–113.

81. In 1922, the NWP launched a specific southern campaign for the ERA and similar state legislation. *See* "Plan Equal Rights Campaign in South: Woman's Party to Seek Enactment in Seven States—Gompers Renews Criticism," *New York Times,* 16 January 1922, 3; For a comprehensive history of the battle among former suffragists over the ERA, see Julie Suk, *We the Women: The Unstoppable Mothers of the Equal Rights Amendment* (New York: Simon & Schuster forthcoming 2020).

82. Those state legislative efforts were very slow and scholars have suggested that slow progress, in part, explains the NWP's drive toward a federal amendment. "Although state branches had succeeded in eliminating some minor discriminations in 1922 and 1923, their slow and erratic progress demonstrated a need for a national amendment." Zimmerman, "The Jurisprudence of Equality," 223. And Nancy Cott notes that after that close of the decade following ratification, some NWP members lamented that " 'the NWP in its direction since 1923 has lost more [and] more of that great feminist

tradition handed to our care from the 18th century. We are bogged down in legal formalism.'" Cott, "Feminist Politics in the 1920s," 67.

Chapter 8

1. Commonwealth v. Welosky, 177 N.E. 656 (Mass. 1931), *cert. denied*, 284 U.S. 684 (1932).

2. Holly J. McCammon, *The U.S. Women's Jury Movements and Strategic Adaptation: A More Just Verdict* (New York: Cambridge University Press, 2012), 111–113. "For much of the 1920s, the Massachusetts Branch of the National Woman's Party (MA-NWP) was . . . working instead on an equal rights bill. In 1930, however, the MA-NWP decided after growing frustration with the legislative response . . . The MA-NWP worked with Boston attorney George E. Roewer to select a 'test case' to take before the Massachusetts Supreme Judicial Court to determine whether this alternative avenue of action could bring the matter to fruition." Ibid., 111. McCammon also identified the Illinois case of Fyfe v. Barnett as one of the few other test cases during the 1920s. The Illinois chapter of the NLWV, in response to failed efforts in the legislature, turned to the courts. "The group's strategic response to the legislative disappointment was to move its battle to an alternative venue, using a tactic Burstein calls 'legal mobilization,' or the pursuit of a test case." Ibid., 60. While they received a favorable ruling in the lower court, that decision was reversed by the Illinois Supreme Court in 1926. "In the end, the jury activists met with a dead end in the Illinois courts and were turned back to the legislature. (This would happen again a few years later in Massachusetts) . . ." Ibid., 61.

3. As to the legal effect of a denial of a writ of certiorari, *see Black's Law Dictionary*, by Henry Campbell Black et al. (St. Paul, MN: West Publishing Co. 6th edition, 1990), 1609. "If the writ is denied, the court refuses to hear the appeal and, in effect, the judgment below stands unchanged."

4. Richard L. Hasen and Leah M. Litman, "Thin and Thick Conceptions of the Nineteenth Amendment Right to Vote and Congress's Power to Enforce It," *Georgetown Law Journal* 19th Amendment Special Edition (forthcoming 2020), draft available at https://papers.ssrn.com/sol3/papers.cfm?abstract_id=3501114, draft at 6.

5. Breedlove v. Suttles, 302 U.S. 277, 284 (1937), *overruled by* Harper v. Virginia State Board of Elections, 383 U.S. 663 (1966). Hasen and Litman note that "[Harper] overruled the portion of *Breedlove* that rejected an equal protection challenge to state poll taxes. As Justice Black pointed out in dissent, however, the *Harper* majority did not overrule the part of *Breedlove* approving gender discrimination in the application of the poll tax. The Court has never returned to the issue, leaving *Breedlove* to be at least nominally good law on the meaning of the Nineteenth Amendment right to vote." Hasen and Litman, "Thin and Thick Conceptions," draft at 6.

6. Hasen and Litman, "Thin and Thick Conceptions," draft at 5, *citing* Justice Harlan's dissent in Gray v. Sanders, 372 U.S. 368 (1963). Some justices in subsequent cases similarly characterized the Nineteenth Amendment, "in isolation, with the Nineteenth

Amendment's enfranchisement of women having nothing to do with the enfranchisement African Americans in the Fifteenth Amendment or the right to equal protection under the Fourteenth." Ibid.

7. J.E.B. v. Alabama *ex rel.* T.B., 511 U.S. 127, 129 (1994); Taylor v. Louisiana, 419 U.S. 522 (1975).

8. A Lexis-Nexis search on 1 January 2020, indicated that there are 622 judicial opinions that cite the Nineteenth Amendment, with 291of those in state courts and 331 in federal courts. The number of US Supreme Court opinions that cite the Nineteenth Amendment is 39. It is interesting to compare that with the same search for the Fifteenth Amendment. That search turns up 2,845 total citations, with 2,734 of those coming after 1920. The split between federal and state courts is more skewed, with 439 state courts and 2,406 federal courts citing the Fifteenth Amendment. Finally, there are 194 citations to the Fifteenth Amendment in US Supreme Court decisions.

9. Alexander Keyssar, *The Right to Vote: The Contested History of Democracy in the United States* (New York: Basic Books Revised Edition, 2009). "For much of American history, the right to vote has been far from universal. Why was this the case? Why were so many Americans, in different places and at different times, denied the right to vote? How could Americans have thought of themselves as democratic while they possessed such a restricted franchise? Most fundamentally, perhaps, how, why and when did the laws governing suffrage change? These questions are central in political history, critical to an understanding of the evolution of democracy; they also are central to our conceptions of what it means to be an American." Ibid., xx.

10. Members of the NWP and NAWSA viewed the Nineteenth Amendment as delivering political rights and liberty to women. That somewhat limited view of the amendment was grounded, in part, in their race and class and in an essentialist view of women. For example, in an interview with Amelia Fry, conducted when Paul was in her eighties, Paul said, "I think men contribute one thing and women another thing, that we're made that way. Women are certainly made as the peace-loving half of the world and the homemaking half of the world, the temperate half of the world. The more power they have, the better world we are going to have." The leading suffragists saw full equality as a continuum. The Nineteenth Amendment was simply a battle in a larger war for equality that would include not only political but civil rights for women and the removal of all legal disabilities under which they suffered. *See* Amelia Fry, "Conversations with Alice Paul: Woman Suffrage and the Equal Rights Amendment" Oral History Project, The Bancroft Library, University of California Berkeley, 1976, http://content.cdlib.org/view?docId=kt6f59n89c&doc.view=entire_text, 266, where Paul referred to moving toward "complete emancipation" after ratification of the Nineteenth Amendment by proposing another amendment, the equal rights amendment. And see correspondence immediately after ratification that referred to having gained "political freedom." Telegram from Bertha W. Fowler to Alice Paul, 27 August 1920, box II: 6, National Woman's Party Records, Manuscript Division, Library of Congress. "The long struggle of American women for political freedom is at and [*sic*] end."

After ratification, the NLWV saw its role as education and advocacy, with state chapters working on specific legislation. "As of 1924, the League of Women Voters reported that its state affiliates had secured enactment of eighty-six bills that would work to remove "legal discrimination against women." National League of Women Voters, *A Record of Four Years in the National League of Women Voters 1920–1924* (1924), *cited* in Reva B. Siegel, "She the People: The Nineteenth Amendment, Sex Equality, Federalism, and the Family," *Harvard Law Review* 115 (2002): 47, 1008 n. 190. The NWP saw its role as lobbying for blanket legislation in states that would strike down all laws that treated women differently from men and for a federal equal rights amendment that would do so. "For an account of the National Woman's Party's legislative aims, see Nat'l Woman's Party, Declaration of Principles, Equal Rights, Feb. 17, 1923, at 5. For an assessment of the movement's legislative accomplishments at the decade's end, see Report of Legislative Work from 1921 to 1929, Equal Rights, Jan. 4, 1930, at 379." Ibid.

Paul clearly saw herself as the leader who played the most significant role in the final push for suffrage. Her position was that, without the militant tactics of the NWP, a federal suffrage amendment would have been much longer in coming. When asked about the role the NWP played, Paul noted that:

> "It was the culmination, of course, of all the efforts that had been made since 1648 [1848], when our first petition was presented. I think the part that the Woman's Party contributed in coming along, toward the end—because we took probably the leading part in the last seven years, but not any before this last seven years because we came into *existence* seven years before the final culmination—I think that the women in the Woman's Party succeeded in increasing the support and arousing the enthusiasm of women all over the United States to an extent that it had been never aroused before. I think that by standing in front of the White House and calling the attention thereby of all political leaders in the country from the President down and, really, calling the attention of the whole *country* to the desire and demand of women for political equality, it gradually brought it to having a foremost place among the different reforms that were being advocated. It impressed upon Congress. It impressed upon the President. When women were actually being imprisoned for it, it made it a still more insistent demand that the country had to give thought to it. Then, I think, by taking it into the field where women who were already voting were lined up with the women who weren't voting, and were using their votes and their political power to make it something that was politically *useful* to members of Congress to be supporting, was one of the biggest things that was done to finally put it across." Fry, "Conversations," 399.

11. Reva B. Siegel, "The Nineteenth Amendment and the Democratization of the Family," *Yale Law Journal Forum* 129 (2020): 450, 451.

12. Neil S. Siegel, "Why the Nineteenth Amendment Matters Today: A Guide to the Centennial," *Duke Journal of Gender Law & Policy* 27: 235, 243–245 (2020).

13. Ibid., 266.

14. Daphne Barak-Erez, "Her-meneutics Feminism and Interpretation," in *Feminist Constitutionalism, Global Perspectives*, edited by Beverley Baines, Daphne Barak-Erez, and Tsvi Kahana (New York: Cambridge University Press, 2012), 85–97, 95.

15. Hasen and Litman, "Thin and Thick Conceptions," draft at 1.

16. Ibid.
17. Ibid.
18. Ibid.
19. Ibid.
20. Ibid., 24–25.
21. Steve Kolbert, "The Nineteenth Amendment Enforcement Power (But First, Which One is the Nineteenth Amendment, Again?)," *Florida State University Law Review* 43 (2017): 507. Kolbert gives a rich historical account of the debates in Congress, prior to passage of the Nineteenth Amendment, around inclusion of section two and its enforcement power. He suggests a number of reasons that Congress saw a central role for itself in enforcing the provisions of the Nineteenth Amendment. These include women's service during World War I, and extensive testimony around women's contributions to society, among others. Kolbert argues that courts should give great deference to any enforcement legislation, since Congress expected that its authority under section two would be broad. Ibid., 559–560. He goes on to make a case for enacting enforcement legislation to remedy constitutional violations of the right to vote by local governments, including voter ID laws, documentary proof of citizenship requirements, improper voter registration database maintenance practices, and cutbacks in access like early voting, election day registration, and restrictions on third-party voter registration groups. Ibid., 564–572.
22. Hasen and Litman, "Thin and Thick Conceptions," 22.
23. Ibid., draft at 19–20. This view of the central role of Congress is made especially clear if one views the Nineteenth as the fourth Reconstruction Amendment. And that role becomes even more significant in enforcing the norms that underlie the ratification of the Nineteenth Amendment in 1920. For scholars who have characterized the Nineteenth Amendment this way, *see* Professor Kimberly Hamlin who also discussed the role that white southern concerns around the Fifteenth Amendment played before enactment of the Nineteenth Amendment. Address at the Center for Constitutional Law Akron's symposium, "The 19th Amendment at 100: From the Vote to Gender Equality: The 19th Amendment: The Fourth Civil War Amendment?" (20 September 2019). *See also* Kimberly A. Hamlin, *Free Thinker: Sex, Suffrage, and the Extraordinary Life of Helen Hamilton Gardener* (New York: W.W. Norton 2020). This reading might suggest that Congress could amend the Voting Rights Act of 1965 (VRA), pursuant to its enforcement power under section two of the Nineteenth Amendment, to include sex as an illegitimate ground for states to limit voting rights. In fact, Steven Kolbert suggests that Congress enact a Nineteenth Amendment Voting Rights Act. *See* Kolbert, "The Nineteenth Amendment Enforcement Power," 564. An amendment of the VRA or a new act might provide the statutory authority to address the disparate impact of laws on poor white, as well as African American, women, as a result of the gender pay gap. One example of such a law is the Florida statute that requires citizens, who have been formerly convicted of felonies, to pay all fees and fines before having their voting rights reinstated. That statute is being contested in the courts and a recent United States District Court decision held that the Nineteenth should be interpreted, similarly to the Fifteenth, to require intentional discrimination. *See* https://www.

splcenter.org/sites/default/files/documents/0420._05-24-2020_opinion_on_the_
merits._signed_by_judge_robert_l_hinkle_on_52420.pdf. *See generally* Southern
Poverty Law Center, "McCoy et al. v. DeSantis et al.," https://www.splcenter.org/
seeking-justice/case-docket/mccoy-et-al-v-desantis-et-al. While unlikely to be
enacted, such a congressional amendment of the VRA, or a new act, would give even
broader reach to the Nineteenth Amendment's underlying norms today. Kolbert
suggests ways in which such an act could meet the congruence and proportionality
standard imposed by the court. Kolbert, "The Nineteenth Amendment Enforcement
Power," 564. *But see* Hasen and Litman's discussion of the limits on such legislation
and the congruence and proportionality standard imposed on congressional legislation under current Supreme Court jurisprudence, and their assessment of whether
legislation that targeted disparate impacts rather than purposeful or intentional discrimination on account of sex would survive judicial scrutiny. Hasen and Litman,
"Thin and Thick Conceptions," 41–45.

24. Siegel, "She the People."
25. Ibid., 949–950.
26. Ibid., 1034.
27. Ibid.
28. Ibid., 1035–1044.
29. In her new essay, Reva Siegel contrasts the attitudinal story around the Nineteenth
    Amendment, which focuses on the "unequal distribution of the franchise at the
    Founding" as a matter of prejudice, with the institutional story of the Nineteenth
    Amendment, which "explains the unequal distribution of the franchise at the
    founding by acknowledging that the founders created a constitutional republic that
    was more egalitarian than its antecedents, yet still deeply hierarchical in structure.
    Unequal distribution of the franchise at the founding was an expression of *institu-
    tional design* as well as attitude. Allocation of the vote empowered some members
    of the community—generally propertied white male heads of households—to con-
    trol other members of the community." Siegel, "The Nineteenth Amendment and the
    Democratization of the Family," 456.
30. Ibid., 450.
31. Ibid., 488–489.
32. Steven G. Calabresi and Julia T. Rickert, "Originalism and Sex Discrimination," *Texas
    Law Review* 90 (2011): 1. Calabresi and Rickert suggest the use of original public
    meaning, which, "can be illuminated by legislative history and by contemporary
    speeches, articles, and dictionaries. Additionally, understanding the original public
    meaning depends on knowing what interpretive methods legislators and informed
    members of the public used to arrive at the meaning of the provisions." Calabresi and
    Rickert note that such an interpretive approach does not necessarily encompass the
    framers' original expected applications. Ibid., 3.
33. Ibid., 99 "We have shown that since 1920 sex discrimination is forbidden as to civil
    rights just as it is to political rights. The Nineteenth Amendment, read together with
    the Fourteenth Amendment, provides a legitimate basis for striking down almost all
    sex-discriminatory laws."

34. Ibid.
35. *See* Tracy A. Thomas, "More Than the Vote: The Nineteenth Amendment as Proxy for Gender Equality," *Stanford Journal of Civil Rights & Civil Liberties* 15 (forthcoming 2020) draft available at https://papers.ssrn.com/sol3/papers.cfm?abstract_id=3364546; Elizabeth D. Katz, "'A Woman Stumps Her State': Nellie G. Robinson and Women's Right to Hold Public Office in Ohio," *Akron Law Review* 53 (2019): 313. Holly McCammon's work provides similar insight into rights like jury service. It also focuses, like this book, on the impact of strategic choices by the former suffragists on the pace of rights reform. McCammon, *The U.S. Women's Jury Movements.*
36. *See* Deborah L. Brake, "On Not Having It Both Ways and Still Losing: Reflections on Fifty Years of Pregnancy Litigation under Title VII," *Boston University Law Review* 95 (2015): 995–1014.
37. Bernadette Cahill, *Alice Paul, the National Woman's Party and the Vote* (Jefferson, NC: McFarland & Co., 2015), 51. As noted in the Introduction, "Native Americans, who were not already eligible to become citizens through other means like marrying white men, did not become citizens until 1924 when President Calvin Coolidge signed the Indian Citizenship Act of 1924. Pub L. No. 68-175, 43 Stat. 253 (1924). Some Asian immigrant women were eligible for naturalization upon passage of the Magnuson Act of 1943 (also known as the Chinese Exclusion Repeal Act of 1943), while others were not eligible for naturalization until the Immigration and Naturalization Act of 1952. Pub. L. No. 82-414, 66 Stat. 163." Introduction (this book), note 5. And African American, Latina, and other women voters of color, while enfranchised as a matter of law, remained disenfranchised as a matter of fact after ratification of the Nineteenth Amendment in 1920.
38. Neil S. Siegel, "Why the Nineteenth Amendment Matters Today," 1 n. 3, *citing* Akhil Reed Amar, *American's Constitution: A Biography* (2005), 419, quoting Amar "[e]ven the most extraordinary feats of the Founding and Reconstruction era had involved the electoral empowerment and/or enfranchisement of hundreds of thousands, not millions."
39. Cahill, *Alice Paul, the National Woman's Party and the Vote*, 51.
40. Gretchen Ritter, "Jury Service and Women's Citizenship before and after the Nineteenth Amendment," *Law and History Review* 20 (2002): 479, 480.
41. The NLWV aligned itself with the social feminists around support for protective legislation and opposition to the ERA. Thus, the NLWV was unlikely after *Adkins* to support a thicker conception since it would likely be used to strike down protective legislation.
42. Gretchen Ritter, *The Constitution as Social Design: Gender and Civic Membership in the American Constitutional Order* (Stanford, CA: Stanford University Press, 2006), 129–130.
43. Vicki Schultz, "Taking Sex Discrimination Seriously," *Denver University Law Review* 91 (2015): 995, 1001.
44. Ritter, *The Constitution as Social Design*, 129. In Ritter's view, "The key problem is not with the narrow construction of the Nineteenth Amendment, but with the construction of the Fourteenth Amendment . . . Unless the terms of civic membership are

substantively reimagined on new constitutional terms . . . then there is little likelihood that "equal" citizenship within the current constitutional order will provide women with a satisfactory civic membership." Ibid., 64.

45. The Supreme Court did not adopt the Fourteenth Amendment as a basis for striking down laws that discriminated on the basis of sex until the 1970s. For the role played by Pauli Murray, Dorothy Kenyon, Ruth Bader Ginsburg, and the ACLU Women's Rights Project, in terms of analogizing to race, see Siegel, "She the People," 954 n. 10. Siegel reasons that:

> "In developing sex discrimination doctrine under the Fourteenth Amendment, the Court seems to have proceeded from the understanding that there is no constitutional history that would support a constitutional commitment to equal citizenship for women—that such a commitment is to be derived, to the extent it can be derived at all, by analogizing race and sex discrimination." Ibid., 1022.

46. See Paula Giddings, When and Where I Enter: The Impact of Black Women on Race and Sex in America (New York: Amistad, 1984), 340. Giddings highlights the often pivotal role that African American women have played in suffrage and the women's movement. "Historical patterns suggest that just as Black women are vital to Black movements, so Black movements are vital to the progress of feminist movements. Feminism has always had the greatest currency in times of Black militancy or immediately thereafter." Giddings links the failure to ratify the equal rights amendment in 1982 to the "race/class myopia" of the leaders of the National Organization of Women (NOW) with regard to the equal rights amendment in the late 1960s and the 1970s. At that time, organized labor was officially opposed to the amendment since it might jeopardize protective legislation, still alive and well at the time. Organized labor was slowly moving away from its support for such legislation, however, and Giddings asserts that class bias by NOW leaders, alienating labor groups, slowed the equal rights amendment in Congress. This delay provided time for effective opposition by "reactionary forces" to form and eventually stop ratification. Giddings also details NOW's failure to engage with African American and other minority women's groups and suggests that failure played a role in the defeat of the equal rights amendment, enacted by Congress in 1972 almost fifty years after it was first introduced. Giddings attributes the amendment's defeat in Illinois, central to the failure of ratification, to this alienation of African Americans in the state legislature. Ibid., 164.

47. Timothy Williams, "Virginia Approves the ERA: Becoming the 38th State to Back It," The New York Times, 15 January 2020, https://www.nytimes.com/2020/01/15/us/era-virginia-vote.html; Robinson Woodward-Burns, "The Equal Rights Amendment Is One State Away from Ratification. Now What?," The Washington Post, 20 June 2018, https://www.washingtonpost.com/news/monkey-cage/wp/2018/06/20/the-equal-rights-amendment-is-one-state-from-ratification-now-what/?noredirect=on&utm_term=.e756115896d2.

48. J. Kevin Corder and Christina Wolbrecht, Counting Women's Ballots: Female Voters from Suffrage through the New Deal (New York: Cambridge University Press, 2016), 281. But see Celeste K. Carruthers and Marianne H. Wanamaker, "Municipal Housekeeping: The Impact of Women's Suffrage on Public Education," NBER

Working Paper No. 20864, January 2015, http://www.nber.org/papers/w20864, attributing up to one-third of the 1920–1940 rise in public school expenditures to the Nineteenth Amendment, yet noting "the continued disenfranchisement of black southerners meant that women's suffrage exacerbated racial inequality in education expenditures and substantially delayed relative gains in black human capital observed later in the century."

49. The gender gap in voting is the difference in the percentage of women and the percentage of men voting for a given candidate. Center for American Women and Politics, *Gender Gap in Voting*, http://www.cawp.rutgers.edu/facts/voters/gender_gap, accessed 8 January 2020. In the 2016 election, the gender gap was as large as it has ever been. Statistician Nate Silver characterized it as "a massive split" in favor of Hillary Clinton, with her advantage among women averaging 15%. Silver concludes that "if Trump loses the election, it will be because women voted against him." Nate Silver, "Election Update: Women Are Defeating Donald Trump," *Five Thirty-Eight*, 11 October 2016, https://fivethirtyeight.com/features/election-update-women-are-defeating-donald-trump/. The Silver post gave rise to the hashtag #RepealtheNineteenth, reflecting his observation that Donald Trump would win if only men voted. Alana Vagianos, "Trump Supporters Tweet #repealthe19th After Poll Shows He'd Win If Only Men Voted," *Huffpost*, 25 October 2016, https://www.huffingtonpost.com/entry/trump-supporters-tweet-repealthe19th-after-poll-shows-hed-win-if-only-men-voted_us_57fea03ce4b05eff55814a75. Of course, Donald Trump did not lose and, in fact, while a majority of all women did vote against him, a majority of white women voted for him. *See* notes 52 and 53.

50. Corder and Wolbrecht, *Counting Women's Ballots*, 272. "[W]ithout the Nineteenth Amendment, Mitt Romney may well have been elected president in 2012. Exit polls showed Romney securing 52 percent of men's votes while 55 percent of the women cast their ballots for Barack Obama." Ibid. In her forthcoming book, *The 19th Amendment and the Politics of Race, 1920–1970*, Liette Gidlow explores the links between the Nineteenth, "and the African American freedom movements of the 1950s and 1960s. Part of the broader reassessment of the 19th Amendment at its centennial, this research finds that a small but significant number of southern African Americans voted after ratification and that their successes, together with unceasing agitation by many who remained disfranchised, transformed not only the black freedom struggle but political parties, election procedures, and social movements on the right and the left." https://www.radcliffe.harvard.edu/people/liette-gidlow.

51. Vanessa Williams, "Black Women Vow to be a Powerful Voting Force Again This Year," *Washington Post*, 10 January 2016, https://www.washingtonpost.com/politics/black-women-vow-to-be-a-powerful-voting-force-again-this-year/2016/01/10/f0c290fc-b324-11e5-a842-0feb51d1d124_story.html?utm_term=.29ad978397cf.

52. Tami Luhby, "How Hillary Clinton Lost," *CNN*, 9 November 2016, http://www.cnn.com/2016/11/09/politics/clinton-votes-african-americans-latinos-women-white-voters/index.html; Greg B. Smith, "Poll Shows Hillary Would Have Won the Election if Women Backed Her Like They Backed Obama," *NY Daily News*, 9 November 2016, http://www.nydailynews.com/news/politics/

poll-shows-women-backed-obama-hillary-clinton-article-1.2866727; Clare Foran, "Women Aren't Responsible for Hillary Clinton's Defeat," *The Atlantic*, 13 November 2016, https://www.theatlantic.com/politics/archive/2016/11/hillary-clinton-white-women-vote/507422/.

53. Jon Henley, "White and Wealthy Voters Give Victory to Donald Trump, Exit Polls Show," *The Guardian*, 9 November 2016, https://www.theguardian.com/us-news/2016/nov/09/white-voters-victory-donald-trump-exit-polls.

54. As Rosalyn Terborg-Penn reminds us, "Feminist history must face the reality: although most suffragists were feminists, many of the white ones were also racists." Rosalyn Terborg-Penn, *African-American Women in the Struggle for the Vote, 1850–1920* (Bloomington: Indiana University Press, 1998), 166.

55. Siegel, "She the People," 1045.

56. Ritter, "Jury Service and Women's Citizenship," 481, *citing* Siegel, "She the People."

57. Siegel, "She the People," 1045.

Bibliography

Archival Collections

Schlesinger Library, Radcliffe Institute, Harvard University. Cambridge, Mass.
   Alice Paul papers.
Library of Congress, Manuscript Division. Washington, DC.
   National Woman's Party records.
ProQuest History Vault. Online.
   NAACP Papers.
   Struggle for Women's Rights, Organizational Records, 1880–1990.

Oral History Collections

Paul, Alice. "Conversations with Alice Paul: Woman Suffrage and the Equal Rights Amendment." An Oral History conducted 1972–1973 by Amelia R. Fry, Regional Oral History Office. The Bancroft Library. UC Berkeley, 1976. http://content.cdlib.org/ark:/13030/kt6f59n89c/. http://content.cdlib.org/view?docId=kt6f59n89c;NAAN=13030&doc.view=frames&chunk.id=d0e18675&toc.depth=1&toc.id=d0e18675&brand=calisphere.

Selected Statutes and Legislative Documents

U.S. Constitution, Article I.
U.S. Constitution, amendment XIV.
U.S. Constitution, amendment XV.
U.S. Constitution, amendment XIX.
U.S. Constitution, amendment XXVI.
H.R. 15018, 66th Cong. (1920).
Hearings of the House Committee on the Judiciary on the Equal Rights Amendment, 68th Congress, 2nd Sess. (Washington 1925).
Extending the Right of Suffrage to Women, Hearings Before the Committee on Woman Suffrage, House of Representatives, 65th Congress, 2d Session on H. J. Res 200. 3, 4, 5, and 7 January 1918 (Washington Government Printing Office 1918).

Cases

Adkins v. Children's Hosp. of the District of Columbia, 261 U.S. 525 (1923).
Akins v. Secretary of State, 904 A.2d 702 (N.H. 2006).

Barbier v. Connolly, 113 U.S. 27 (1885).

Breedlove v. Suttles, 302 U.S. 277 (1937).

Brown v. City of Atlanta, 109 S.E. 666 (Ga. 1921).

Children's Hospital of District of Columbia v. Adkins, 284 F. 613 (D.C. 1922).

Cleveland, C., C. & St. L. Ry. Co, 170 N.E. 27 (Ohio. Ct. App. 1929).

Commonwealth v. Maxwell, 114 A. 825 (Pa. 1921).

Commonwealth v. Welosky, 177 N.E. 656 (Mass. 1931).

Davis v. Warde, 118 S.E. 378 (Ga. 1923).

Fairchild v. Hughes, 258 U.S. 126 (1922).

Graves v. Eubank, 87 So. 587 (Ala. 1921).

Guinn v. United States, 238 U.S. 347 (1915).

Harper v. State Board of Elections, 383 U.S. 663 (1966).

Hawke v. Smith, 253 U.S. 221 (1920).

Hawthorne v. Turkey Creek School District, 134 S.E. 103 (Ga. 1926).

In re Graves, 30 S.W.2d 149 (Mo. 1930).

In re Opinion of the Justices, 62 Me. 596 (1873).

In re Opinion of the Justices, 135 N.E. 173 (Mass. 1922).

In re Opinion of the Justices, 130 N.E. 685 (Mass. 1921).

In re Opinion of the Justices, 139 A. 180 (N.H. 1927).

J.E.B. v. Alabama *ex rel.* T.B., 511 U.S. 127 (1994).

Leser v. Garnett, 258 U.S. 130 (1922).

Leser v. Garnett, 114 A. 840 (Md. 1921).

Lochner v. New York, 198 U.S. 45 (1905).

Marbury v. Madison, 5 U.S. (1 Cranch) 137 (1803).

McComb v. Robelen, 116 A. 745 (Del. Ch. 1922).

Minor v. Happersett, 88 U.S. 162 (1875).

Muller v. Oregon, 208 U.S. 412 (1908).

Myers v. Anderson, 238 U.S. 368 (1915).

Neal v. Delaware, 103 U.S. 370 (1881).

Palmer v. State, 150 N.E. 917 (Ind. 1926).

People *ex rel.* Fyfe v. Barnett, 150 N.E. 290 (Ill. 1925).

People *ex rel.* Murray v. Holmes, 173 N.E. 145 (Ill. 1930).

People v. Barltz, 180 N.W. 423 (Mich. 1920).

Preston v. Roberts, 110 S.E. 586 (N.C. 1922).

Radice v. New York, 264 U.S. 292 (1924).

Reed v. Reed, 404 U.S. 71 (1971).

Rice v. Board of Aldermen of City of Woonsocket, 112 A. 175 (R.I. 1920).

Rosencrantz v. Territory, 5 P. 305 (Wash. Terr. 1884).

The Slaughter-House Cases, 83 U.S. 36 (1873).

Solon v. State, 114 S.W. 349 (Tex. Crim. App. 1908).

State v. Bray, 95 So. 417 (La. 1923).

State v. Dreher, 118 So. 85 (La. 1928).

State v. James, 114 A. 553 (N.J. Err. & App. 1921).

State v. Mittle, 113 S.E. 335 (S.C. 1922).

Stephens v. Ball Ground School District, 113 S.E. 85 (Ga. 1922).

Stewart v. Cartwright, 118 S.E. 859 (Ga. 1923).

Strauder v. West Virginia, 100 U.S. 303 (1880).

Stuard v. Thompson, 251 S.W. 277 (Tex. Civ. App. 1923).

Taaffe v. Sanderson, 294 S.W. 74 (Ark. 1927).
Taylor v. Louisiana, 419 U.S. 522 (1975).
United States v. Cruikshank, 92 U.S. 542 (1876).
United States v. Cruikshank, 25 Fed. Cas. 707, 710 (D. La. 1874) (No. 14, 897).
United States v. Virginia, 518 U.S. 515 (1996).
Uphoff v. Industrial Board of Illinois, 111 N.E. 128 (Ill. 1915).
West Coast Hotel Co. v. Parrish, 300 U.S. 379 (1937).
Wilkinson v. State, 151 N.E. 690 (Ind. 1926).
Young v. United Parcel Service, Inc., 575 U.S. 206 (2015).

Selected Books and Articles

Adams, Katherine H. and Michael L. Keene. *Alice Paul and the American Suffrage Campaign*. Urbana and Chicago: University of Illinois Press, 2008.
Albert, Richard. *Constitutional Amendment: Making, Breaking, and Changing Constitutions*. New York: Oxford University Press, 2019.
Amar, Akhil Reed. *America's Constitution: A Biography*. New York: Random House, 2005.
Amar, Akhil Reed. "The Bill of Rights as a Constitution." *Yale Law Journal* 100 (1991): 1131–1210.
Amar, Vikram. "Jury Service as Political Participation Akin to Voting." *Cornell Law Review* 80 (1995): 203–259.
Amar, Vikram David. "The 100-Year Anniversary of the First State Ratification of the Nineteenth Amendment: Reflections on the Breadth of Freedom from Discrimination in the 'Right to Vote.'" *Verdict Justia*, 27 June 2019. https://verdict.justia.com/2019/06/27/the-100-year-anniversary-of-the-first-state-ratification-of-the-nineteenth-amendment.
American Civil Liberties Union, "Crystal Eastman," https://www.aclu.org/other/crystal-eastman.
Babcock, Barbara Allen. "A Place in the Palladium: Women's Rights and Jury Service." *University of Cincinnati Law Review* 61 (1993): 1139–1180.
Barak-Erez, Daphne. "Her-meneutics Feminism and Interpretation." In *Feminist Constitutionalism, Global Perspectives*, edited by Beverley Baines, Daphne Barak-Erez, and Tsvi Kahana, 85–97. New York: Cambridge University Press, 2012.
Batlan, Felice. "Notes from the Margins: Florence Kelley and the Making of Sociological Jurisprudence." In *Transformations in American Legal History: Law, Ideology, and Methods*, edited by Daniel W. Hamilton and Alfred L. Brophy, vol. 2, 239–253. Cambridge, MA: Harvard University Press, 2010.
Berenson, Barbara F. *Massachusetts in the Woman Suffrage Movement*. Charleston, SC: The History Press, 2018.
Bernstein, David E. "Class Legislation, Fundamental Rights, and the Origins of Lochner and Liberty of Contract." *George Mason Law Review* 26 (2019): 1023–1047.
Bluestein, Frayda. "Self-Executing Constitutional Provisions." *Coates' Canons: NC Local Government Law*, 23 March 2011. https://canons.sog.unc.edu/self-executing-constitutional-provisions.
Brake, Deborah L. "On Not Having It Both Ways and Still Losing: Reflections on Fifty Years of Pregnancy Litigation under Title VII." *Boston University Law Review* 95 (2015): 995–1014.

Brown, Jennifer K. "The Nineteenth Amendment and Women's Equality." *Yale Law Journal* 102 (1993): 2175–2204.

Butler, Amy E. *Two Paths to Equality: Alice Paul and Ethel M. Smith in the ERA Debate, 1921–1929.* Albany: State University of New York Press, 2002.

Cahill, Bernadette. *Alice Paul, the National Woman's Party and the Vote: The First Civil Rights Struggle of the 20th Century.* Jefferson, NC: McFarland & Co., 2015.

Calabresi, Steven G. and Julia T. Rickert. "Originalism and Sex Discrimination." *Texas Law Review* 90 (2011): 1–102.

Carruthers, Celeste K. and Marianne H. Wanamaker. "Municipal Housekeeping: The Impact of Women's Suffrage on Public Education." NBER Working Paper No. 20864, January 2015. http://www.nber.org/papers/w20864.

Center for American Women and Politics, *Gender Gap in Voting.* http://www.cawp. rutgers.edu/facts/voters/gender_gap, accessed 8 January 2020.

Chused, Richard and Wendy Williams. *Gendered Law in American History.* Durham, NC: Carolina Academic Press, 2016.

Corder, J. Kevin and Christina Wolbrecht. *Counting Women's Ballots: Female Voters from Suffrage through the New Deal.* New York: Cambridge University Press, 2016.

Cott, Nancy F. "Feminist Politics in the 1920s: The National Woman's Party." *Journal of American History* 71 (1984): 43–68.

Currie, David P. "The Constitution in the Supreme Court: 1921–1930." *Duke Law Journal* (1986): 65–144.

Eastman, Crystal. "What Next." *The Suffragist: Official Organ of the National Woman's Party* 3 No. 10 (November 1920): 278–286.

Ernst, Dan. "Frankfurter and DC Minimum Wage Case: The View from the Adkins Papers." *Legal History Blog,* 28 June 2012. http://legalhistoryblog.blogspot.com/2012/06/frankfurter-and-dc-minimum-wage-case.html.

Ferguson, Andrew Guthrie. "The Jury as Constitutional Identity." *UC Davis Law Review* 47 (2014): 1105–1172.

Foran, Clare. "Women Aren't Responsible for Hillary Clinton's Defeat." *The Atlantic,* 13 November 2016. https://www.theatlantic.com/politics/archive/2016/11/hillary-clinton-white-women-vote/507422/.

Frankfurter, Felix. "The Case of Sacco and Vanzetti." *Atlantic Monthly* 139 (March 1927): 409–432.

Frankfurter, Felix. *The Case of Sacco and Vanzetti: A Critical Analysis for Lawyers and Laymen.* Boston: Little, Brown and Co., 1927.

Free, Laura. *Suffrage Reconstructed: Gender, Race and Voting Rights in the Civil War Era.* Ithaca, NY: Cornell University Press, 2015.

Frierson, William L. "Amending the Constitution of the United States." *Harvard Law Review* 33 (1920): 659–666.

Giddings, Paula. *When and Where I Enter: The Impact of Black Women on Race and Sex in America.* New York: Amistad, 1984.

Gillman, Howard. *The Constitution Besieged: The Rise and Demise of Lochner Era Police Powers Jurisprudence.* Durham, NC: Duke University Press, 1993.

Gordon, Ann D. (ed.) et. al., *African American Women and the Vote: 1837–1965.* (Amherst: University of Massachusetts Press 1997).

Gosnell, Harold F. *Why Europe Votes.* Chicago: University of Chicago Press, 1930.

Grossman, Joanna. "Women's Jury Service: Right of Citizenship or Privilege of Difference?" *Stanford Law Review* 46 (1994): 1115–1160.

Hamlin, Kimberly A. *Free Thinker: Sex, Suffrage, and the Extraordinary Life of Helen Hamilton Gardener.* New York: W.W. Norton, 2020.

Hart, Vivien. *Bound by Our Constitution: Women Workers and the Minimum Wage.* Princeton, NJ: Princeton University Press, 1994.

Hartley, Roger C. *How Failed Attempts to Amend the Constitution Mobilize Political Change.* Nashville, TN: Vanderbilt University Press, 2017.

Hasen, Richard L. and Leah M. Litman. "Thin and Thick Conceptions of the Nineteenth Amendment Right to Vote and Congress's Power to Enforce It." *Georgetown Law Journal* 19th Amendment Special Edition (forthcoming 2020), draft at https://papers.ssrn.com/sol3/papers.cfm?abstract_id=3501114.

Holloway, Vanessa A. *In Search of Federal Enforcement: The Moral Authority of the Fifteenth Amendment and the Integrity of the Black Ballot, 1870–1965.* Lanham, MD: University Press of America, 2015.

Hubbard, B.V. *Socialism, Feminism, and Suffragism: The Terrible Triplets, Connected by the Same Umbilical Cord, and Fed from the Same Nursing Bottle.* Chicago: American Publishing Company, 1915. Library of Congress Rare Book Collection. https://www.loc.gov/item/15016027/.

Johnson, Helen Kendrick. *Woman and the Republic: A Survey of the Woman-Suffrage Movement in the United States and a Discussion of the Claims and Arguments of its Foremost Advocates.* New York: The Guidon Club, 1913.

Katz, Elizabeth D. "'A Woman Stumps Her State': Nellie G. Robinson and Women's Right to Hold Public Office in Ohio." *Akron Law Review* 53 (2019): 313–357.

Kerber, Linda. *No Constitutional Right to Be Ladies: Women and the Obligations of Citizenship.* New York: Hill and Wang, 1998.

Keyssar, Alexander. *The Right to Vote: The Contested History of Democracy in the United States.* New York: Basic Books Revised Edition, 2009.

Kolbert, Steve. "The Nineteenth Amendment Enforcement Power (But First, Which One Is the Nineteenth Amendment, Again?)." *Florida State University Law Review* 43 (2017): 507–572.

Kraditor, Aileen S. *The Ideas of the Woman Suffrage Movement /1890–1920.* New York: Columbia University Press, 1965.

Library of Congress, "NAACP Victory in Guinn v. United States," *NAACP: A Century in the Fight for Freedom.* http://www.loc.gov/exhibits/naacp/founding-and-early-years.html#obj23.

Lopach, James J. and Jean A. Luckowski. *Jeannette Rankin: A Political Woman.* Boulder: University Press of Colorado, 2005.

Lunardini, Christine. *From Equal Suffrage to Equal Rights: Alice Paul and the National Woman's Party, 1920–1928.* Lincoln, NE: toExcel Press, 1986, 2000.

Lupton, John A. "Illinois Supreme Court History: Women and Juries." *Illinois Courts Connect,* 26 March 2019. https://courts.illinois.gov/Media/eNews/2019/032619_SCHistory.asp.

Marbury, William L. "The Limitations upon the Amending Power." *Harvard Law Review* 33 (1919): 223–235.

Marbury, William L. "The Nineteenth Amendment and After." *Virginia Law Review* 7 (1920): 1–29.

Mathews, John M. *Legislative and Judicial History of the Fifteenth Amendment.* Baltimore: Johns Hopkins Press, 1909.

McCammon, Holly J. *The U.S. Women's Jury Movements and Strategic Adaptation: A More Just Verdict.* New York: Cambridge University Press, 2014.

Mitchell, Jonathan F. "Textualism and the Fourteenth Amendment," *Stanford Law Review* 69 (2017): 1237–1322.

Monopoli, Paula A. "Gender and Constitutional Design." *Yale Law Journal* 115 (2006): 2643–2651.

Monopoli, Paula A. "Inheritance Law and the Marital Presumption after Obergefell." *Estate Planning & Community Property Law Journal* 8 (2016): 437–459.

Murphy, Bruce Allen. *The Brandeis/Frankfurter Connection: The Secret Political Activities of Two Supreme Court Justices*. New York: Oxford University Press, 1982.

National American Woman Suffrage Association, *Victory: How Women Won It, a Centennial Symposium, 1840–1940* (New York: H. W. Wilson, 1940).

National League of Women Voters. *A Record of Four Years in the National League of Women Voters 1920–1924* (1924).

National Woman's Party. Declaration of Principles, Equal Rights, 17 February 1923.

Novkov, Julie. *Constituting Workers, Protecting Women: Gender, Law, and Labor in the Progressive Era and New Deal Years*. Ann Arbor: University of Michigan Press, 2001.

Ogden, Frederic D. *The Poll Tax in the South*. Tuscaloosa: University of Alabama Press, 1958.

Park, Maud Wood. *Front Door Lobby*, edited by Edna Lamprey Stantial. Boston: Beacon Press, 1960.

Pauley, Garth. *LBJ's American Promise: The 1965 Voting Rights Address*. College Station: Texas A&M University Press, 2007.

Pope, James Gray. "Snubbed Landmark: Why United States v. Cruikshank (1870) Belongs at the Heart of the American Constitutional Canon." *Harvard Civil Rights-Civil Liberties Law Review* 49 (2014): 385–447.

Power, Garrett. "Eugenics, Jim Crow and Baltimore's Best." *Maryland Bar Journal*, December 2016, 4.

Rhode, Deborah L. *Justice and Gender: Sex Discrimination and the Law*. Cambridge, MA: Harvard University Press, 1989.

Ritter, Gretchen. "Jury Service and Women's Citizenship before and after the Nineteenth Amendment." *Law and History Review* 20 (2002): 479–516.

Ritter, Gretchen. *The Constitution as Social Design: Gender and Civic Membership in the American Constitutional Order*. Stanford, CA: Stanford University Press, 2006.

Rodriguez, Cristina M. "Clearing the Smoke-Filled Room: Women Jurors and the Disruption of an Old-Boys' Network in Nineteenth-Century America." *Yale Law Journal* 108 (1999): 1805–1844.

Schearer, Michael. "No Ma'm: Progressive Reform as an Obstacle to Gender Equality," SSRN (April 2014). https://papers.ssrn.com/sol3/papers.cfm?abstract_id=2573791.

Schmidt, Caroline S. "What Killed the Violence Against Women Act's Civil Rights Remedy before the Supreme Court Did?" *Virginia Law Review* 101 (2015): 530–533.

Schultz, Vicki. "Taking Sex Discrimination Seriously." *Denver University Law Review* 91 (2015): 995–1120.

Scott, Anne Firor. "After Suffrage: Southern Women in the Twenties." *The Journal of Southern History* 30, No. 3 (1964): 298–318.

Scott, Anne Firor. "Epilogue," in *Votes for Women: The Struggle for Suffrage Revisited*, Jean H. Baker, ed. New York: Oxford University Press, 2002.

Siegel, Neil S. "Why the Nineteenth Amendment Matters Today: A Guide to the Centennial." *Duke Journal of Gender Law & Policy* 27 (2020): 235–268.

Siegel, Reva B. "Collective Memory and the Nineteenth Amendment: Reasoning about the 'Woman Question' in the Discourse of Sex Discrimination." In *History, Memory, and the Law*, edited by Austin Sarat and Thomas R. Kearns (Ann Arbor: University of Michigan Press, 1999).

Siegel, Reva B. "She the People: The Nineteenth Amendment, Sex Equality, Federalism, and the Family." *Harvard Law Review* 115 (2002): 947–1046.

Siegel, Reva B. "The Nineteenth Amendment and the Democratization of the Family." *Yale Law Journal Forum* 129 (2020): 450–495.

Sklar, Kathryn Kish. *Florence Kelley and the Nation's Work: The Rise of Women's Political Culture, 1830–1900*. New Haven, CT: Yale University Press, 1995.

Southern Poverty Law Center. "McCoy et al., v. DeSantis et al." https://www.splcenter.org/seeking-justice/case-docket/mccoy-et-al-v-desantis-et-al.

Suk, Julie. *We the Women: The Unstoppable Mothers of the Equal Rights Amendment* (New York: Simon & Schuster forthcoming 2020).

Swinney, Everette. "Enforcing the Fifteenth Amendment, 1870–1877." *The Journal of Southern History* 28 (1962): 202–218.

Terborg-Penn, Rosalyn. *African-American Women in the Struggle for the Vote, 1850–1920*. Bloomington: Indiana University Press, 1998.

Thomas, Tracy A. *Elizabeth Cady Stanton and the Feminist Foundations of Family Law*. New York: New York University Press, 2016.

Thomas, Tracy A. "More than the Vote: The Nineteenth Amendment as Proxy for Gender Equality." *Stanford Journal of Civil Rights and Civil Liberties* 15 (forthcoming 2020), draft at https://papers.ssrn.com/sol3/papers.cfm?abstract_id=3364546.

Van Voris, Jacqueline. *Carrie Chapman Catt: A Public Life*. New York: The Feminist Press, 1987.

Vose, Clement E. *Constitutional Change: Amendment Politics and Supreme Court Litigation Since 1900*. Lexington, MA: Lexington Books, 1972.

Walton, Mary. *A Woman's Crusade: Alice Paul and the Battle for the Ballot*. New York: Palgrave Macmillan, 2010.

Ward, Geoffrey C. and Ken Burns. *Not for Ourselves Alone: The Story of Elizabeth Cady Stanton and Susan B. Anthony*. New York: Alfred A. Knopf, 1999.

Weiss, Elaine. *The Woman's Hour: The Great Fight to Win the Vote*. New York: Viking/Penguin, 2018.

Woloch, Nancy. *A Class by Herself: Protective Laws for Women Workers, 1880s–1960s*. Princeton, NJ: Princeton University Press, 2015.

Young, Louise M. *In the Public Interest: The League of Women Voters, 1920–1970*. Westport, CT: Greenwood Press, 1989.

Zahniser, J.D. and Amelia R. Fry. *Alice Paul: Claiming Power*. New York: Oxford University Press, 2014.

Zimmerman, Joan. "The Jurisprudence of Equality: The Women's Minimum Wage, the First Equal Rights Amendment, and Adkins v. Children's Hospital, 1905–1923." *Journal of American History* 78 (1991): 188–225.

Index

For the benefit of digital users, indexed terms that span two pages (e.g., 52–53) may, on occasion, appear on only one of those pages.